People of Faith, People of Jeong (Qing)

"This book is a must-read for Asian North American pastors, church leaders, concerned laypeople, and multicultural leaders who are committed to their own ethnic loyalties and Jeong (indivisible compassion)/Qing (a beautiful heart)."

—**Andrew Sung Park**, United Theological Seminary, Ohio, USA

"Uniquely Canadian and yet speaking a language of faith that resonates with many immigrant Christian communities across the globe, this book explores insightful ways how churches in Canada offer a spiritual home for Asian diaspora communities as they cultivate the Christian ethic of serving others and affirm their distinct hybrid and diverse linguistic identities."

—**HyeRan Kim-Cragg**, Emmanuel College, University of Toronto

"Praiseworthy is the perceptivity of Dr. Song and her research team into the problem compounded by different languages and cultures amid different generations and their constructive proposals in dealing with the complexity of these issues."

—**Wes Chan**, ordained minister, Trinity Mandarin Presbyterian Church, Toronto

"This book brilliantly illumines the life of Asian immigrant churches in Canada today and what their ministries might look like tomorrow."

—**John Vissers**, University of Toronto

"This work provides a valuable (and missing) chapter in the history of Christianity in Canada in addition to identifying possibilities for the Christian church as it lives into an unfamiliar social and cultural landscape."

—**Dorcas Gordon**, University of Toronto

People of Faith, People of Jeong (Qing)

The Asian Canadian Churches of Today for Tomorrow

EDITED BY
Nam Soon Song
Ben C. H. Kuo
Dong-Ha Kim

AND

In Kee Kim

FOREWORD BY
Greer Anne Wenh-In Ng

WIPF & STOCK · Eugene, Oregon

PEOPLE OF FAITH, PEOPLE OF JEONG (QING)
The Asian Canadian Churches of Today for Tomorrow

Copyright © 2020 Wipf and Stock Publishers. All rights reserved. Except for brief quotations in critical publications or reviews, no part of this book may be reproduced in any manner without prior written permission from the publisher. Write: Permissions, Wipf and Stock Publishers, 199 W. 8th Ave., Suite 3, Eugene, OR 97401.

Wipf & Stock
An Imprint of Wipf and Stock Publishers
199 W. 8th Ave., Suite 3
Eugene, OR 97401

www.wipfandstock.com

PAPERBACK ISBN: 978-1-7252-5318-6
HARDCOVER ISBN: 978-1-7252-5319-3
EBOOK ISBN: 978-1-7252-5320-9

Scripture quotations are from New Revised Standard Version Bible, copyright © 1989 National Council of the Churches of Christ in the United States of America. Used by permission. All rights reserved worldwide.

Manufactured in the U.S.A.　　　　　　　　　　　　　　　　　　　　07/06/20

Contents

Foreword by Greer Anne Wenh-In Ng | vii
Preface | xiii
Acknowledgements | xv
Abbreviations | xvii
Introduction | xix

Part I: Past Story

Chapter 1   A Brief History of the Chinese Immigrant Church in Canada
—Alan Ka Lun Lai | 3

Chapter 2   A Brief History of the Taiwanese Immigrant Church in Canada
—Luis Liang and Ben C. H. Kuo | 17

Chapter 3   A Brief History of the Korean Immigrant Church in Canada
—In Kee Kim | 30

Part II: Present Story

Chapter 4   People of Faith (I)—Nam Soon Song | 43
Chapter 5   People of Faith (II)—Nam Soon Song | 60
Chapter 6   People of *Jeong* (*Qing*)—Nam Soon Song | 80

Part III: Future Story

Chapter 7   Future Story—Nam Soon Song | 103

Part IV: For Better Stories

Chapter 8   Building One United Church—In Kee Kim | 123

Chapter 9   Communicating and Bridging Relationship Gaps across Language, Generational, and Cultural Divides: A Case of Asian Canadian Immigrant Churches in Toronto —Ben C. H. Kuo | 138

Chapter 10   Empowering Second-Generation Leadership —Dong-Ha Kim | 160

Chapter 11   Moving towards a Multicultural Church —Nam Soon Song | 177

Conclusion | 199

Bibliography | 203

Foreword

Significance of the Present Volume

BEGINNING WITH WORDS OF congratulations is always a joy. Congratulations are in order for the publication of *People of Faith, People of Jeong* for the successful conducting of significant research with three East Asian faith communities, each with its own immigration history, and for the publication of its findings. By making available so many direct quotes from the multitude of persons interviewed, the editors have provided access into the minds and struggles of Christians young and mature in a rich tapestry of authenticity. By recruiting writers from disciplines ranging from religious education and psychology to theology, pastoral ministry, and ecclesiology, they have enabled access to expertise and insight in the analysis of the study's findings.

For myself as a Canadian, in particular, a special significance of this volume resides in the fact that it deals explicitly with faith communities in Canada without any apology. No longer is it necessary to fit Canada under the umbrella of "North America" in order to gain legitimacy or recognition, as when *People on the Way* appeared with the subtitle: *Asian North Americans Discovering Christ, Culture and Community*.[1] Or, as used to be the case, to subsume Canadian contributions under "Asian American," as Julia Ching's was in *Journeys at the Margin: Toward an Autobiographical Theology in American-Asian Perspective*,[2] or mine, in *Realizing the America of Our Hearts: Theological Voices of Asia Americans*.[3] My fervent hope is that, with the recent appearance of *Reading-in Between: How Minoritized Cultural Communities Interpret the Bible in Canada*,[4] Canadian voices and realities will increasingly come to shape ideas on ministry and mission,

1. Ng, *People on the Way*.
2. See Ching, "House of Self," 41–61.
3. See Ng, "Land of Maple and Lands of Bamboo," 99–114.
4. Medina et al., *Reading In-Between*.

theological reflection and biblical interpretation, assuming a rightful if still modest place in the complex totality of Christian religious endeavor continentally and globally.

The Canadian Context

Much as the experience of people of Asian heritage in Canada share with their counterparts to the south—racialization as "visible minorities," histories of exclusion by the imposition of a head tax followed by immigration acts until after World War II, the internment of Japanese residents during that world war, and so on, there is sufficient specificity in Canada's history and current context to warrant paying to it its own attention. This goes beyond Canada having its own national formation—first colonizers from France followed by those from England. For its relevance to the lives of the "people of faith, people of *jeong*" of this volume, however, I lift up first Canada's official multiculturalism policy of 1971, followed by the multiculturalism Act of 1988. The development of Chinese, Taiwanese, and Korean immigrant congregations in all their variety has probably gained by this country's multiculturalism policy and its intentional multicultural makeup.

The meticulously documented accounts of three ethno-cultural communities making up the "people of faith, people of *jeong*" studied in this volume—Chinese, Korean, and Taiwanese—present case studies of East Asian immigrant groups trying to build viable communities of faith in their specific circumstances. Their stories of facing internal challenges socially, linguistically, and generationally invoke in myself, as a first-generation Chinese Canadian, similar experiences spent in one such Asian Canadian congregation several decades ago in a downtown urban setting. Issues such as how to keep together in the same congregation three generations of members functioning better in either Chinese or English—and in more than one dialect within the Chinese one, how to persuade existing "pillars of the church" to share some of their long-held power and intentionally nurture leadership with younger members, sound familiar indeed. Plus, in my case, the additional challenge of how to make a viable place as a minoritized segment within a major Canadian Protestant denomination—the United Church of Canada—and finding that a simultaneous translation system between English and Chinese—Cantonese in this case—greatly facilitated such an aspiration.

At the same time, the study reminds us vividly of the diversity within even these three Asian communities themselves, and not just in their distinctive histories of emigration to and settlement in Canada so well documented by the respective writers of the historical chapters. Looking, for instance, at language use, a major area of contention between generations, Korean congregations need to deal with only Korean-speaking first-generation immigrants and their younger, mostly English-speaking 1.5 plus subsequent younger members. On top of this major divide, the Chinese and Taiwanese congregations need at the same time to contend with a variety of dialects, thus resulting in a multiple of dialect-specific faith communities such as Cantonese and Mandarin, and Mandarin and Taiwanese. And even though these two similar ethno-cultural communities share the same written language, the scripts they employ for identical Chinese characters are split between a traditional form still used in Taiwan and Hong Kong, and a simplified form used by those who grew up in the People's Republic after that script was introduced post-1949. Such diversity becomes relevant in the recent phenomenon of ever stronger immigration numbers from mainland China, shown by the establishment of Mandarin-speaking "missions" within Anglican parishes, as I learned from an Anglican colleague on the west coast.

In spite of the resonance with my own past experience in a Chinese congregation, I am also realizing that there are other East Asian faith communities that have moved on to what might foreshadow possible scenarios emerging in the future as immigration patterns evolve. For instance, Japanese Canadian faith communities seem to have moved on to a stage where their Japanese-language components are decreasing due to a lack of first-generation migration from Japan, resulting in a predominance of English-speaking subsequent-generation members. Such congregations have begun merging with mainstream Caucasian ones to form predominantly English-speaking congregations that, while monolingual, are ethnically multicultural, as in the current Bayview United Church of Toronto, evolved from Centennial Japanese United Church, itself a merging of the Issei—second-generation—Japanese congregation with coresident "ethnomajority" Centennial United Church earlier on.

Invitation to People of Faith in Canada and Beyond

Thus I find myself asking: to what extent do the findings of this volume apply to faith communities apart from Korean, Chinese, or Taiwanese ones, in or outside the Canadian Diaspora? How can some of the wisdom gleaned from this study benefit—or act as cautions, which is just as important—and be appropriated? Furthermore, which new situations offer other areas for research, or at least suggest possible responses to the questions raised, for which this study has given a template to investigate?

It seems to me that much potential lies in widening the scope of research beyond the three ethno-cultural faith communities identified here, beyond the main Christian Protestant denominations to which these three faith communities belong, and beyond the historical and current contexts of migration that have shaped them. As migration becomes much more global in these and following decades of the twenty-first century, to what extent can the experience of the congregations of these three Asian Canadian immigrant faith communities offer a mirror for emerging migrant Christian groups to Canada, keeping in mind differences in geopolitical and economic realities as well as cultural differences? What we find is that changing global migration patterns are bringing more variety into such "missions" both within the wider Asian faith communities and beyond. From the New Ministries national staff person in my own denomination, for instance, I learn that non-Catholic Christians from South and Southeast Asia, as well as from Africa, have led to the formation of Tamil and Filipino, Ugandan and Ghanaian "missions" as new migrant congregations. While the socio-economic and migration status of these more recently formed faith communities to Canada might differ from those of earlier East Asian groups, all share the attempt to retain heritage languages and cultural and liturgical traditions from their countries of origin. Like their East Asian counterparts, these more recent arrivals often trace their need for leaving home to political circumstances. As these faith communities become more established, it will be interesting to see what impact they might have on current trends to becoming not just multicultural, but "intercultural" churches.

This brings me to another feature shared by these "latecomer" immigrant faith communities with their East Asian counterparts. No matter how "minoritized" these communities are when compared to their Euro-origin compatriots, all non-indigenous Canadians share a "settler" status where Canada's indigenous peoples—First Nations, Metis, and Inuit—are concerned. Along with their more established Euro-origin immigrants, no matter how many generations ago their ancestors first set foot in Canada, these more recent immigrants also participate in Canada's longstanding colonial relationship with its native populations. As Christian faith communities, they are tainted with the "truth" of Canada's oppressive, often abusive, "Indian" residential school system. Even as, like all immigrants, they aspire to become as "Canadian" as possible, they will need to face the shared challenge vis-à-vis the need to work towards "reconciliation" with indigenous communities as part and parcel of their faith journey. The recent work of the Truth and Reconciliation Commission in its final report of 2015 has issued forth a clarion call. Some of the report's ninety-four "Calls to Action" are specifically addressed to those Christian bodies which had helped Canada's federal government implement its sorry history of abuse perpetuated on the students of the residential schools, a history these newer faith communities have unknowingly inherited. How they now pay attention in recognizing their relationship with indigenous communities and move toward reconciliation as an aspect of their faith development will pose a steep learning curve, a learning curve they can try to tackle with earlier immigrant faith communities, including the "people of faith, people of *jeong*" studied in the present volume.

Conclusion: *Qing* 情 and *Xin* 信, Signs of Humanity

One of the gifts the present volume has given me is its very title. It is pushing the "linguistic detective" side of me to search for insights which the two umbrella concepts *qing* 情 and *xin* 信 might unearth. My "sleuthing" is based on the premise that Chinese terms and concepts are made up of individual ideograms or "characters" that combine to yield newer, deeper, and more nuanced meanings. I share my very preliminary findings below for any contribution they might bring or add to your own understanding. I will employ the traditional script for the characters here, though fortunately in these examples all the characters happen to share a common script.

Concepts which the Chinese character *qing* can yield when combined with another character range from *ren qing* 人情, "human feeling," to *gan qing* 感情, "have a feeling for." More colloquially, *you qing* 有情, "have feeling/with feeling," refers to "with compassion," hence, "compassionate": its opposite, *wu qing* 無情, "without feeling or pity," is therefore the term for being "heartless."

In the same way, when combined with other characters, the character *xin* 信, "believe/acknowledge," can create terms with a range of related meanings. In its active verb use, to *xiang xin* 相信 is "to believe something is true." Combined with *xin* 心, "heart," it yields the term for "faith," *xinxin* 信心. Combined with *yang*, "looking up," *xin yang* 信仰 is the Chinese term for—religious—faith, with an emphasis on belief and doctrine. Then there is *xin ren* 信任, "trust," and *xin kao* 信靠, "to depend on." Incidentally, I have always been fascinated by the fact that *mi xin* 迷信, "blindly believing," is the Chinese term for "superstition."

All this makes me realize that, since people of any faith—*xin yang*—share one basic humanity—*ren xing* 人性—they exhibit *ren qing*—human feeling—among themselves, and usually share *gan qing*—feeling, *jeong*—for one another. The challenge going forward, it seems to me, is whether such *jeong/qing* remains confined to communities made up only of people like themselves, or could extend to individuals and communities unlike them. In a world ravaged by pandemics and climate crises, how could people begin to develop *xin ren*—trust—in many and different others, and even come to *xin kao*—depend on—them?

As one member of this universal community of faith, this universal people of *jeong/qing*, I look forward to seeing some of these explorations being taken up in the not-too-distant years ahead.

Greer Anne Wenh-In Ng 吳詠嫣

Emmanuel College Emerita
Victoria University in the University of Toronto

Preface

SOME YEARS AGO, A group of Asian Canadian Christians—the Chinese, Taiwanese, and Korean first-generation congregants of Asian Canadian immigrant churches (ACIC)—began to have conversations about the future of our churches at the Center for Asian Canadian Theology and Ministry at Knox College (i.e., "Asian Center"), University of Toronto, where I served as the director for more than fifteen years. I am currently serving as the director of the Research Center of the Asian Center. Although the Chinese Canadian congregants were among the first Asian groups to arrive in Canada around a hundred years ago, their struggles in the church were similar to those in the Korean and Taiwanese immigrant churches. We found commonalities between these three Asian groups based on shared experiences and comparable immigrant history in Canada; we also discovered that these groups share similar concerns about the present as well as the future of their ethnic-specific churches, such as "What does the future hold for immigrant churches in Canada?" and "Where is God leading these ethnic-specific churches?" Accordingly, they have grown uneasy about the prospect of losing their "home" in Canada. Over the years, we have held numerous discussions about our concerns not only through such public forums at the Asian Center, but also at other informal venues including clergy meetings, small group gatherings of laity, and so on.

This book was born out of our shared concerns for the future of ACIC. The Asian Center decided to respond in a way that has never been done before, conducting a research study on ACIC that offer two or three language services on Sunday. The Asian Center had previously conducted a research study on the Asian Canadian young adults in the Greater Toronto Area (GTA) under the title, "Religious Commitment and Attitudes of Second and 1.5 Asian Canadian Protestant Young Adults in GTA." This study was published under the title "Demythologizing the 'Silent Exodus': Asian-Canadian Protestant Young Adults" in the *Journal of Youth Ministry* in the fall of 2019.

For the purpose of this research, the Asian Center was able to extend the limits of the study to include the whole church, specifically the ethnic-language-speaking and English-speaking congregants and clergy at one of three types of Asian ethnic churches (i.e., Chinese, Korean or Taiwanese) with various denominational affiliations. The focus of this research was to diagnose where we are now, while envisaging our future direction, how we see our future, and where and how we need to move forward.

This book is woven with the real lived experiences and voices of the ethnic Chinese, Taiwanese, and Korean interviewees, and English-speaking interviewees, who were either laity or clergy. It is based on the raw data from interviews we conducted, beginning with why we choose ethnic-specific churches—considering that for our second generation English is the first language—what challenges we face as a church, how we can turn our challenges into opportunities, and what kind of future church we envisage. While reading this book, you may sometimes hear your own voice from the voices of our interviewees; sometimes you may find yourself laughing at what someone said because that is what you have been thinking all along; sometimes you may or may not agree with what others said; and towards the end, you may reach an "Aha" moment for your own church: "Aha, there is a way!"

We hope that the leaders of your church will have an opportunity to pick up this book, and perhaps read it with you before having a discussion on relevant issues and challenges affecting your church. There are a set of discussion and reflection questions after each chapter, excluding church history chapters, which you may find helpful. We sincerely hope that this book will prove helpful to Asian Canadian churches in navigating their future directions, and serve as a practical guide as they find the way God is leading each church to be.

Principal Editor

Nam Soon Song

Acknowledgements

NOTHING COMES AUTOMATICALLY BY itself. All things come from visible and invisible efforts, minds, and contributions. The first book on Asian Canadian (immigrant) churches was born thanks to many generous people supporting financially, psychologically, and spiritually in faith, and with their various gifts and talents.

First, we gratefully acknowledge the funding support by Louisville Institute Project Grant for Researchers, which made this research possible. Your generous grant bore fruits in the form of this book. We deeply appreciate your generosity that will surely make a difference in the future of Asian Christian churches in North America.

Second, we recognize Knox College, particularly Principal Rev. and Dr. John Vissers and Principal Emeritus Rev. and Dr. Dorcas Gordon. Your enthusiasm, words of encouragement, and generous financial support for our research helped bring this book to life. We express our sincere appreciation to many friends and colleagues at Knox College, who have shown their enthusiasm and interest in this research on Asian Canadian churches. From the beginning of this project, all of you have been a part of our team.

Third, we recognize the council members of the Center for Asian Canadian Theology and Ministry for walking with us on this project, sharing our concerns, supporting financially and emotionally, and waiting for the book to be born. We recognize our shard jeong (Qing) as friends. Thank you for being patient with us.

Fourth, we thank the research participants, both lay and clergy, for making yourselves available for the interview, sharing your thoughts and concerns candidly, and selflessly loving Asian Canadian churches.

Fifth, we recognize and appreciate all of our friends and individual colleagues, who have been supportive in many ways, and for helping us stay motivated until the end. We especially appreciate that Dr. and Rev. Greer Anne Wenh-In Ng, Professor emeritus at Emmanuel College, agreed to write the foreword to this book; Dr. and Rev. Alan Lai, who contributed to this book with a chapter on the Chinese Canadian church history; and Rev. Luis Liang, who coauthored a chapter on the Taiwanese Canadian church history with Dr. Ben Kuo. I appreciate the coeditors of this book, Prof. and Dr. Ben Kuo, Rev. In Kee Kim, and Dr. Dong-Ha Kim, who worked as a team from the beginning to the end, interviewing, writing, and editing chapters as a gift to the Center for Asian Canadian Theology and Ministry and for our Asian Canadian Churches (any profit from this book will be given to the Center for Asian Canadian Theology and Ministry at Knox College). We also want to thank Rev. Wes Chang, who interviewed Mandarin and Taiwanese speaking interviewees and transcribed the recordings word by word; Sarah Yoo, one of our PhD candidates at Knox College, University of Toronto, who transcribed some interview materials. We offer our thanks to othe anonymous interviewers and transcribers who do not wish to be named. We are grateful to Lorna Hutchison, who read and edited some of our manuscripts; Rev. Simon Park, who read manuscripts from the second-generation perspective, and for making valuable input; and last but not least, Eun Ju Chung, one of our PhD candidates at Knox College, University of Toronto, who walked with us from the very beginning to the end, making sure everything is in order with our research and our book, such as editing and formatting chapters, researching some data, and analyzing demographics. Words cannot describe how much you have done for this book. Thank you very much.

It would not be possible to count all the visible and invisible hands that have accompanied and supported us on this journey. We would like to take this opportunity to thank each and every one of you. We glorify God who is the source of life!

Principal Editor

Nam Soon Song

Abbreviations

ACIC	Asian Canadian Immigrant Churches
AD	Anno Dominu (in the year of the Lord)
am	ante meridiem (before noon)
aka	as known as
CBC	Canadian-born Chinese
CCM	Contemporary Christian Music
CM	Chinese Ministry
1 Cor	first book of Corinthians (Scripture)
CPC	Chinese Presbyterian Church
EM	English Ministry
Eph	book of Ephesians (Scripture)
etc.	et cetera (and)
FCCT	Formosan Christian Church in Toronto
FGCCT	Formosan Grace Christian Church in Toronto
Gal	book of Galatians (Scripture)
GTA	Greater Toronto Area
i.e.	id est (this is)
KM	Korean Ministry
N.B.	nota bene (note well)
NLGCT	New Life Gospel Church in Toronto
NRSV	New Revised Standard Version (Bible version)
PCC	The Presbyterian Church in Canada
PhD	Doctor of Philosophy

QT	Quiet Time
Rev.	The Reverend
Rev	book of Revelation (Scripture)
Rom	book of Romans (Scripture)
TCTPC	Toronto Central Taiwanese Presbyterian Church
TFCCFHL	Toronto Formosan Christian Church in Faith, Hope and Love
TFPC	Toronto Formosan Presbyterian Church
TJGCCT	Taiwan Justice and Grace Christian Church in Toronto
TM	Taiwanese Ministry
TTMPC	Toronto Trinity Mandarin Presbyterian Church
TUCT	Taiwanese United Church in Toronto
U.S.	United States
vs.	versus

Introduction

WHY DO ASIAN CANADIAN immigrant church congregants keep returning to our ethnic-specific churches, sometimes driving several tens or even a hundred plus miles to do so? On their way they might pass many other churches, even those of same denomination, yet they keep doing this every Sunday for decades after they have moved far away, perhaps. Let us consider Biming's ministry story:[1]

> No matter what happens on Sunday they would come to church, even under rainstorms or blizzards. They are so loyal to this church. They love the church so much, which means they love God so much . . . This church is known for keeping the loyalty they have for their faith, for fostering the neighbourly love they have for one another.

It is indeed a strong faith that is represented by Asian Canadian congregants: How strongly we trust in God, and how loyal we are to God. Faith is our shelter in this strange land, and God was and is our refuge from the hardship we experience as ethnic immigrants in a land so different from where we have come from.

Given that for second- and third-generation congregants of Asian Canadian immigrant churches, English is their first language, why do they choose to stay in our ethnic churches instead of worshiping in a fully English-speaking "Canadian" church? Ann and Susan tell their stories, explaining why they stay in our ethnic-specific churches.

> At church it's easier to connect with people just because, well, like you're the same ethnicity and there's already a sense of closeness. I feel it's easier to connect to people of the same

---

1. All names of interviewees and churches have been changed to ensure their anonymity. We assigned English names for the second-generation interviewees and ethnic-specific names to ethnic Asian language interviewees.

ethnic culture because you have the same ethnic values, more or less and like.

I think even if I were to switch churches, like if I were to switch churches when you get married or whatever, I think I would still choose a Korean church, just cause like there's something, I don't know what it is. I can't really put my finger on it, but there's something familiar and core to me that I want to keep.

We discern *jeong* in what Ann says: "a sense of closeness I feel," and in Susan's words, "there's something . . . something familiar and core." *Jeong* (*qing*)[2] can be found in these words: Something the interviewees can't put a finger on, but something nevertheless core to them; that ease of being connected and of already possessing a sense of closeness. We sense the flow of jeong, from not only these stories, but also from all other stories we heard. *Qing* (情), the Chinese character, is more or less equivalent of *jeong*; literally it means a "beautiful heart." *Jeong* is like a stream of water, flowing from one person to another, particularly amongst the people of same ethnicity, or those living in the same nation or ethnic enclaves. It is because of *jeong* that even the second- and third-generation Asian Canadian congregants remain in our respective ethnic-specific churches.

From all the stories we heard during our interviews, we were able to sense the flow of these two distinctive elements—faith and *jeong* (*qing*)—characterizing what Asian Canadian immigrant churches are and who Asian Canadian Christians are.

In this book we use "faith" in the sense of a gift from God, meaning our trust in and loyalty to God. The word "*jeong* (Korean phonetic), and *qing* (Chinese and Taiwanese phonetic)" are both impossible to replicate in English, as they carry unique Asian cultural emotions including a feeling of connectedness, attachment, and togetherness, all of which lead to a sense of closeness and belonging. It is an associated feeling of compassion, a natural tendency of caring for others, and a feeling of warmth, affection, solidarity, and relationality. Because of *jeong* and faith, we stay in our own ethnic-specific churches, even in the face of challenges and difficulties. Because of *jeong*, we come back to our Asian immigrant churches even if we leave for a while after hurtful experiences. Because of *jeong*, we sense a feeling of warmth only at certain ethnic-specific churches. Because of *jeong*, we feel part of a larger Asian community. And because of *jeong*, we feel a sense of belonging to our ethnic-specific churches that stand by with us. Drawing on these two terms, faith and *jeong* (*qing*), this book presents

2. *Jeong* or *jung* is a Korean word, *qing* is a Chinese word, which comes originally from the Chinese 情.

a clear narrative of the Asian Immigrant churches in Canada—a story that has never been written before.

Asian Canadian Immigrant Churches (ACIC) have played a significant role in immigrant history in Canada, with the Chinese (over one hundred years), Taiwanese, and Korean immigrant churches (over fifty years),[3] in particular, functioning not only as spiritual homes, but also as social, cultural, and psychological homes for these ethnic Asian communities. The church is the so-called "home away from home," and the "home for homeless at home." Over the last two decades, ACIC have witnessed rapid demographic changes to their communities and congregants. This has resulted in many having to conduct separate services with different languages so that we might accommodate the needs of first- and second-generation members respectively: typically a service in the mother tongue for the benefit of the first generation and in the English language for the second- and third-generation congregants and beyond. That is, two or more language services with members of varying generational statuses are held weekly under the same roof of a single Asian ethnic immigrant church.

In fact, the demographics of Asian Canadian immigrants have switched in recent decades. There are now fewer newly arrived and first-generation immigrants, and increasingly more of the second or third generation within Asian communities. The population of the first-generation congregants has thus either stagnated or declined in ACIC in recent years. Furthermore, the populations of the second-generation congregants in these same churches are not increasing on par with the growth of this generation group nationally, despite the efforts by these churches to offer services in English for second-generation and beyond members. This evolving demographic shift, though gradual, has and will continue to have momentous impact on ACIC and our congregants in the present and into the future.

Henceforth, ACIC are faced with a crucial, emerging concern about whether or not our churches will remain "Asian" or "immigrant" in the decades to come. There is currently not much known about how our churches are affected by and responding to these critical sociodemographic changes. ACIC have gone through many significant immigrant experiences in Canada, and yet their experiences have not been critically assessed, told,

---

3. According to Anthony B. Chan, "In 1858, Chinese immigrants began arriving in the Fraser River valley from San Francisco, as gold prospectors. Barkerville, British Columbia, became the first Chinese community in Canada." See Chan, "Chinese Canadians," para. 4.

An official Chinese immigrant church, the Chinese Methodist Church, was established on Dupont St., Vancouver in 1889. See "Church Records: Methodist," para. 2.

Koreans and Taiwanese began to immigrate to Canada after the reforms of the Canadian Immigration Act of 1966.

and documented over this long history. Our unique experiences need to be critically addressed, not only sociologically and psychologically, but also theologically and spiritually. Ministry can only be implemented effectively when the context of the congregation is understood fully and critically. Doing general ministry is not enough; for ministry to be effective, it has to be specific, and address the issues of the people in a particular context. Asian Canadian immigrant churches need to diagnose this particular context by listening to the stories of congregants and clergy, in order to engage in effective and relevant ministries.

As a new response to the current situation of ACIC, the Research Team of the Centre for Asian Canadian Theology and Ministry conducted qualitative research that included lay and clergy, men and women from both Asian ethnic and English-speaking congregants in the Greater Toronto Area (GTA). The research included interviews with thirty laypeople and twenty members of the clergy, aged between twenty and eighty, from the Chinese, Taiwanese, and Korean churches across the GTA. The following question was at the core of the research: "What are the opportunities and challenges for Asian Canadian Immigrant churches (ACIC) that are simultaneously housing first and second generation congregants in two separate language services?" Interviewees were recruited from a variety of churches from each of the target ethnic groups, based on diverse church sizes, denominations, and their location in the GTA. The main purpose of the study was to help Asian Canadian immigrant churches discern future pathways and identify critical implications for both generations in ACIC and Asian Canadian churches, respectively.

Coming out of the research, this present book has four parts, each consisting of a story: The past, present, and future stories of Asian immigrant churches in Canada, plus the implications for better stories. Part I, the first story as the past story, is a brief history of the Chinese, Taiwanese, and Korean churches. How did the Asian immigrant churches arrive at this point in Canada, where we have two or more services under the same roof? Each history is written by each respective ethnic church minister: The Chinese immigrant history is by Alan Lai, minister at South Arm United Church, Richmond, British Columbia; the Taiwanese immigrant church history is coauthored by Luis Liang, minister at Formosan Grace Christian Church in Toronto, Ontario, and Ben C. H. Kuo, a professor of University of Windor; while the Korean immigrant church history is by In Kee Kim, minister at St. Timothy's Presbyterian Church in Toronto, Ontario. Part II, the second story as the present story, concerning people of faith, and people of *jeong*, is contemporary immigrant church stories told in the voices of the people who were interviewed—both lay and clergy. It is the descriptive story of what is currently happening in Asian immigrant churches: their presence, characteristics, advantages, and the challenges they face. Part III, the third story, is the descriptive predictions concerning the future of Asian Canadian immigrant churches as told by interviewees. What future do they envisage for the church? What is their unique vision of the church twenty-five years from today? Part VI, the fourth story, aims at better stories in the future, and here the original research team members respond to the churches of today for tomorrow, under four separate themes: how to become one unified church, by In Kee Kim; how to enhance communication between people of different languages, generations, and cultures, by Ben Kuo; how to empower English ministry leaders, by Dong-Ha Kim; and how to move towards a multicultural church, by Nam Soon Song.

This book is a collaborative effort between local churches and academia. The coeditors and contributors are currently ministers of the church with long-term experience, and current professors in theological seminaries and a general university. The Rev. In Kee Kim weaves his ministry experience with the research findings, drawing out implications for churches from a ministerial perspective. Professor Ben Kuo, as clinical psychology professor at the University of Windsor, specializes in quantitative and qualitative research with ethnically and culturally diverse populations in Canada, Asia, and around the world. Here he provides valuable Taiwanese, Chinese, and crosscultural perspectives in applying the research findings about communication to different cultures. Being of 1.5 Korean descent and a trained theologian, Professor Dong-Ha Kim contributes to this book by conceptualizing findings from a theological and spiritual perspective and promotes empowerment of English ministry leaders. As the chief editor, I, Nam Soon Song, write the current and future stories of Asian churches based on these interviews. I also draw out the practical implications for moving towards a multicultural church by weaving in my own multicultural church experiences.

Born out of qualitative research, this book offers an opportunity for ACIC to engage with each other in critical dialogue, reflection, and self-examination about their present demographic, social, cultural, and spiritual realities, and to further envision their future at a practical level. This unique book will benefit other ethnic immigrant churches in Canada and the United States that concurrently house two or more language services for diverse generation groups. ACIC's unique experiences will shed critical light on Asian churches or immigrant churches in North America at large. Stories of ACIC's experiences will help others identify the issues immigrant churches face and how these might be practically resolved in the present. They also point to what immigrant churches might look like in the future. This book can therefore benefit Canadian/US churches generally, by helping them to envisage their future in new ways. Not only various recently-founded immigrant churches, but also long-time settler churches in North America can learn how to accommodate young people who, as a result of rapid social change, are now culturally different. Although Asian Canadian churches struggle with cultural and generational differences along with language differences between their ethnic and English language congregants, they still have young people in the church. This book will therefore also help non-Asian churches learn how to bring young people back through their doors.

While reading the stories of both generations of lay and clergy folk, an image came to my mind—that of the storeroom key, which was common in post-war Korea. When I was a child, almost every house in the village had a storeroom for all the crops, vegetables, and fruits the whole family would then live on. The contents of such storerooms would sustain families for an entire year, particularly through long cold winters, so managing this room-keeping key was critical for whole family. In most families, the mother was the key-bearer. After bringing in a new daughter-in-law, the mother-in-law would retain the key to the storeroom for a period. She would wait for the right time to turn it over to the new daughter-in-law. A wise mother-in-law would turn the key over at just the right time, which would be determined by taking internal family matters into account. From that point on, the mother-in-law would take a back-seat and become an adviser to her daughter-in-law, who was at that point given responsibility for the whole household. From this image I grappled with the following question: When will it be the right time for Asian immigrant churches in Canada to turn over their keys to the English ministry? I hope this book helps each Asian immigrant church discern the right time to do so.

Part I
Past Story

1

A Brief History of the Chinese Immigrant Church in Canada

Alan Ka Lun Lai

Imagine there was no shortage of low-wages workers in Canada to build the Canadian railway, no gold was ever discovered in the Fraser Valley and California, and there was no economic hardship in southern China before the turn of the twentieth century. If that were the case, the history of Chinese in Canada would have a different story to tell. Based on what we know, the earliest Chinese came with the simplest goal of survival not only for themselves, but for their starving families back home. Little did those people know at the time of their departure, they may never return. On the other side of the ocean, the country now called Canada was not ready to receive them as permanent citizens either. Crossing the Pacific Ocean was no less significant for both sides of the Pacific.

In this chapter, I provide a brief retelling of Chinese in Canada and to get a glimpse of the growth of Chinese Canadian churches. I recount important historic events such as building the national railway, the discriminatory experiences of the early Chinese settlers, and the subsequent immigration waves in the post-war period. These are the key events that form the background of how the Chinese settled in Canada. This background also provides a social fabric that helps to explain the challenges and concerns facing Chinese congregations in Canada today. The chapter's closing focus is on how the growing needs of second and subsequent generations of Canadian-born Chinese (aka. CBC) challenges congregational life.

Chinese in Canada: A Brief Migration History

Chinese started coming to Canada in 1858; with large numbers coming between 1881 and 1885.[1] Several factors triggered their coming: The domestic economic hardship at home, the discovery of gold in California, and the consequent gold rush in the Fraser Valley of British Columbia. Behind the migration there was a larger historical context. The Qing dynasty had been ruling China since 1644. In 1838, China suddenly found herself witnessing the domination of Western powers, especially when China lost to the British in the Opium War (1839–42). China was forced to sign the Treaty of Nanjing in 1842, which led to Hong Kong Island being conceded to the British; in addition, China was forced to open up five coastal ports for trade. Subsequently, between 1838 and 1990, British, France, Germany, Austria, Japan, the United States, Italy, and Russia fought in a series of wars in China and succeeded in obtaining concessions from the weak Qing government. China became a huge and attractive market to the European capitalists.

About the same time, domestically, China suffered declining productivity in the farming sectors. This troubling fact multiplied when natural disasters such as floods and famines hit. At the time when Chinese feudal systems were still intact, natural calamities made the lives of peasants miserable when absentee landlords controlled much of the profits. The incredible hardship farmers faced explains why some southern Chinese thought of venturing abroad to seek a better life, despite the fact that the imperial state had imposed a stiff penalty when leaving the empire without a special permit.[2] Many coastal provinces of Guangdong and Fujian, due to their proximity to the sea, made it easier for the peasants to emigrate. Around 1884 to 1885, there was an estimate that about 23 percent of the Chinese in British Columbia originated from Toishan. Many of these Chinese workers came via a coolie trade system that involved European ships with the assistance of Chinese middlemen. These commercial companies would pay the passage ticket for and a small amount of money to the prospective emigrant, who in return would accept employment arranged by the company, with a portion of monthly wage being deducted.[3] This system of contract labor was widely used in the United States at the time to procure Chinese workers whereby they shipped large numbers of Chinese workers to America, West Indies, and South Pacific islands. Hong Kong and Macao, being controlled by the British and Portuguese respectively, became

1. Li, *Chinese in Canada*, 16.
2. Li, *Chinese in Canada*, 19.
3. Li, *Chinese in Canada*, 21.

crucial ports for such transports. An estimation of 89 percent of Chinese workers were shipped from these two cities.[4]

Early Chinese came to Canada to work in mining, salmon canning industries, and as cheap laborers to build the Canadian Pacific Railway. Others came to search for gold in the Fraser Valley in British Columbia. These Chinese lived in small ghettoes in Victoria, Vancouver, and Toronto, and were scattered somewhere in between. These laborers usually came from the poorer sector of southern Chinese society and often with no knowledge of English at all. These people were sometimes called *sojourners*, because they were not *immigrants* in the way we understand the social phenomenon of "migration" today; they did not intend to settle; instead, they came with a dream of returning home rich.[5] However, their dreams were seldom realized. Their financial situations were so precarious that most of them ended up staying as unintended permanent residents.

Around 1860, the number of Chinese populations in Vancouver Island and the mainland of British Columbia was about four thousand. During the heydays of building the national railway, there were about sixteen thousand between 1881 and 1884.[6] After the railroad was completed, these Chinese sojourners moved eastward to the prairies, Ontario, and Quebec to look for work. Some opened restaurants, laundries, and developed vegetable farms.[7] One can imagine how the Canadian economy was stagnant in the early twentieth century; agitation against Chinese laborers became severe.[8] Since Chinese laborers would accept lower wage for menial tasks, they were seen as competitors in the struggling job market. In addition, utilitarian attitudes among Western industrialists depicted Chinese as useful laborers but undesirable citizens. Anti-oriental sentiment was high. From 1884 to 1923, the British Columbia legislature passed numerous bills restricting the political and social rights of Chinese.[9] To prevent more Chinese from coming, the federal government imposed a head tax of fifty dollars, which was later raised to five hundred dollars in 1903.[10] Racist names such as *Chinamen* and *Stream engine* were imposed onto these settlers. Seeing that none of these maneuvers

---

4. Li, *Chinese in Canada*, 20.
5. Yang, *Chinese Christians in America*, 29.
6. Ye, "Protestant Missionary Work," 8.
7. Ye, "Protestant Missionary Work," 9.
8. Li, *Chinese in Canada*, 24.
9. Li, *Chinese in Canada*, 32.
10. Wang, "Organised Protestant Missions," 697.

worked, the Canadian Immigration Act was passed in 1923 to prevent "Orientals" from entering Canada. This act was not repealed until 1947.[11]

More favorable social conditions began to emerge in 1965 when Canada amended its immigration laws. Immigration acts were actually repealed right after World War II, but it was not until 1965 when a further amendment of the immigration laws allowed the expansion of migration which led to an influx of family members and relatives.[12] Most of the Chinese immigrants at this time were skilled workers or international students in their prime working years, between the age of fifteen and thirty-four, and many of them intended to stay as permanent residents. Some immigrants were family members of earlier immigrants. This was also the period when the Civil Rights movement in the United States began to take shape. Because of the influx of first-generation immigrants, the concerns over intergeneration gaps and Chinese identities became important issues.[13]

In 1985 and onward, another wave of Chinese immigration occurred; this time, they came as entrepreneurs and investors. During that time, most of these Chinese immigrants were Chinese from Hong Kong, but some also came from Taiwan and Singapore. These immigrants were mostly well-educated and cosmopolitan people who had substantial amounts of capital. As professionals and skilled workers, they were able to establish themselves in middle-class neighborhoods and the suburbs in Canada. Chinatowns, which were mostly established years ago, used to be places of commerce and sites for tourists; they later became less significant for the daily life of these new immigrants. The significance of Chinatown for these professionals diminished as they built Chinese infrastructure in suburbs, as in the case of Richmond in Vancouver, and Scarborough in Toronto. In the years leading up to 1997, when British-held Hong Kong was to be handed over to Mainland China, the uncertainty due to the fear of Communist China caused many Hong Kong Chinese to migrate to Western countries. An estimated 260,000 Hong Kong residents migrated to Canada between 1980 and 1989.[14]

Before the turn of the twenty-first century, which coincided with an economic boom in Asia, many Hong Kong Chinese were able to establish themselves in the wealthy middle-class strata of Canadian society. In Vancouver, the term *monster houses* refers to the phenomenon of Asian immigrants building mansion-style houses in prestigious neighborhoods

---

11. Li, *Chinese in Canada*, 89.
12. Li, *Chinese in Canada*, 93.
13. See Ng, "Pacific-Asian North American," 195.
14. See Lai et al., "Unrecognized Religion," 89–90.

that were not in harmony with traditional Canadian-style houses. In the late 1990s, there was a general perception in Vancouver that the wealthy Hong Kong buyers were the chief cause of skyrocketing real estate prices and a radical change in the architecture of houses.[15] Sociologist Peter Li argues that "the 'monster houses' controversy illustrates how a negative racial image of the Chinese was socially constructed in the contemporary context, and how the Chinese were being stigmatized as wealthy foreigners who had little regard for the aesthetic values and traditional life-style of Canada."[16] The massive influx of well-to-do immigrants from Hong Kong in this period created another wave of anti-Asian sentiments. It seems a similar situation is currently repeating as contemporary housing markets in Vancouver and Toronto are skyrocketing; except this time, the sentiments are imposed onto mainland Chinese buyers.

For the past ten years or more, with the economic boom of Mainland China, a significant number of Chinese from China has resettled in Canada. Since 2000, China has become one of the fastest economies in the globe. One may speculate that because of the country's constant contact with the West due to its economic open-door policy, Western culture and lifestyle are increasingly popular.

The Birth of Chinese Immigrant Churches in Canada

In the late nineteenth and early twentieth century, anti-Chinese immigrants' social sentiments from the dominant English-speaking Canadian was high. Through popular literature, public speeches, and even religious sermons, there have been many efforts to keep Chinese immigrants out of the social and economic life of Canadian society.[17] But not all Canadians exhibited discrimination toward Chinese. Some English-speaking Christians realized that these Chinese immigrants would stay in the country permanently, and soon found them favorable in their newfound missions. To these Caucasian Christians, they thought that Christianizing Chinese was the best way to solve the "Chinese problem." Mainline Protestant denominations such as Methodists began to offer English as a Second Language (ESL) classes for Chinese and evangelistic work among Chinese communities.[18] The Methodist Church was among the first to organize mission work for Chinese in 1885, followed by the Presbyterians in 1892, and the Anglicans in 1917. However, in this

15. Li, *Chinese in Canada*, 148.
16. Li, *Chinese in Canada*, 149.
17. Wang, "Organised Protestant Missions," 692.
18. Wang, "Organised Protestant Missions," 692.

period, missionary efforts to convert Chinese by local churches were not particularly successful. Churches functioned more as community centers for new immigrants. They were places where English language classes were held for adults, and cultural heritage classes were provided for children. Social services were accessed through the churches.[19]

In the case of the Methodist's mission to the Chinese in Victoria, a Presbyterian missionary's son, John E. Gardiner, was particularly significant in reaching out to the Chinese. Gardiner was born in China, and he could speak Cantonese fluently. In a trip where he traveled from San Francisco to Victoria to be an interpreter for a Chinese trial, it was Gardiner's first time becoming knowledgeable about the social conditions where Chinese workers lived. After a lack of success trying on his own, Gardiner was able to persuade the Methodist church to open a Chinese mission school, where English language classes, Bible study classes, and religious services were offered. This mission was proven to be successful as there were an estimated six to seven hundred people present at one of the worship services.[20] Subsequent missions were set up in Vancouver and other British Columbia cities with the help of Chan Sing Kai. Chan was born to a Christian family in Hong Kong, and his father was instrumental in translating the Bible into Chinese. Chan later became the first Chinese ordained minister of the Methodist Church of Canada.[21] By 1923, the Methodist Church had missions set up in almost every community in Canada.[22]

Gardiner's ability to speak Cantonese was a key factor in Methodist's mission to Chinese in Victoria and Vancouver. Seeing the positive outcome of that mission, the Presbyterians appointed Alexander B. Winchester as their first missionary to reach out to the Chinese immigrants.[23] Prior to this mission, Winchester had worked in China for a number of years. Winchester knew the Chinese language, but it was not Cantonese. That proved to be a significant language factor at the time deciding whether the mission was a success or failure. Winchester later went to Canton to learn the language. On his return, Winchester brought with him Ng Mon Hing, a Chinese assistant. Ng was a graduate of the American Presbyterian Theological School in Canton, and had worked among Chinese before coming to Canada. Ng played an important role in attracting Chinese immigrants to churches in

19. Yang, *Chinese Christians in America*, 38.
20. Wang, "Organised Protestant Missions," 694.
21. Wang, "Organised Protestant Missions," 605.
22. Wang, "Organised Protestant Missions," 702.
23. Wang, "Organised Protestant Missions," 704.

Victoria, Vancouver, and Toronto during his twenty-five years of tenure as a minister of the Presbyterian Church.[24]

In the decades leading toward the Second World War, Chinese church membership began to decline when new waves of anti-Chinese agitation started in the early twentieth century.[25] The social environment at this time was unfavorable for Chinese mission. Missionaries had a hard time convincing Chinese to convert to Christianity, a faith that represented the core values of the country, when many English-speaking considered Chinese as superstitious and ignorant. In 1913, affected by the anti-Chinese sentiment, a group of about thirty Chinese Christians broke away from a Presbyterian mission in Vancouver, and established their own independent congregation, the Christ Church of China.[26] Lack of mutual trust made mission almost impossible. Many missionaries of the time believed that the purpose of the mission was to challenge the discriminatory attitude toward Chinese.

Growth of Chinese Immigrant Churches in Canada

In the early sixties, Chinese congregations experienced steady growth and development as a favorable political environment emerged when the Canadian government made multiculturalism and immigration more favorable in 1967. As pointed out by Chung-Yan Chan's work, Canadian Baptists had significant mission work among Chinese immigrants even back in the sixties.[27] The mission at the time can be characterized by two major streams: to develop Chinese ministry within the English-speaking churches and independent Chinese congregations. The first is associated with the Baptist Union of Western Canada and the Fellowship of Evangelical Baptist, where the second is associated with the Canadian Convention of Southern Baptist.[28] Many congregations offered ESL classes to immigrants, and much efforts were made to integrate Chinese-speaking and English-speaking people in the same worship service. Ward Memorial Baptist Church and Marpole Baptist Church in Vancouver belong to this type of mission. A vision of a "House of Prayer for All Nations" prompted Ward Memorial Church to begin a Chinese ministry, although only about ten people attended the

---

24. Wang, "Organised Protestant Missions," 794.
25. Wang, "Organised Protestant Missions," 697.
26. Wang, "Organised Protestant Missions," 712.
27. Chan, "Recovering a Missing Trail," 20–35.
28. Chan, "Recovering a Missing Trail," 23.

service.²⁹ For those who came, they were new immigrants trying to blend into the Canadian mainstream society.

In the 1960s, activities of Chinese congregations exceeded that of regular Sunday worship, Bible study class, and ESL classes. The steady growing of church attendance with the increased number of Canadian-born Chinese allowed churches to offer a number of outreach initiatives such as Chinese language school, sport ministries, and daycare services. As in the case of Toronto Chinese United Church, which was formed in 1918, the congregation established a Chinese language school in 1959. Later renamed T. H. Chan Memorial Chinese School in 1988, the school was aimed at educating young local-born Chinese in the traditional Chinese cultures and languages. Subsequently, mathematics tutorial classes were added to meet the demand of Chinese parents. When the congregation relocated to Scarborough in 1986, the congregation established a nonprofit daycare center; and with the addition of a new gym, the church tried out several sport outreach ministries such as badminton and floor hockey. The social dimensions of community life took shape.³⁰

As in the case of the Chinese Presbyterian Church (CPC), one example was to organize a Chinese mission in Toronto in 1903, which involved Rev. Moon Hing Ng coming from Vancouver to be the minister of this mission. Thus, that was the beginning of the Toronto Chinese Presbyterian Church. Upon graduating from Toronto Bile College, Rev. Ng's successor Rev. Ma started working with the CPC with a desire to reach out to young Chinese boys and men. Ma's idea of organizing Bible study classes, English languages classes, and dinner events were meant to keep these men away from the Mah Jong gambling houses.³¹

The Chinese population in Toronto had grown from two thousand in 1916 to more than six thousand in 1956; yet, the number of ethnic recreational programs for Canadian-born Chinese was lacking. Seeing the need to do more in terms of outreach, Elder William Wong and Deaconess Margaret Near started a Boys and Girls Club on Saturday morning; that was an add-on to their involvement of teaching Chinese language school every weeknight from 5:00 to 7:00 pm. Some of the Canadian-born teenagers who lived near the church on Beverly Street were given church keys so they could drop in during the week to do homework or just hang out. As mentioned before, the community life of Chinese congregations was

---

29. Chan, "Recovering a Missing Trail," 23.
30. Toronto Chinese Church 1918–2018 Centennial Yearbook, 36.
31. Yu, *Chinese Presbyterian Church 100th Anniversary*, 14.

taking shape. The congregation continued to grow with the coming of Rev. Thomas Ng from Chicago in 1987.[32]

From around the late seventies until the mid-eighties, a large number of international students from Hong Kong played a significant role in the development of Chinese congregations in Canada. Chinese people value education as one of the key paths leading toward success in life. But back in the eighties, Hong Kong had only two universities, Hong Kong University and the Chinese University of Hong Kong. Competition was severe, and only a small number of highly achieved applicants were admitted. The majority of students either attended the two-years trading colleges or needed to find work. Some determined folks from financially capable families went overseas as a viable option. Many Chinese Canadian local churches saw this as the golden opportunity to evangelize; it was not uncommon to find many Chinese congregations in Canada that had a large number of international students attending Friday night fellowship groups, and Sunday worship services. Logos Chinese Baptist Church in Toronto, for example, had a significant number of international students coming from Hong Kong. Although many of the students came with the goal to earn university degrees with no plan to apply for immigration, many congregations welcomed them as Logos Chinese Baptist Church did. These churches provided them with spiritual homes and solid Bible knowledge training. Such visionary acts eventually empowered those students to serve churches after they returned to Hong Kong. With the uncertainty regarding the future of Hong Kong growing in the late eighties, some of these well-trained students stayed and became permanent residents after graduation. These Christians were the solid base for future church development in Canada.

In the late 1980s, Canada saw a large number of Chinese immigrants coming from Hong Kong. This time it was no longer just students who came, but whole families were emigrating. This massive immigration scene was the result of the changeover of the British-ruled Hong Kong back to China. This may have been the defining factor in stimulating the rapid growth in Chinese churches in Canada. Similar rapid growth of Chinese churches was also observed in the United States, Great Britain, and Australia. With the 1989 Tiananmen Square student crackdown by the Chinese Communist government still vivid in their memories, some financially well-to-do Hong Kong people decided to go abroad for a more stable life.

The early nineties were the golden time to do church planting. Many Christian denominations created outreach strategies for the Chinese immigrants. New congregations were formed every year with gratifying results.

---

32. Yu, *Chinese Presbyterian Church 100th Anniversary*, 18

Many of these immigrants were mature lay Christians who were able to lead congregations. While formerly Chinese immigrants who attended Baptist integrating churches were minorities in those congregations, the huge numbers of new Chinese immigrants allowed them to build their own mega ethnic congregations. Some of the largest Chinese Baptist congregations such as Vancouver Chinese Baptist Church, Surrey Chinese Baptist Church, and Coquitlam Chinese Baptist Church in Port Coquitlam, British Columbia remain strong in financial and human resources. Regular weekly activities such as Sunday worship, Sunday school for both children and adults, fellowship groups, retreats, and prayer meetings are offered.[33]

The Christian and Missionary Alliance was one of the most outreach-minded Christian denominations to reach out to Chinese immigrants. With this denomination's strong emphasis on mission and evangelism, much effort had been put to articulating a missional theology for doing mission to the diaspora.[34] Ethnic associations such as the Canadian Chinese Alliance Churches Association were formed to further strategize outreach. Denominational theological schools such as the formerly named Canadian Theological Seminary and Canadian Bible College in Regina, Saskatchewan developed a Center for Chinese Studies, and later it evolved into the Center for Inter-Cultural Studies. However, it is unfortunately now defunct. This shows how the denomination envisioned the fabric of Canadian urban centers would be changed. Such awareness allowed healthy mission to be developed and materialized.

The rapid growth of Chinese churches in Canada is not an accident. It was the result of intentional, studied, and strategized mission to develop Chinese churches. In 2006, researcher Jing Ye published a paper detailing the early mission work among Chinese in the Toronto area and reported that there are 150 Chinese Christian churches in the Greater Toronto Area and over 350 in Canada.[35] She suggests that Christianity has become the most practiced religion among Chinese in Canada. Over the recent years, Cantonese-speaking congregations experienced stagnation in terms of membership numbers as the majority of newcomers are from mainland China. Some churches added Mandarin interpretation and social groups as a result. Now, with mainland Chinese coming to Canada in such great force, Mandarin-speaking congregations have been growing rapidly for the past ten years. However, with the 2019 pro-democracy crisis in Hong Kong, many predict another immigration wave is on the way. If it materializes,

---

33. Chan, "Recovering a Missing Trail," 27.
34. Tira, "Local Church and Mission," 5.
35. Ye, "Protestant Missionary Work," 6.

Cantonese-speaking congregations will have a rebirth. This reinforces the fact we already know: unstable domestic social environment contributes to the growth and development of Chinese communities in Canada.

Social Roles of Chinese Immigrant Churches in Canada

Many first-generation Chinese Canadians felt that they were marginalized because they carried different cultural values and norms. As a result, they tried hard to keep their cultures and languages. As members of visible minorities, their visible *racial uniform* hindered them from being fully assimilated in the dominant society. No matter how good their English abilities were and how much they identified themselves as Canadians, first-generation Chinese immigrants were often seen as *others*. At the same time, they often experienced rejection in their communities of origin for being too Westernized. Chinese Canadians were caught *in-between* two worlds. As the late Professor Jung Young Lee says, "To be in-between two worlds mean to be fully in neither. The marginal person who is placed between this two-world boundary feels like a non-being."[36]

There were additional internal factors. The "1.5 generation" (those who came to North America at very young age) posed intergenerational issues. Having grown up mostly in Canada, the 1.5 generation shared the burdens of their parents, but not the traumatic experiences. Such an intergenerational gap contributed to a sense of estrangement among the one-point-five generation not only from the dominant Canadian culture, but also from their Chinese families and heritage.[37] Also, because of the high rate of influx of Chinese immigrants and their closer tie with China, it further jeopardized their relationship with the native-born Canadians, who did not share to the same degree the experiences of their "oversea-born" parents.[38]

In light of this social phenomenon, what role could Chinese Canadian churches play? Could the church help Chinese to cope with the racial tension? Even less considered were what ways the church could assist in helping Chinese people to be Canadians. Given the fact that issues of assimilation, racism, and the quest for identity occupied Chinese Canadians, they had also been struggling to define the role of the Chinese church for Chinese in Canada.

There were psychological as well as social needs for Chinese in Canada. In the case of Chinese immigrants, coming to Canada meant uprooting

36. Lee, *Marginality*, 45.
37. Lee, *Marginality*, 68.
38. Lee, *Marginality*, 67.

and reestablishing. This journey of resettlement was usually tense and uncertain, thus it produces "the intensification of the psychic basis of religious commitment."[39] Such needs pushed new immigrants to appreciate anew the Chinese cultural values and at the same time look for means to affirm those values in the new country. Another need was to find ways to enter the social, legal, and economic realm of their host country.

Even though Chinese churches in Canada were not considered the major agents of acculturation, at least not consciously, their adoption of the English language (for some) and Euro-Canadian lifestyle helped their members to live harmoniously in Canada. As I indicated earlier, facing a multicultural, pluralistic, fast-paced, and uncertain society, many Chinese Christians found Christianity attractive. Many of them attended Evangelical churches, as it offers ways to read the Bible that affirm the cultural desire for personal integrity and spiritual growth. Chinese Christians living in Canada were drawn to the Evangelical idea of conservative values and certainty. To clasp onto a faith tradition that teaches Christians alone know the way of eternal truth offers its adherents a secure sense of acceptance and achievement. The Christian message of hope thus empowers many Chinese to deal with their premigration traumas and postmigration uncertainties in Canada. It also met their longing desire to be accepted and valued. These Chinese churches emphasized personal Bible study and small study groups. Bible study forms part of their spiritual practices as well as strengthens their religious life and this, in turn, enriches their relationship with other members. It was not surprising to see many Chinese churches approach the Bible predominantly through the lens of morality. Sermons tended to be focusing on personal faith issues and individual integrity. And the Chinese cultural lens of *face* and *shame* continue to be the guiding force in regarding how Chinese Christians conduct their assumed moral lives in churches and in Canada.[40]

Chinese churches, at least from the perspective of Chinese parents, preserved Chinese cultural values while participating in religious activities that had shaped the civilization of Western world. As some researchers point out, Chinese Canadian churches function as a hub where churches offer social bonding and psychological support. Ethnic churches became places where cultural values and languages were being educated and upheld, and men were able to restore their social status through exercising congregational leadership that they used to occupy in their countries of origins.[41] In addition, Chinese

---

39. Yang, *Chinese Christians in America*, 30.
40. See Poon et al., "Pastoral Counseling," 402.
41. Wong et al., *Listening to Their Voices*, 3.

churches had been and continue to function as safe havens and provide the prophetic voices of the marginalized Chinese people, who may have been discriminated against or experienced inequality in Canada.

Development of Two or Three Language Churches under One Roof

Subsequent generations of Chinese Canadian Christians were, however, showing signs of change. As much as the first generation Chinese Christian immigrants wanted their children to practice faith the same way as they do, these local-born Chinese Christians, having grown up in Canada, had daily exposure to different ways of thinking and being. They grew up with diverse ethnic classmates who exercise different religions and beliefs. While from the outset they showed obedience, it was not easy to expect strict conformation to their parents' wishes.

Many Chinese congregations in Canada began as Chinese-speaking exclusive congregations. As in the case of Toronto Chinese United Church and many others, during Sunday worship, young children and teens often were offered Sunday school in English in separate rooms. This model ran well when children were small. But it soon became unsatisfying when those teens were no longer children. Even with many years of attending Chinese language schools, Chinese teenagers were not getting the spiritual nourishment they needed when the act of worship and sermons were conducted in Chinese only. To accommodate the needs of the local-born Chinese Canadians and the 1.5 generation, some Chinese congregations offered side-by-side English interpretation, and sometimes via headphones, as worship under the same roof was important to many of the Chinese parents. From the point of view of the Chinese parents, the problem was solved, but from the perspective of many English-speaking youth, they found this accommodation to be less than ideal. The heart of the matter was more than language, although miscommunication between generations played a key factor in the dissatisfaction; it was the cultural mindset and modes of thinking that matters. Despite many Chinese youth growing up in Chinese homes, their education in Canada provided them the abilities to engage fully in the Canadian society, which included language and culture, plus the Canadian ideal of social integration and various concepts of equality. And that was why this so-called "parent-child" model where the Chinese adults occupied the driver seats to decide issues for all members of the congregation proved to be problematic. Local-born Chinese Canadians felt they were treated with inferior attitudes. Church boards were usually filled with first-generation leaders and English-speaking adults had only a small representation. It was not uncommon to find that the language spoken in those board meetings was Chinese.

While developing English-speaking ministry within a Chinese congregation was a logical next step (or French-speaking in Quebec), there was a struggling period where several ideological issues needed to be sorted out. The greatest one was identity. Many first-generation Chinese immigrants were proud of their achievements, that is, having built Chinese congregations in Canada. By their hard work, Chinese traditional values, language, and customs were being preserved. The fact that they were building a *Chinese* church permeated the mission and dedication of these worshippers. In recent years, some discussions about the possibility of dropping the word *Chinese* in their church names in order to reach out to all Canadians were often met with negative comments. Many first-generation Chinese Christians saw their churches as *Chinese* thoroughly. In the early negotiations about setting up English-speaking ministries, some first-generation immigrants insisted that the mission of Chinese congregations, although they understand that it was not the whole picture; the mission also includes Chinese churches as being the cultural vehicles to pass on Chinese language and cultures. This view was soon met with opposition as the other side which insisted the mission of the church was to spread the gospel. One the one hand, the two do not need to be mutually exclusive, yet, stressing too strong for the former could be counterproductive, or even miserably fail when the cultural identity card stood in the way of meaningful religious engagement.

To complicate the matter further, some insisted the meaning of *Chineseness* must include the ability to speak and understand Chinese. If one is not capable in this regard, one may not be regarded as a *real* Chinese. From the minds of many first-generation Chinese, English-speaking Chinese Canadians are less than Chinese. Often, the latter are being called as *bananas* (yellow outside but white inside) or *bamboo sticks* (hollow inside), by their Chinese family members. This may sound insulting, and it is; but many English-speaking Chinese Canadians would not call themselves Chinese but simply Canadians. Thus, some wouldn't refer themselves as Canadian-Born Chinese (aka. CBC). The debate concerning who is Chinese, and what constitutes *Chineseness*, continues.

2

A Brief History of the Taiwanese Immigrant Church in Canada

Luis Liang and Ben C. H. Kuo

THE HISTORY OF TAIWANESE immigrant churches in Canada is comparatively recent and brief as compared to other immigrant churches featured in this book. The root of Taiwanese Canadian churches in Toronto, for example, can be traced back to the 1960s—a history spanning slightly over five decades. Besides having a relatively short past, the examination of Taiwanese Canadian church history is made particularly challenging due to the fact that, to the authors' knowledge, there have not been any comprehensive, published records, documentations, or literature on the church history of this immigrant group in Canada. According to the information available on the website of Taiwanese Christian Council of North America, multiple Taiwanese Christian churches exist across major cities in Canada. Based on that information, there are a total of five Taiwanese Presbyterian churches (two in Toronto, two in Vancouver, and one in Montreal), five Taiwanese United churches (one in Toronto, one in Calgary, and three in Vancouver), and four independent or nondenominational Taiwanese churches (one in Toronto, one in Montreal, and two in Vancouver) across Canada.[1] Despite that, little has been written and reported about these Taiwanese immigrant churches in Canada and their history. On the basis of the authors' personal knowledge, however, there are and have been other additional Taiwanese Canadian churches not accounted for on this list.

Considering the limited documentation on Taiwanese churches in Canada, in this chapter we intend to organize, describe, and present a general review and account of the development and the characteristics

---

1. See the Taiwanese Christian Council of North America website at http://tccna.org/TheChurch/CA/CA-others.htm.

of Taiwanese Canadian churches, particularly by focusing on those in the Greater Toronto Area, which correspond to the target of the *Asian Canadian Churches of Today for Tomorrow* project and of this book. Due to the absence of official records and literatures on the history of Taiwanese Canadian churches, much of the information in this chapter is based on selected reports and anniversary publications of various Taiwanese churches in Toronto, personal interviews with and accounts of knowledgeable members within the Taiwanese Christian community, and our own research and cumulative observations of these churches and the larger community. Hence, in the following sections, we share our knowledge and experiences from the perspective of being along-standing members of this Taiwanese Christian community in Toronto and members of the ministry teams in these Taiwanese Canadian churches.

Historical Contexts of Taiwanese Immigrants and Immigrant Churches in Canada

Ever since God created the world, he has conveyed his messages to all people in a profound manner from generation to generation. In the time of the early church, the gospel of Jesus Christ was spread out across lands and seas despite and due to the persecutions and dispersions of the Apostles and the Christians. During the eighteenth to nineteenth centuries, the Gospel was introduced to the Asian regions as an extension of those early movements of Christian faith. In the case of Taiwan, the Gospel was officially introduced to this island national by the early missionaries including Dr. James Laidlaw Maxwell from Scotland in 1865 and Dr. George Leslie MacKay from Canada in 1871 respectively. Hence, there have been strong spiritual and historical ties between churches in Canada and those in Taiwan. Overall, according to the government statistics of the Republic of China, Christians comprised only 3.9 percent of the total population in Taiwan; the Christian population in Taiwan is roughly equally divided between Protestants and Catholics.

Early Immigrants from Taiwan to North America

Taiwanese are defined as people who were either born or resided in Taiwan with the cognition of their identity being "Taiwanese" as opposed to "Chinese," even though "Han" Taiwanese ancestors originally migrated from China. The history of Taiwanese immigrants to North America can be traced back to the time period before the Second World War while Taiwan was still the Colony of Japan (AD 1895–1945). Many wealthy Taiwanese families sent their children overseas to Japan, China, Europe or North America for education during those times. This trend was intensified after the war was over, when a great number of Taiwanese people started to migrate to North America, particularly the United States. These new immigrants started their new lives on this new continent with hardworking spirit and determination, and later on they settled in many different cities and states/provinces across both the United States and Canada.

The 1950s was "the era of Taiwanese overseas students" as many international students from Taiwan decided to travel and pursue graduate studies mostly in North America. Many of these students decided to stay, to work, and even to marry in North America after completing their studies. These students in the 1950s became the "first wave" of Taiwanese immigrants to North America. After having established a stable livelihood with regular jobs, incomes, and families, many of these first group of Taiwanese immigrants became well-established in the United States and Canada with good careers and social statuses by end of the 1960s. In 1967, Canada adopted a new immigration rules bringing a "points" system for immigrants and opened its doors to people of all race and ethnicity. Under this new immigration policy, Taiwanese was among the first, new wave of immigrants to Canada.

It is important to know that the major motivations of Taiwanese to migrate to the United States and Canada in the 1960s and 1970s were due to four main events: a) the Cultural Revolution of China in 1967; b) the Vietnam War, started in 1968; c) the withdrawal of Taiwan from the United Nations in 1971; and d) the break of diplomatic relation between the United States and Taiwan in 1972. These historical events caused an intense sense of insecurity and anxiety among the people in Taiwan. In the beginning of this migration movement, the majority of Taiwanese immigrants resettled mainly in the west coast of the United States (e.g., California), but later Taiwanese immigrants began to spread out and move to the east coast of the United States and Canada, enticed by education and career opportunities. From the 1970s, there were even more new immigrants moving from Taiwan to the United States and Canada. These nonstudent Taiwanese immigrant newcomers were financially more well-off than the previous cohorts of Taiwanese immigrants, who were mostly students.[2] Taiwanese Canadian churches were established during this particular era. In the following sections, we will describe three periods of development over this history of

---

2. Hwang, *Development of Taiwanese Christian Churches*, 1–5, 13–18.

Taiwanese Canadian churches in Toronto: the birth of the churches, the growth of the churches, and the present status of the churches.

Birth of the Taiwanese Immigrant Church in Toronto

The first Christian worship gathering began in Toronto in 1965 and 1966. At the time there were about thirty-five Taiwanese people knew each other and lived in the City of Toronto around Christmastime. Among these new Taiwanese immigrants there were businessmen, medical professionals, and students, with most of them being Christians. Prior to their gathering for worship, these Taiwanese Christians were scattered and worshiped at different churches, speaking a variety of dialects including Japanese, Cantonese, and English. However, as the feeling of wishing to worship God in their own mother tongue grew stronger, Dr. Joseph Tai initiated a Bible-study meeting on the weekend in the beginning of 1966. Subsequently, the first worship in Taiwanese dialect was held on June 19th, 1966 at Knox Presbyterian Church at 640 Spadina Ave. and it was hosted by Rev. James Ira Dickson. This was a historical event for Taiwanese Christians in Toronto.

Taiwanese Bible study meetings continued to be held on the weekends in different family homes by rotation throughout 1966. This Bible study group later leased from the University Lutheran Church on Friday evenings for regular meetings. At the end of 1966 the first official Taiwanese church in Toronto was established under the name of "Formosan Christian Church in Toronto" (FCCT), an independent and nondenominational church. As the number of the Taiwanese immigrants grew during this time period, the congregation of FCCT also expanded.

With the assistance of ministry from Rev. Sydney Chang, Dr. C. T. Tai, and Rev. S. Y. Liu, the members of FCCT had grown over sixty. The church later moved to Leaside Presbyterian Church in Toronto (at 670 Eglinton Avenue E.) on February 10th, 1974. In the same year, while some members suggested FCCT to join the Presbyterian Church in Canada (PCC), neither the church board nor the result of the congregational meeting had led to a firm decision even after several meetings. This occurrence unfortunately promoted the eventual split of the congregation of the FCCT.[3] As will be seen in the later development the Taiwanese Canadian Christian community, congregational tensions, conflicts, and disharmonies had sadly reoccurred throughout its short history.

---

3. Formosan Christian Church in Toronto, *Establishment and Development*, 8.

Growth of Taiwanese Immigrant Churches in Toronto

The period from the mid-1960s to the early-1970s was followed by a phase of expansion for Taiwanese churches in Toronto. The development and changes of the following nine individual Taiwanese Canadian churches are briefly profiled and reviewed in the ensuing sections.

Formosan Christian Church in Toronto (FCCT)

After several meetings of discussion regarding joining PCC without any firmed outcome, the church board set up a committee to handle this issue. Following a congregational meeting held on December of 1974, eleven new board members were elected and instituted into the constitution of FCCT. FCCT later moved over to worship at the Glebe Road United Church in Toronto (20 Glebe Road E.). Under the ministry of Rev. David Chen the number of FCCT grew to over a hundred. Later Rev. Larry Chou was called to be the first full-time minister of FCCT for a three-year term. In the following decades, FCCT experienced both blessings in terms of membership growth as well as fractions due to differences of views due to denominational, political, and administrative affiliations and conflicts among its Taiwanese immigrant members. On November of 1995 FCCT started English service for its English-speaking congregants. The first Sunday of each month was devoted to a joint service between Taiwanese ministry and English ministry in the church.[4] Rev. Jeff MacMillan was called to be the first full-time minister for English ministry for FCCT in June, 1999. A notable reunification of previously split congregations occurred on March 6th, 2005, with members of FCCT and of Taiwan Justice and Grace Christian Church in Toronto (TJGCCT; formerly Justice and Grace Fellowship) coming together as one church for the purpose of witnessing the Christian faith and spirit of "united as one in Christ."[5]

Toronto Formosan Presbyterian Church (TFPC)

Led by a group of pastors and elders who departed from FCCT with the wish to join the Presbyterian Church in Canada, the Toronto Formosan Presbyterian Church (TFPC) was formerly established on March 2nd, 1975. It began with forty-one members and held the Sunday afternoon service

---

4. Formosan Christian Church in Toronto, *Establishment and Development*, 8–9.
5. Formosan Grace Christian Church in Toronto, *Church History*, 12–14.

by leasing from Leaside Presbyterian Church, a part of the East Toronto Presbytery. On January 4th, 1976 TFPC formed its first session by electing five elders. Initially, in the absence of a full-time minister, the East Toronto Presbytery appointed Rev. James Jack to be the inter-moderator for TFPC. On August 1st, 1982 Rev. N.J. Wang was installed as the first full-time minister of TFPC and remained serving at the church until 1994. TFPC began its English ministry in late 80s. After moving to its current location at 31 Eastwood Road in Toronto, the English service was ministered by several English-speaking pastors over the years. The English service is held separately at a separate time from the Taiwanese service.

Taiwanese United Church in Toronto (TUCT)

Also originating from initial FCCT, a group of church members from that church were highly involved and active in the political affairs of Taiwanese, in particular, about the sociopolitical future, human rights, sovereignty and independence of Taiwan, began gathering for their own worship at the Newtonbrook United Church in North York (Toronto) on March, 1983. The church later became the "Taiwanese United Church in Toronto" (TUCT), which officially joined the United Church in Canada (UCC) on February 26th, 1983. The emergence of TUCT pointed to the complex intersections among Christian faith, cultural identity, and political persuasion/activism among Taiwanese immigrants in Canada, the United States, and elsewhere in the world.

A church member of TUCT, Mr. Danny Huang was called by God to study theology and he graduated in September of 1987 from Emmanuel College. Pastor Danny Huang then served as the first full-time minister of TUCT for many years until 2003.[6] Due to TUCT's strong political stance on human rights and the Taiwan independence movement, conflicts emerged among the Taiwanese-speaking congregation which led to a subsequent split. As a result, the congregation had been downsized to about two-thirds of the original number. This and other events had unfortunately led to reduction of TUCT's church members. For example, the members of the younger English-speaking generation no longer attend and participate in the church due to different culture backgrounds, mindsets, thoughts, and values, etc., from those of their first-generation Taiwanese parents.

---

6. Taiwanese United Church in Toronto, *Church History*, 3.

Toronto Formosan Christian Church in Faith, Hope, and Love (TFCCFHL)

The "Toronto Formosan Christian Church in Faith, Hope and Love" (TFCCFHL), an independent and nondenominational church, was established in 1983 by Rev. Larry Chou, who formerly served as the pastor of FCCT from 1980 to 1983. The church was comprised of some former FCCT members, who departed FCCT along with Rev. Chou. Rev. Chou served at TFCCFHL until 1989 and then was succeeded by Rev. David Pan, who was called to be the second full-time minister for the church. Eventually TFCCFHL joined PCC to become a Presbyterian church. With this development, the church took on a new name in 1997, as "Toronto Trinity Mandarin Presbyterian Church" (TTMPC). The TTMPC will be reviewed in the later section.

Toronto Central Taiwanese Presbyterian Church (TCTPC)

"Toronto Central Taiwanese Presbyterian Church" (TCTPC) originated from TFPC, discussed previously. It is one of the three Taiwanese Canadian churches that joined the Presbyterian Church in Canada. This church began with a fellowship through monthly family services that began in October, 1982 and led by Rev. Stephen Chen. As the number of this group increased to over fifty members, the members established the "Church Establishment Committee" and formally adopted the name TCTPC on February 5th, 1983. TCTPC was then admitted to the East Toronto Presbytery as a member church of PCC in the following year, on June 12th, 1984. Initially, Rev. Stephen Chen served as the inter-moderator of the church. With a growing congregation, in 1985 TCTPC moved to Leaside Presbyterian Church. Appointed by East Toronto Presbytery, in PCC. In 1987, Rev. Chen became the official full-time minister of TCTPC. At its peak membership, TCTPC hosted many new Taiwanese immigrants and visa students. The church, however, experienced significant decline in its congregation in the subsequent decade after 1997. Interestingly, with the encouragement and the facilitation of the East Toronto Presbytery, the Presbytery tabled a proposal of "merging TFPC and TCTPC as one." This proposal was actualized on October 26th, 2008 as the congregations of both churches came together for a joint service.[7] The two Taiwanese Presbyterian churches in Toronto were eventually amalgamated.

---

7. Toronto Central Taiwanese Presbyterian Church, *Church History*, 1–9.

Taiwan Justice and Grace Christian Church in Toronto (TJGCCT)

In 1990, led by a group of former elder and members of FCCT, the "Justice and Grace Fellowship" was formed—it was a nondenominational Taiwanese church. The movement began in November of 1989. Owing to various reasons, this group of Taiwanese Christian immigrants met and started the idea of forming a new fellowship. They set out the following two purposes for the fellowship: a) to be prepared for establishing a Taiwanese spoken church in the near future; and b) to care for the new immigrants and visa students from Taiwan in order to bring them to the church to know God. The first worship service of TJGCCT was then held on April 22nd, 1990, at Blythwood Baptist Church in Toronto at 80 Blythwood Road with about thirty people in attendance. The English-speaking youth group then started its first meeting in the month of September. Later a group of former church members of TFPC joined TJGCCT in 1992. The history of TJGCCT was blessed with God's grace through having many well-respected Taiwanese and Taiwanese Canadian pastors to shepherd and support the spirituality of the congregation.

On June 30th of 1996, Rev. Han-Luan Chih was installed as the first full-time minister of TJGCCT. During his term, Rev. Han-Luan Chih liaisoned between FCCT and TJGCCTwith many joint activities, winter retreats, joint services, youth Bible studies, family gatherings, and Christmas celebrations between the two Taiwanese churches. This had helped laid the critical foundation for merger and unification between FCCT and TJGCCT in later years.[8] The unification of the two churches was finally realized on March of 2005 under the leadership of Rev. Jen-Li Tsai, who was the second full-time minister of TJGCCT.

New Life Gospel Church in Toronto (NLGCT)

New Life Gospel Church in Toronto (NLGCT) was established in April 1992 by the calling of God and led by Dr. Kenneth Tung with other six youths from TFPC. Unlike other Taiwanese Canadian churches in Toronto, NLGCT belonged to the Evangelical Formosan Church (EFC) as the church joined this denomination in May 1995—a denomination established by Taiwanese American Christian immigrants with root in

---

8. Taiwan Justice and Grace Christian Church in Toronto, *Church History: Taiwan Justice*, 7–9.

Presbyterian Church in Taiwan and originated in the Orange County Evangelical Formosan Church in the United States.

The first pastor of NLGCT was Pastor Chung-Lun Hu, who was ordained in September 1999. What is also unique about NLGCT among the Taiwanese Canadian Churches in Toronto is that the church began with a ministry focusing on youth and young adults of Taiwanese and Mainland Chinese backgrounds as well as second-generation children of immigrants. Under this objective, NLGCT has built and maintained a Mandarin ministry as well as a robust English ministry. Currently NLGCT has four pastors, including one pastor for English ministry (Rev. Joe Tung), one pastor for Mandarin ministry (Rev. Men-Wen Tsai), one caring pastor (Rev. David Pan), and a senior pastor (Rev. Joshua Yao). In terms of its membership number, NLGCT has about three hundred members, the largest among all Taiwanese churches in Toronto. Its active ministries include short-term missions, camps of various age levels, fellowship for college students, sports activities indoor and/or outdoor, and Chinese school. Consequently, NLGCT has attracted many young families, children, and youth and it is growing steadily with younger generations.[9]

Toronto Trinity Mandarin Presbyterian Church (TTMPC)

As mentioned in the previous section on the Toronto Formosan Christian Church in Faith, Hope and Love (TFCCFHL), after this church joined PCC the name was changed to "Toronto Trinity Mandarin Presbyterian Church" (TTMPC) in 1997, with Rev. Dennis Ngien being appointed as the first full-time minister. One of the major transitions with this change to TTMPC was the use of Mandarin as the medium of its ministry as opposed to Taiwanese, as under TFCCFHL. In 2002, Rev. Dennis Ngien passed the baton to Rev. Wes Chang, who graduated Knox College, and later was ordinated as a Presbyterian minister.

Formosan Grace Christian Church in Toronto (FGCCT)

The Formosan Grace Christian Church in Toronto (FGCCT) is an amalgamation of FCCT and TJGCCT. The merge and unification discussion was held for the first time on November 2nd, 2003 at FCCT, followed by five prayer and amalgamation meetings held in 2004. With the grace of God, there was an

---

9. See the New Life Gospel Church website at http://www.findglocal.com/CA/Toronto/515937381787419/New-Life-Gospel-Church.

overwhelmingly support for unification. The new unified church was named "Formosan Grace Christian Church in Toronto"(FGCCT).[10]

FGCCT has been a marvelous testimony of God's will, as it showed that God allowed Taiwanese churches to willingly make adjustment a new situation as the turn of a new century. Under the leadership of Rev. Peter Ho, the first full-time minister of FGCCT, the church moved into a new church building at its current address on Progress Road in Scarborough on April 29th, 2012. An unfortunate situation, however, occurred among the congregation a few years later in 2016, which resulted in the departure of some church members of FGCCT. A separate church under the name of "New Hope Gospel Christian Church" (NHGCC) was formed by Rev. John Ko. Currently FGCCT has two streams of ministries: a) a Taiwanese-speaking ministry served by Rev. Luis Liang and b) an English-speaking ministry by Rev. Tim Li.

In additional to the above mentioned Taiwanese churches, two churches existed for a brief period of time. "Formosan Agape Church of Toronto" established in 1989 by Rev. Larry Chou ended the ministry in 1996. "Toronto Taiwanese Revival Mennonite Church" established by Mr. Frank Liao launched a fellowship group consisted of Taiwanese immigrants and families in 1988, but the church ended in 2001.

Of note, for the purposes of promoting fellowship and partnership in the same faith and sharing cultural identity and heritage, several Taiwanese churches in Toronto came together and formed the Taiwanese Christian Churches Association in Toronto in 1995. The current members of the Association include Toronto Formosan Presbyterian Church (TFPC), Taiwanese United Church in Toronto (TUCT), Formosan Grace Christian Church (FGCCT), and New Life Gospel Church in Toronto (NLGCT). The activities of the Association comprise of holding four joint services among member churches annually, joint spiritual retreat, and, also in the past, having a joint Taiwanese Christian choir. The spirit of the Association exemplifies Taiwanese churches' vision and effort to strive for unity and fellowship among churches, despite their differences.

Multiple Roles of Taiwanese Immigrant Churches in Canada

As seen in this brief survey and account of the development of Taiwanese immigrant churches in Toronto, while the churches played a critical role in the lives of newcomers from Taiwan since the 1960s, the journey up to this point has been bittersweet. Specifically, the history of Taiwanese Canadian

---

10. Formosan Grace Christian Church in Toronto, *Church History*, 15–17.

churches was filled with both moments of hope, optimism, grace, and coming together, as well sadly flawed with incidents of repeated conflicts, bickering, and divisions over time. Nevertheless, with the mercy and the grace of the Lord Almighty, Taiwanese Canadian churches stood as a crucial entity in the lives of many newcomers from Taiwan since 1960s. The churches have served in many roles and capacities for new immigrants, which include a place of spiritual worship, cultural preservation, social support, and a key source of information for their adaption and adjustment in Canada. On this note, Taiwanese immigrant churches normally hold their worship services in the Taiwanese dialect, which help preserve their mother tongue, culture, and cultural identity. Most Taiwanese Canadian churches also maintain a close connection with other Taiwanese Canadian groups, organizations, or associations to help support and provide services for visitors or newcomers from Taiwan. For example, New Life Gospel Church in Toronto (NLGCT), discussed previously, holds worship services in both Mandarin (the official language spoken in Taiwan) and English. As a result, they set up a Chinese Mandarin school program within the church to offering lessons for children of both new immigrants and the second generation.

However, as the second-generation Taiwanese Canadians continue to grow and become more distant from the Taiwanese cultural heritage and roots of their parents, the role of Taiwanese Canadian churches has been forced to change and evolve. To the authors' knowledge, among the current active Taiwanese Canadian churches in Toronto, three churches have designated English ministry for the second-generation, including the Formosan Grace Christian Church in Toronto (FGCCT), the Toronto Formosan Presbyterian Church (TFPC), and New Life Gospel Church in Toronto (NLGCT). These second-generation ministries are of critical importance for the future of Taiwanese immigrant churches in Canada. However, the Taiwanese churches in Toronto are facing and witnessing the phenomenon of "silent exodus," as described by Helen Lee, among the younger generation of Taiwanese immigrant youth and young adults. Lee observed "silent exodus" as the rapid loss of second-generation children of immigrant in the intergenerational Korean immigrant churches in the United States. Furthermore, similar to other Asian ethnic churches, Taiwanese Canadian churches are faced with diminishing membership among its first generation congregants due to aging and decreased number of new immigrants and immigrant families from Taiwan. There remain many critical issues confronting Taiwanese Canadian churches today and into the future. We believe that these issues and their solutions call for not only steadfast faith in Lord's power and will for his churches, but also for open, honest, thoughtful, and proactive responses from the Taiwanese immigrant Christian community itself, including laypeople and church leadership, first-generation and second generation congregants.

Paths to the Future of Taiwanese Canadian Churches: Addressing Critical Questions

To conclude this chapter on the history of Taiwanese Canadian churches, we would like to raise and offer a few crucial questions and issues, as "food for thought" for the readers—challenges that face Taiwanese Canadian churches today as well as marching into the future. Firstly, with respect to the future directions of Taiwanese immigrant churches in Canada, immigrant churches must ask: "What purposes and roles would Taiwanese immigrant churches serve and play into the coming decades?" For instance, given the diminishing new Taiwanese immigrant and international student populations to Canada, to what extent is a Taiwanese-speaking congregation within the immigrant churches relevant and necessary? Should Taiwanese Canadian churches be expanded to include Mandarin congregants, as in the case of Toronto Trinity Mandarin Presbyterian Church (TTMPC) and New Life Gospel Church in Toronto (NLGCT)? If yes, what implications would this hold for Taiwanese Canadian churches in promoting, safeguarding, and preserving its intrinsic "Taiwanese identity"?

Secondly, in regard to the second generation Taiwanese Canadians, one critical issue bearing upon the future of this group in the church is: "What are the roles and the expectations of the second generation within the Taiwanese churches?" Will they continue to be viewed as "children" by their first generation immigrant "parents," who continue to operate and hold the administrative and structural leadership of the church? How might this parent-child cultural and relational hierarchy that exists in traditional family but also is transposed to immigrant churches be contested and modified? How might the intergenerational communication and relationship be improved and enhanced to foster more open dialogues, understanding, and collaboration between the first- and the second-generation congregants?

Thirdly, if the "baton" of leadership were indeed to be passed onto the second-generation Taiwanese Canadian members and congregant: "How might the transition look, in terms of preparation, training, and sharing of visions?" As with any major changeover and transformation, the churches will need significant amount of Christ-centered courage, wisdom, patience, and humility in charting through these unknown water.

Fourthly, it is equally imperative for the currently existing Taiwanese Canadian churches to ask: "What will it take to not only achieve congregational and community peace and unity within the Taiwanese immigrant Christian community, but also to maintain and ensure such a unity for the long run?" If the review of Taiwanese Canadian church history in Toronto in this chapter has taught us anything, it is that the unity of the church is most fragile and vulnerable when its people lost their Christ-centered focus and spiritual vision. In time of conflicts, personal pride, hurt, and disillusionment between and among clergies, leadership, and congregational members can amount to fraction and dishonor. The future of Taiwanese immigrants, as with all universal churches, rests upon learning and acting on Christ-like humility, compassion, and critical skills to resolve conflicts as characterized by the very essence of who he is—the *Prince of Peace*.

3

A Brief History of the Korean Immigrant Church in Canada

In Kee Kim

Early Korean Immigrants to Canada

KOREAN IMMIGRATION IN TORONTO officially started in the 1960s. During the early 1900s, there were a number of Korean students studying in Canada, thanks to sponsorships of Canadian missionaries serving in Korea. However, such activities increased significantly after the Korean War and more Koreans were able to come to Canada as foreign students, supported by nongovernment and civilian aid agencies. Some of these students remained in Canada as professionals and pastors. The official ties between Canada and Korea, established in 1963, marks the beginning of Korean immigration to Canada in earliest. As Canada opened its doors wider in 1967 by enacting the Immigration Act to accept more visible minorities, officially Koreans began to immigrate to Canada. According to Korea's Ministry of Foreign Affairs and Trade, two Koreans living permanently in Canada in 1962 increased to 507 in 1967.[1] Koreans were still only a hundred in number in Toronto at that time. They knew each other very well and they were like a big extended family. Often, they invited each other to their homes for a meal and enjoyed a picnic at the park with other families. They helped each other to settle in this foreign land. They came to Canada for a better future for themselves and for their children.

The first Korean immigrants came to Canada with great expectation and hope. But immigrant life was not as easy as they anticipated. What they discovered when they landed in this foreign land was a very harsh reality. They encountered a very different culture and more than anything else, they

1. Korean Canadian Cultural Association, *History of Korean Canadians*, 67–78.

experienced a huge language barrier. Most of them had a high level of education, having a university degree back in Korea, but because of language limitations and a lack of education and training here in Canada, they had no choice but to find menial labour that did not require English language abilities. My mother was a homemaker all her life, living comfortably back in Korea. But here in Canada, to get a job she had to knock on the door of every factory with one sentence she memorized: "I need a job." One person told me that he sent hundreds of job applications to construction companies since he worked in a construction company as an engineer back in Korea and yet he said he did not get any response from those companies. Koreans were not physically as strong as average Canadians and yet they had to try their best to survive and to make a living. They had no choice. Many of them worked double shifts. Some of them went far away into small towns because the pay was good and they could get more hours to work, including overtime. But living in a small town where the majority population was white Caucasians was challenging socially, culturally, and psychologically. They were basically isolated in their homes. They suffered from loneliness and depression. After a few years of working, they saved enough money to start their own small businesses such as convenience stores and drycleaning businesses. They did not have enough money to hire helpers in the beginning, and so they had to take care of their business all by themselves. That meant working from early in the morning until closing time, which was usually 11:00 pm. They could not afford to take a vacation and worked 365 days a year, including Christmas Day. This was a very dehumanizing environment and experience.

One of the elders at the church said to me that even though life was hard, they never complained about their situation. They were just thankful that they had work to make a living. Also, they all felt very hopeful about their future. They had a conviction that in this country, if they would work hard, they could survive. They came with a high expectation but they were pushed into a very dehumanizing environment for their survival. However, they never lost hope that they could survive. What helped them deal with their dehumanizing environment was the church. The church was like an oasis in a desert.

Birth of the Korean Immigrant Church in Canada

The first community the Korean immigrants established was the church. It is not an exaggeration to say that Korean immigrant history is church history. There were no other significant communities they had in the beginning. The impetus for the early Korean communities to be centered on churches may have something to do with the fact that the earliest Koreans arriving in Canada were seminary students sponsored by Canada's Christian missionaries. A steady increase in population, including those who were actively involved in church activities in Korea, and finding that there existed a number of seminary students and graduates ready to offer their services, led naturally to an increase in the demand for more churches.

The first Korean church in Canada was established in Montreal. In 1963, Father Matthew Koh was appointed as the first Korean priest to minister to the St. Louis de France Catholic church's Korean congregation, as well as to serve as assistant minister to the whole congregation. At that time about seventy Korean immigrants resided in Montreal, including fewer than ten of the Catholic faith. In 1965, Montreal Korean United Church was established.[2] The second church was founded in Vancouver. Rev. Sangchul Lee, who had studied at the Union Seminary in 1961, was appointed as minister for the Steveston United Church for both the Caucasian and the Japanese Canadian congregation. From 1966, Rev. Lee also conducted the worship service for the Korean congregation once a month at the Union Seminary, which led to the establishment of the Vancouver Korean United Church.[3] The third church was established in Toronto. In March of 1963, the number of Koreans living in the Toronto area was about 150. Most of these were Christians and they desired to have service in their own language, leading naturally to the establishment of their own church. Among those, there was a group that preferred a Presbyterian service, as well as another group who argued for a more ecumenical service. The latter was quicker to begin their service in April of 1967, and they called their congregation the Korean Church; its name was changed to Toronto Korean United Church in June of that same year; and later, in September, seventy-five worshipers gathered to start the first Korean Presbyterian church in Toronto.[4] In Korean Canadian church history, it is significant to note that the churches were founded by Korean Canadians themselves, including the ordained Korean Canadian pastors.

Growth of Korean Immigrants Churches in Canada

They gathered together every week and often more than once a week. The church was not just a church. Church was like their home. They loved to gather together every week. There was no other Korean community that met

2. Korean Canadian Cultural Association, *History of Korean Canadians*, 305.
3. Korean Canadian Cultural Association, *History of Korean Canadians*, 41–42.
4. Korean Canadian Cultural Association, *History of Korean Canadians*, 316–18.

so regularly. This regular meeting became the routine of their immigrant life. Not only did they work hard for the church community but they also received social and psychological benefits from the church community. The church was for them not only a spiritual place but also a home away from home. With this significant role of being centered in the community, the church grew in accordance with the increasing number of immigrants.

During the early 1970s, many Korean miners and nurses who were working in West Germany migrated to Canada after their contracts were finished and began the formation of Korean Canadian communities. Most of these people had post-secondary degrees but had accepted three-year work assignments to go to Germany because of high unemployment rate at the time in Korea.[5] Along with the groups of Koreans from Germany, more Koreans arrived from other countries and also directly from Korea so that Korean immigration to Canada steadily increased during the early parts of the 1970s. As the example only in Toronto, Korean churches that were largely concentrated in and around the Bloor Koreatown in Toronto during the 1960s began to spread out to the suburbs in the 1970s with more Korean immigrants arriving. Furthermore, more Korean Christians started to arrive in Canada who had no ties to Canadian denominations and this led to establishment of Methodist, Baptist, Full Gospel, Pentecostal churches, etc. within the Korean communities.

The number of Korean immigrants in the Greater Toronto Area exceeded thirty thousand in the early 1980s and this also led to more Korean churches opening their doors and the general expansion of the Korean Christian community. The number of Korean churches stood at more than two hundred at this time. Koreans came to Canada because of business from the late 1980s and the number of immigrants with financial ability increased rapidly during and after the 1997 economic crisis in Korea which needed the IMF (International Monetary Fund) to intervene.[6] This saw a rapid expansion of Korea's economy and many immigrants and foreign students who came to Canada had sufficient funds to live and study comfortably. Many of these people, rather than start their own churches, were more prone to attend existing churches. One effect of this was the growth of a number of churches into megachurches. Many Korean churches who rented space from Canadian churches began to raise funds to have their own buildings. Services aimed at the second generation also increased significantly during this time.[7]

5. Korean Canadian Cultural Association, *History of Korean Canadians*, 67–78.
6. Korean Canadian Cultural Association, *History of Korean Canadians*, 72.
7. Korean Canadian Cultural Association, *History of Korean Canadians*, 316–28.

Important Roles of Korean Immigrant Churches in Canada

The church played an important role to help the first Korean immigrants. Through the church, they helped each other. Earlier immigrants helped new arrivals by picking them up at the airport and taking them to their home until they were able to find their own place. Some people went to the airport where Korean Airlines arrived, without knowing who would come. Even though they were strangers to them, they took them to their home until they found their own place to live. They were all eager to help each other. People tended to do exactly the same business as what the people they met the first time did. Who picked them up at the airport was important because that determined their future in their immigrant life. If the people who picked them up at the airport ran a convenience store, they also ran a convenience store. If they ran a dry-cleaning business, they also ran a dry-cleaning business. In this foreign land, that was the only information available to them. They also went to the same church. The ministers' job was not just to take care of the church such as preaching, leading worship and Bible studies, and doing the pastoral visits but also to take care of the first immigrants by helping them settle in. They went to Manpower (a government organization to provide jobs) to help them get a job. They did interpretation for them. They helped them find low-income housing. They were not only ministers but also social workers.

Korean immigrants worked in Canadian society but their "real" life happened in the church. They were in this society to survive but they were in the church to enjoy "life." The first Korean immigrants did not have a social life in Canadian society. They could not make friends with people other than Koreans. They hardly went out to eat at fancy restaurants because they were either intimidated or just not interested. They didn't go to see movies because they couldn't understand the language. They were intimidated to do anything in this society. This fear of being in a foreign land affected them in every aspect of their lives. This fear basically isolated them from the rest of their society. It was confirmed and intensified when they were ridiculed by children and teenagers who came to the store. They never experienced being called "Chinks" or any other name. They had to adjust to this new foreign and hostile environment. They held relatively high positions in their homeland but here in Canada, they were "nobody" who could not even speak the language. Church was the only place where they could live like decent human beings with respect.

The way they dealt with their fear was to insulate themselves more within their church. In that sense, the church was not just a home away from home but a refuge that can protect them from the hostile environment. Even though Canada was a "Christian" country, to Korean immigrants, the secular Canadian society was not a safe place. Spiritually and culturally they wanted to protect themselves and their children from the surrounding culture, which was a threat to them. The church played a very important role to provide them with a safe environment. They also wanted their children to grow in the church so that they would not be influenced by this secular Canadian culture. This fear made them obsessively focus on survival. So they used the church to be a refuge but at the same time, church also helped them overcome their fear to a certain degree.

The church was not just a home away from home and a refuge. The church also helped them understand the spiritual reason for their existence here in Canada. Ministers tried to show them that their immigrant life was a sense of calling from God for God's holy purpose. They believed that the suffering they went through was not just for their own survival but it was for God's holy purpose. Every week, through sermons, the ministers gave them spiritual interpretation for their harsh immigrant situation. They used biblical figures, saying that they were also immigrants. Abraham was a good example. Abraham left his home town because God called him to the promised land for a holy purpose. Abraham was an immigrant. They identified with Abraham. Even Jesus was an immigrant from heaven to earth. That was how they related to the Scripture and how they interpreted their immigrant existence. They believed that they were sent by God to this land to be blessed. They believed that this blessing would pass on from one generation to the next generation. They were also called for blessing others as they were blessed. They had formulated the idea that the existence of the Korean immigrant churches just for themselves was not enough and there should be a higher and more noble purpose for the church. They started opening their eyes to live out God's purpose for them here in Canada. They started getting interested in doing mission. The church sent these short-term mission teams overseas every summer. Churches spent tens of thousands of dollars to do this mission. Some churches were also very interested in the mission for North Korea. Many immigrants in Canada were born in North Korea before the Korean War. They had a strong desire to pray for the home they left and also for the situation in North Korea. Interestingly, their mission was not for the land they were living in (Canada). They focused on mission overseas, especially the poorer countries. It was because Canada was an affluent country and they were not quite sure what they could do for this country. However, they saw the urgent needs in other parts of the world. With the offering they collected, they were able to do much more in poorer countries than what they could do here in Canada. Also, they wanted to live out Jesus' commission to be witnesses in Jerusalem, in all Judea and Samaria, and to the ends of the earth. So, in the name of a global mission, they started reaching out to other countries. This gave them a clear picture of their purpose in this country. God sent them here so that they could be used for reaching out to the world.

But church was not a utopia. The church had to deal with her own problems. The church community helped them by providing them a home away from home, giving them practical help to deal with their harsh immigrant situations, and giving a sense of greater purpose to suffer in the dehumanizing situation. But at the same time, the church community also suffered from fights and division. Their "real" life happened in the church and the "real" life included conflicts. Not only did they share a lot of good things with each other, but they also experienced deep conflicts. The church was a small world for them. The recognition they could not get from the Canadian society, they wanted to get from the church, their immediate world. They tried to compensate their diminished status in the society by having some status at church. Their pains, hurts, and struggles in the society were poured out into the church. The church tried her best to absorb their pain but sometimes it was too much for the church to bear their burdens. The church was not well-established or equipped to accommodate different opinions to help them learn how to live together with each other's differences in peace and harmony. The church experienced many splits, and every time a new church was formed. One of the contentious issues was eldership. Who becomes an elder was a big issue. Being elected as an elder gave them a sense of worth, recognition, and respect which they didn't get in the society. When they didn't get elected as elders, they felt devalued, hurt, and deeply disappointed. This shows how diminished their existence had been in their immigrant life. In the early part of the Korean immigrant life, Korea was in turmoil politically. Some churches strongly spoke against the human rights violations in their homeland which they left. Others felt uncomfortable to hear political messages from the pulpit every week. This was another cause for the church split. Canadian politics were never a cause for their conflicts. Even now, their main political interest is what is going on in Korea. Church conflicts and division have exposed how much stress they had to bear in their everyday life.

Church Split and Second-generation Korean Canadians

Unfortunately, the church split affected the second generation Korean Canadians deeply at their personal level. They made friends at the church. But since their parents were in conflict with each other, with no choice, they had to leave the church where all their friends remained. Overnight, they had to be separated from their friends. This caused them confusion, sadness and sometimes even anger. But more than anything else, this created the mistrust for the church and for Christians in the minds of the second-generation Korean Canadians. They thought their parents were so devoted to their church and to God and yet they did not know how to live in peace and harmony like good Christians. They saw their religious zeal on the one hand, and on the other hand, they also saw the hypocrisy and the immaturity that brought conflicts and fights. This caused disillusionment in second-generation Korean Canadians about the church and furthermore about Christianity in general. So, some second-generation Korean Canadians left the church and never came back. Even if they come to church now, they don't want to get heavily involved. They have a very passive attitude. They do not have a high view of the church.

The conflicts and division were not the only reason for the second-generation Koreans to have lost interest in the church. The first-generation Koreans did not build up the church leadership for second-generation Korean Canadians. They did not prepare them to deal with spiritual challenges they would face in the upcoming Canadian culture. Simply, Korean immigrant churches were not equipped to prepare their children because they themselves did not know the Canadian society in depth. The first-generation Korean immigrants' prime concerns were twofold: one, their survival in their present situation, and two, the future of their children. One first-generation elder told me that it was their mistake not to have trained the future church leaders. Even though the church played such an important role for them, they did not think of building up the leadership for the future church. Their main concern was to survive and to prepare their children for their own future at the personal level. They did not focus much on the future leadership of the second and third generation for the church. Their main concern for their children was not to help them carry on the ministry they started but it was solely focused on their personal well-being and their children's. This was caused by their fear for survival. They emphasized their children's education not for education's sake but for survival. They believed that the only way to survive in this hostile Canadian environment was to be well-educated and even better educated than other Caucasian people. They felt that if their children were not better than other Caucasian friends, they would not be able to survive because of racism that was embedded in this society. Many second-generation Korean Canadians indeed did very well as their parents wished. Many of them have received high education and gotten good jobs. They are highly successful. They do not need to worry about their survival as their parents did. However, there are not enough leaders for the church because they have never been encouraged to participate in the church leadership. Many second-generation Korean Canadians never had ownership for their church. They were simply going to their parents' church. Even though they had many friends in the church, it was never their own community. They were very dependent on their parents to run the church. Their understanding of Christianity is very limited at the level of Sunday school. Most of them do not have a deep root in Christianity. They did not want to deal with deep theological issues on their own. Church is very much a social place where they meet their friends. It is a place where they turn their minds off after stressful work during the week. Instead of, as Abraham Heschel said, the six days existing for Sabbath's sake, for second-generation Korean Canadians, Sabbath existed for six days.[8] Church is not a home away from home to them. They did not need church to provide a safe place for them because to them Canadian society is no longer a dangerous place where they needed to protect themselves from. In that sense, what the church meant to the first-generation Korean immigrants was very different from what it meant to the second-generation Korean Canadians. They are very much a part of this Canadian society. They are comfortable in the Canadian society. Even though they have kept certain Korean traditions like food, some mannerisms, and cultural understandings, they enjoy being a part of the Canadian society. Unlike their parents, they are very familiar with the Canadian ways of living. They go see movies, they go to theaters and concerts, find good restaurants, and often go out to eat at fancy restaurants, and take vacations anywhere in the world. They do not need the church to provide them with social outlets. The church is not that crucial for their survival.

Second-generation Korean Canadians are not interested in politics in Korea like their parents. They have no idea of what is going on in Korea. However, many of them are not interested in Canadian politics either. They are comfortable being in Canadian society and yet they are not really involved in it either. Their main interest is in their work and their immediate family. Everything else is secondary, including the church. Church is not their home and their community at the deepest level. They are merely interested in the services the church provides for them. Many of them left the church because of both disillusionment for Korean immigrant churches and the secularization of Canadian culture.

---

8. Heschel, "Sabbath," 14.

Development of Two Services in Different Languages

At one point, there were more than three hundred Korean immigrant churches in Toronto alone. Korean immigrants in Canada experienced something unique which is different from that of neighbors down south. After the early immigrants in the 1960s, the majority of Korean immigrants came in between 1973 and 1979. From 1980, Korean immigration in Canada almost stopped until it started again in late 1990s. This affected the church in an interesting way. Korean churches could not grow through new immigrants during that time. Their future existence had to do with the second-generation Korean Canadians. During that time, thirty thousand Korean immigrants landed every year on US soil in three major cities: New York, Los Angeles, and Chicago. Korean churches in the United States didn't have to deal with the existence of second-generation English-speaking members. Without them, churches were growing because of new immigrants. The second-generation English-speaking members silently left the church. But in Canada, the Korean churches had no choice but to face the reality of their future. They sensed that they didn't have a future without the second-generation English-speaking members as far as the church is concerned. Every church in the Korean immigrant community had to deal with second-generation ministry. Many churches did not have a formal English-speaking worship service. Their worship was like Sunday school worship. Now they all tried to build formal English-speaking worship services. Unfortunately, there weren't many second-generation English-speaking ministers and so it was hard to build the formal English-speaking worship services. Korean immigrant churches looked for leaders who could both speak English and understand the Korean culture. Some churches have a bigger English-speaking worship but others have only a small service for high school students. Only a few have the proper English-speaking self-sustaining congregation.

Part II
Present Story

4

People of Faith (I)

Nam Soon Song

> Now faith is the assurance of things hoped for, the conviction of things not seen. (Heb 11:1, NRSV)

THIS IS A STORY of our church, Asian Canadian Churches, or that of people of faith journeying in a strange land. In God's grace, our church story continues today in Canada. Although a handful of our churches have been present in this land for over a hundred years, our stories have not been heard until now. We acknowledge that our church story can also be your church story, given that we as Christians are connected to one another. While we may worship God in different places in Canada based on our language preferences or ethnic backgrounds, all of us are still one in faith of Christ and share the story of Jesus Christ. We share some common ethnic cultures—Chinese, Taiwanese or Korean—yet we don't all speak the same language. Some of us speak Cantonese, some Mandarin, some Korean, some Taiwanese, and of course many of us as second, third, and fourth generations speak English, but there is no "us and them," only "we."

Our church buildings come in various shapes and sizes: Some are very old buildings purchased from other Caucasian churches that have closed or relocated, while others are brand-new buildings designed and built to accommodate multiple congregations at once. Still some churches rent worship spaces from other churches, mostly mainline Caucasian churches. Let us consider the signposts outside the church buildings first. In many of our churches, the church name is displayed outside in the ethnic language only. In other words, there are a very few Asian immigrant churches whose church name in English and English service time are displayed outside. It is interesting to note that over time some of our churches have changed the church name to shed ethnic identification. For example, one church used to be called the Maple Chinese Church. Now it is known as the Maple Christian Church. Likewise, Matthew Korean Church dropped its ethnic identification and officially goes by the name Matthew Community Church.

Some of our churches have two or three language worship services under the same roof; some have only one ethnic-language service constrained by finance and space availability. Let us now delve into the stories of congregations with two or three language services.

We, the first-generation Asian Christians living in Canada, choose to attend ethnic-specific churches given the fact that they offer what we grew up with, and hence there is an increased level of comfort and familiarity with the language and culture therein. We do not have to change or adjust ourselves at the ethnic specific churches. Currently there is an ongoing demand for ethnic-language service for the first generation, ethnic-language-speaking congregants, and for the newcomers from our homelands. A separate English-language worship service is necessary for our English-speaking second generation without any language-related hurdles, in addition to serving as an invitation to our English-speaking neighbours. Our current arrangement—having separate services in two or three languages under the same roof—seeks to accommodate both the ethnic-language-speaking first generation and English-speaking second generation, as well as others who might be interested in coming to our church. Therefore, the English congregation is comprised of mostly English-speaking young adults and working professionals, whereas the ethnic-language congregation is predominantly an older, aging group of first-generation adults.

Recently, there has been an increase in the number of worship services offered in Mandarin in order to accommodate the growing number of Mandarin-speaking immigrants from mainland China. A select few Chinese and Taiwanese churches in the GTA have begun offering three main services to address the different needs and language preferences of their multi-generational congregants. For example, Mandarin is the official language of present-day Taiwan, thus the young, recently immigrated Taiwanese members speak only Mandarin, not Taiwanese. This is why some Taiwanese churches are offering separate services in three languages: One in Taiwanese, one in Mandarin, and one in English. Many of us prefer to attend one church as a family, albeit separate services at the same time, space permitting, in order to join our family members for fellowship or even communal lunch afterwards. If separate services are held at the same time, the ethnic-language congregation usually worships in the main sanctuary, and the English congregation in the gym or the basement. If services take place at different time slots, the ethnic-language congregation usually worships at the prime time slot (i.e., 10:30 am or 11:00 am) with the English congregation worshiping in the early morning or afternoon time slot. Chinese churches with three separate worship services in Cantonese, Mandarin, and English, then the Cantonese congregation—the older, dominant group of the church—would take the main sanctuary at the prime time slot for worship. Out of all the churches offering two main services on Sunday, only one church offered the prime time slot of worship to the younger English congregation in preparation of the future of the church.

A number of well-resourced Asian Canadian churches in the GTA offer three main services on Sunday in order to cater for the generation-specific taste and language preferences of their congregants. In such cases, the first main service takes place early Sunday morning for the mostly older ethnic-language-speaking congregants, who prefer the traditional style of ethnic-language worship with traditional hymns. This is followed by the second main service, which is offered in English and is vastly different from that of the ethnic-language service in terms of style, organizational structure, music, and so on. The third and final main service at noon is unique from the rest as it takes a nontraditional approach, incorporating contemporary Christian music (CCM) and concerted prayers in between.

In most ethnic-specific churches the English congregation is yet to become the dominant group owing to its financial dependence on the ethnic-language congregation. In other words, even if each congregation makes its own budget, the ethnic-language congregation often supports the English congregation financially and otherwise. However, the proportion of financial support from the ethnic-language congregation is different for every English congregation, and largely depends on the English congregation's own financial capability; out of fifteen churches, two churches had an arrangement where the English congregation voluntarily paid a monthly fee in lieu of rent, as a token of independence. Many English congregations expressed amazement at their ethnic-language counterpart's offering surpluses. They considered it as a blessing for the whole church. By offering separate services in two or three languages, we pray that our faith in Christ is passed down from generation to generation in Canada, our new homeland. We may look like one church with two or three self-governing bodies or departments. Let us look deeper into the current inner workings of our churches.

Church as Spiritual Home

As Biming, a Chinese language minister, observes: "No matter what happens on Sunday we would come to church, even under rainstorms or blizzards. We are so loyal to this church. We love the church so much. Which means we love God so much . . . this church is called for up-keeping the loyalty we have for our faith, for fostering our neighborly love we have for one another." An English minister, Moses, claims the presence of a distinct kind of spirituality at the ethnic specific churches: "It would be safe to predict better future outcomes for this church under the condition that the distinct Korean spirituality, and strengths of Korean immigrant church, are preserved and further enhanced."

Our churches have been serving as "spiritual homes" for immigrants who arrived in a new land hoping for a better life but without much information, just as Abraham left his homeland with nothing but God's promise and "built there an altar to the Lord" (Gen 12:7, NRSV). Some of us were not Christians back in our homeland; however, after having arrived in Canada and becoming lost and overwhelmed in a completely new environment, we needed to rely on God for a sense of security and belonging. Chen Yi puts it this way: "Mainly because I accepted the Lord in this church, baptized here and joined this congregation, then I feel this is my spiritual home. There is no reason to depart from your home . . . We don't choose our spiritual home, just like you have no choice for where to be born." Some of us were already Christians in our homeland and found ourselves growing even closer to God and deeply involved with the church after coming to Canada. So Young describes just how much we cling to God in our daily life here in Canada:

> The first-generation immigrants have no one else to turn to but God. We desperately rely on God in our daily lives for guidance and comfort. Indeed, some first-generation members have had active church life back in Korea, but in navigating a new life as immigrants we learn to rely on God more than ever. In other words, the first-generation member's environment brings out their desperation and sincerity toward God. So, it is no accident just how much they are invested in the church life.

Jae Min, who began attending the church for the first time after coming to Canada, echoes her sentiments:

> We are passionate about worshiping God every Sunday and very invested in the church life in general. There is an early morning service every day at my church. There is also a Wednesday worship service and Saturday worship service.

Every year, church members take turns fasting. Dedicating as much time out of our lives to serve the church and worship God is very important. We become full of the Holy Spirit and get closer to God. As such, I try to attend as many early morning worship services during the week. Personally, I found that attending worship services during the week in addition to the Sunday service helps me to engage in a time of self-reflection. And more importantly, my own faith matures.

Ming Dao agrees with Jae Min: "We know how we can go, how we can face the future, how we meet the challenges, difficulties. We always need to pray, we need to pray to the Lord who gives us opportunities, so we can foresee that we need to keep going. No matter what we encounter here, we always feel we have the support from God." Being able to worship in one's own ethnic language helps immensely, especially considering the language barrier—or lack thereof—at the ethnic-specific churches and many first-generation worshipers' inability to comprehend the sermon in English. Case in point: The first-generation worshipers would not be able to fully engage in the English worship service due to their limited English proficiency, and their compromised worship experience would become a hurdle to receiving grace in worship. It is no accident that many ethnic-language-speaking first-generation adults live a church-centered life in Canada with the help of their ethnic specific churches—one that seeks to address a very specific spiritual "hunger." To put it simply, our ethnic-specific churches have made us feel at home and more comfortable being ourselves due to the ease of communication, as Chen Cheng echoes: "We the first-generation immigrants feel at home when we were able to use Taiwanese for our worship." Seok Ho agrees with Chen Cheng: "The Korean language service helps create a strong sense of community amongst older members of the church. Specifically, older Korean members of the church can feel at home during Korean language worship service and nurture their relationship with God and with each other." Several others echo their sentiments on how the current arrangement of providing at least two worship services separated by language preferences can help make them feel right at home during worship, which in turn helps nurture their faith. Given the ease of communication amongst ethnic-language congregation, we can freely discuss our spirituality, pray together, listen to sermons in the language we feel most comfortable, and sing hymns in our ethnic language. What this means is that being able to speak the same language at least within our ethnic-specific churches can help enhance our spiritual growth. We are able to get the most out of sermons and actively participate in the worship service in the absence of a language barrier, both of which are critical to our personal spiritual growth and maturity.

The ethnic-specific churches have been serving as spiritual homes not only for the ethnic-language-speaking first-generation, but also for the English-speaking second generation and beyond. Jasmin, a second-generation interviewee, says that this is a spiritual blessing: "I feel very comfortable coming and going, because I have travelled quite an amount over the years, and coming back to my present roots each time is a blessing spiritually. It's like a comfort blanket." Lian, another second-generation interviewee, puts it this way: "The beauty of having two generations of congregants in two different languages is to provide them a place for worship, gathering and fellowship, especially for the second generation . . . We have provided them an environment in which to feel comfortable to grow spiritually. Having friends is one of the important advantages for them, in finding companions for this spiritual walk."

God's Call to This Church

Attending our current ethnic-specific church and serving the Lord and the community through the church we believe is God's call. A second-generation interviewee, Melia, tells her story as follows:

> I've always grown up in the Chinese community and so it's been a very natural process to be um in a Chinese church. Even though, yes, I'm second generation, but I grew up with lots of friends that are also like second generation. We both speak English and Cantonese, or English and a Chinese dialect. I never really thought about stepping outside to go to another church, like not a Chinese church. I think God's call for the Oak Tree church was pretty strong for me. In terms of uh, in terms of desiring for him to establish a house of prayer at the Oak Tree church.

Another second-generation interviewee, Sam, echoes her sentiments: "Over twenty-nine years I've seen people come and people go, I've seen a lot of that. I'd say myself, I'm a loyal. I feel like there's really not a perfect reason to leave the church that God has called you to, unless you completely disagree on certain doctrines and it's uh affecting your ministry." Again, another second-generation interviewee, Robert, confirms God's call to his church, saying: "Yes, I [initially] joined the Korean ministry, which I really liked. But [there was] the generation gap. When I went on missions, I realized what it actually means to follow God: To put down everything you have and follow him. When I went on the foreign missions, I really came to love being in this church [and now] consider this place as my own."

Jin Hee, a first generation interviewee, says the following about responding to God's call to her current church:

> In retrospect, I think it was a part of God's plan to send my family to this church. When I was in the process of deciding which church to attend in Canada, I prayed for one thing: That I would be able to focus on the word of God above all else. I asked God to send my family to a Bible-centered church. I think this church was God's response to my prayer. I have never thought of attending another church.

So Young, another first generation interviewee, agrees, "I believe that coming to this church was a part of God's plan. I knew that this church was the one for my family. We prayed about it for a long time and God would show us that this was the one for us. And everything else worked out, we moved to a new home, opened up a new business, and settled into our new lives around the church."

No Excuse for Church Absence

What we have is a certain spiritual need that can only be addressed at our ethnic-specific churches, thus we are naturally committed to the church and worshiping God every Sunday. There is no excuse for skipping church, whether rain, shine, extreme cold, or illness. We are at the church no matter what happens to us, under any circumstances. Susan tells her story as follows:

> Oh, this (going to church) is very important and this is something we do as a family, even though we're not physically in the same worship. But literally they will take me every time and it's like something like engrained in you. Like for my family, even if you're deathly sick, like you still go to church, it's just not a question . . . the first-generation Koreans, definitely their sense of prayer and like certain spiritual disciplines is very strong . . . Even though it's difficult and really early in the morning you still go. It's a good role model of certain disciplines, like prayer, it's amazing.

Ruth also shares her story, which is quite similar:

> But, it was never an option. It was one of the few things in my life that was a constant. I knew that I had to go to church with

my family on Sunday. So that was kind of engrained into me at a young age. Which I'm thankful for now when I'm older. Um, so a lot of it has to do with just something that was expected and then became a habit, but eventually the understanding and desire to be here kind of followed. So I think I had to be here for all of it to click, so I'm glad I had to be here.

Ruth continues firmly: "This is my church and I love it very much. This is going to be my church for better and for worse and I'll trust that God is going to work here and I'll try to do my part while I'm here." She has developed a special bond to the church and is deeply committed to her church-centered life; her love for the church grew stronger even after experiencing hurtful, conflict-ridden church splits in the past.

Jia Xing, a first-generation interviewee, remembers how committed she was to her church-centered life, and the ways in which she coerced her children into church activities in the past: "When we were young, we pulled our children to Sunday worships, no matter how busy we were. As long as there were church activities, we tried to participate, but now we don't have that kind of spirit as we are getting old." What we have is a strong sense of community around our church, built on having not only multiple services per week, but also fellowship through communal meals and activities after service. This kind of continued engagement after service helps our church family stay in touch during the week.

For many immigrants attending ethnic-specific churches, the church itself has become the center of life. So our lives often revolve around the church, following a faith-based, church-centered lifestyle. Therefore, as Seok Ho claims, "The church community also becomes our source of strength." The culture of devotion amongst Asian immigrant churches in Canada, particularly amongst Korean immigrant churches, is quite unique. For example, a number of Korean immigrant churches in the GTA offer church-sponsored services and activities on a daily basis, such as QT (i.e., a meditative reflection exercise on Bible passages), Wednesday worship service, Friday evening prayer meeting, and early morning worship services, all of which are typically not offered at a mainline, English-speaking church. The Korean Canadian congregants in particular tend to prioritize church attendance and are quite invested in the church life; they are the epitome of church-centered lifestyle. These different church-sponsored services and activities help foster a sense of connectedness among members, eventually leading to communities of faith to grow together in Christ.

Faith as a Part of Who We Are

We cannot separate faith from who we are as a person and a community. While faith is a gift from God, we are called to nurture it continuously in our home, church, and society. Faith is a part of our daily life, not just our church life, especially for those of us attending ethnic immigrant churches. The ethnic immigrant churches help connect both the ethnic-language congregants and English-speaking congregants to their roots through sharing common experiences, ethnic food, and cultural holiday traditions (e.g., the Lunar New Year and August Full Moon). For example, one Korean immigrant church in the GTA holds a New Year's Eve service around midnight every year. Before the New Year's Eve service commences, the first-generation Korean members prepare a communal meal for the whole church, which is typically a traditional Korean dish like red bean soup (i.e., Potjuk). The members of the church also gather together to play a traditional Korean game (i.e., Yutnori) before having the communal meal. This is considered a wonderful time of gathering and celebration for the whole church, with both the Korean-speaking first-generation members and English-speaking members present. The younger English-speaking children in particular, most of whom are third-generation attending the Korean language school, show a keen interest in the Korean culture after such church-wide cultural events. These children also perform a New Year's bow (i.e., Sebae) to the elderly Korean members as a part of Lunar New Year celebration at the church. In return, the elderly Korean members present a monetary gift (i.e., Sebetdon) for children. The Chinese and Taiwanese churches also celebrate the Lunar New Year and August full moon as a whole church, with special traditional food and rituals at the church. Such church-sponsored cultural events often attract the unchurched Chinese and Taiwanese people from the local community, especially the international students seeking a taste of their homelands.

The ethnic church community is one of the few places where children of second or third generation can receive validation for their ethnic identity. Most children really do not have any other places to go for constant support and validation. They come to accept their ethnic identity with the support from members of church community. We observe this especially amongst small children at church, who show a heightened interest in their ethnic culture after participating in different church-wide cultural events. Perhaps the right kind of push is all that is needed for children to become more than bystanders in these events, which will in turn help them make peace with their ethnic identity.

Being able to connect to our ethnic roots is integral to the creation of a hybrid identity, which helps the ethnic-language congregants and English-speaking congregants alike as they navigate their lives in Canada outside the church. Ruth says that her church is the only place where she can receive cultural learning, which is an added bonus that comes from attending ethnic specific churches. She spoke of "a love for my Korean heritage, but it's definitely tied into church, because that's the only place where I get my cultural influence from . . . that extra bonus of being part of a Korean church." Stuart echoes her point, speaking about the importance of "learning the significance about family and just keeping some of that [Taiwanese] culture." Likewise, Ming Dao claims that: "We can still enjoy understanding life together, so we know where we are coming from."

Ji Hun has witnessed a wide array of benefits of having two worship services separated by language preferences at his Korean immigrant church, one of which is helping the second- and third-generation children build themselves up with a distinct hybrid identity:

> They end up with a hybrid identity. As we go from one generation to the subsequent generation, the Korean immigrant churches can help make sense of this hybrid identity from combined cultural experiences—the good, the bad, what to accept, and what to discard . . . If they want to take root, they must first understand the roots of their parents. I am not saying the second generation ought to adopt the ways of their parents. It is about making sense of who they are as second-generation Korean Canadians.

Passing on Faith from Generation to Generation

The most frequently mentioned reason for providing a separate English service at the ethnic specific churches was the transmission of faith from generation to generation. The ethnic-language-speaking first-generation members in particular are encouraged to share the stems of faith and pass on that faith to the next generation. As noted above, we cannot separate faith from who we are as a person; it is an integral part of ourselves. Although our churches offer separate worship services to cater to language preferences, it is still an ethnic immigrant church at the core with the majority of its members continuing to identify with the ethnic cultural heritage, traditions, and practices. Therefore, one of the most important roles of ethnic immigrant churches is helping its members retain the ethnic cultural aspect of their faith. What this means is that our current arrangement of having separate services in two or three languages under the same roof is necessary for a number of reasons: First, for retention of ethnic cultural elements in our faith; second, for fostering camaraderie between different generations; and third, for solidifying the ethnic Canadian community ties. As Jin Hee puts it: "We can share stems of faith by staying together as a family in the same church, just as faith was passed on from generation to generation in the Bible."

The vast majority of ministers agree that the transmission of faith from generation to generation is one of the most valuable assets of offering multiple services under the same roof. Jane echoes this, saying: "I think it is a way that the first generation is able to sow [seeds] into the next generation, by leading through example, serving as credible witnesses, but also at the same time not enforcing their own language that might no longer speak to the second generation . . . It is biblical to be multigenerational, or for that relationship to continue—fostering this continuum is very important." When the next generation of believers are allowed to grow up in the same church as their families, the family ties and values are strengthened. Min Woo concurs with this observation regarding family values, saying: "Passing on the values, roles and lessons of the Korean immigrant churches to the next generation of worshippers is real benefit for ethnic churches. As the older parent generation, we plant a seed of faith in our children to continue the work of God's kingdom. Our children will do the same for the succeeding generation. This is a cycle upon which the Korean immigrant church is preserved."

This is one of the reasons why the first generation devotes themselves to the church financially and spiritually, which includes giving generously to the church, and praying diligently for the next generation of Christian leaders and believers. Jin Hee continues to tell her church story, which is relevant here:

> My current church life helps to preserve the church itself, by guiding the next generation of worshipers to the faith-centered lifestyle. Just as the faith had been passed down from Abraham to Isaac in the Bible, so we can only pass on our faith to our children by staying together in peaceful coexistence. If ethnic immigrant churches can successfully help upcoming generations' faith life, they will continue to exist within their respective ethnic enclaves. We can make necessary sacrifices to preserve our faith into the next generation.

Kate agrees, as follows: "The parents go to the adult congregation and the children can be in the youth service or the English congregation. They are still together even though there are different services; they're still able to worship together in one church in a sense. It might be different services, but it is one building, one church." Stuart expresses his joy of worshiping with his parents in the same church as follows:

> I love worshiping with my parents. It is a very family-oriented thing. The other second generation [members] have some of their parents in the church as well . . . My parents' friends are like my friends; they are almost like my [own] parents. They saw me grow up. I saw them grow older. And I grew up with their kids and we have seen [each other] getting married and growing our families with our own kids. So we are all one big family. As the first-generation congregation sacrifices for English congregation, there is expectation and hope for second generation congregation.

Jae Min says, "We have a relatively strong KM, with many active first-generation members passionate about worshiping God and serving the church community. Following their lead, I hope that the second-generation members in the EM can be reenergized and become more passionate about church life."

In general, the English-speaking second-generation congregants are cautiously hopeful about the future of their ethnic immigrant church. Despite the claims of "mass exodus" of second-generation Christians from their respective ethnic immigrant churches, there has been a renewed optimism and hope for the next generation and what lies ahead in the future of the church. Ruth envisions that her ethnic immigrant church would be strong and resilient into the next generation, saying: "It's the people, I think. When I see the next generation, so the younger kids, it's the high school ministry. When I see them, really good kids, you know. And they love church, they love God, and when I see that it just makes me very hopeful, hopeful for our church. Even though it struggles, it does, by no means feel like a dying . . . when I say, it's not, it still feels like our church is, it just feels new for some reason."

At one ethnic immigrant church in the GTA, all generations of English-speaking members would have a joint Good Friday service every year, bringing together everyone from kindergarten children to young adults. It is interesting to hear that every generation takes part in the preparation, organization, and execution of this annual joint Good Friday service. Ruth describes it as follows: "It was very exciting . . . at the core of it, still, is our Christian faith and what we believe and what we want to celebrate. It was exciting to see everyone working together to make that happen. So at the core of it, there's still people at this church, that want to give everything to make sure that God's will be served."

Some English-speaking second-generation members are vocally appreciative of all that the first-generation members do to support the church, and even look up to them as role models. For example, Susan, a second-generation interviewee, appreciates the positive influence her mother has had in her life, saying: "Um, I think, like, my mom is a huge role [model] to me in terms of how she does church and how she does faith. And I'm like a little scared to think of the day when I am in her shoes and like she prays like so fervently and like she's so close to the Word and I don't know if I can live up to that. And just seeing her heart for, she has a huge heart for Christian education and just seeing how much she does for it." This tells us that the active prayer life of the first generation has had an immeasurable impact on both the church life and home life of the second generation and beyond, inspiring them to pray regularly and fulfill their potential as Christians.

Another related opportunity arising from having multiple worship services under the same roof is potential intergenerational learning opportunities that can bridge the gap between different generations and language groups sharing the same cultural roots. In addition, the ethnic immigrant church can help resolve generational differences between family members by building mutual understanding and respect. For instance, members of the first generation are called to guide and mentor members of the second generation, and not simply instruct them, through sharing common experiences, offering support, and praying together. Again, Jin Hee observes that "[t]he Korean-speaking first-generation members have a chance to learn about the younger generation's views and values through a mutual interaction at close quarters. The Korean-speaking first-generation members can benefit further from learning about English-speaking second-generation members' views and values, most of which overlap with those of the mainstream Canadian culture."

Ann echoes the above sentiments as follows: "Because of different values growing up, it's nice to be able to come and talk to the kids and feel connected and find a solution together. Also, some of the adults in the Chinese congregation are second generation, so talking to them really helps, because they went through it and they can give us a better perspective on our parents while relating to us." Ga Eun and So Young stress the importance of the role of bridge builders at their ethnic immigrant church housing multiple services in different languages. Ga Eun says, "I think being able to attend the same church and worship God together even in separate worship rooms helps bridge the gap between the first generation and second generation." So Young agrees, saying: "Older members can serve as a model of faith to younger members, and I think that is a plus. But if we have a complete separation of EM and KM, that connection will be lost, and it will be like two separate entities." Susan refers to her own learning opportunity that came from observing the older generation praying at her church: "When I see the older generation pray and the amount of prayer things that they have, it just reminds me of how important that is, and even though, yes, it's difficult and really early in the morning, you still go. So yes, I think there's things to be learned, you just have to look very carefully."

Also, the majority of ministers serving the ethnic immigrant churches in both language ministries concur that the transmission of faith from generation to generation is one of the most valuable assets of offering multiple services under the same roof. Jane supports this, saying, "I think it is a way that the first generation is able to sow [seeds] into the next generation, by leading through example, serving as credible witnesses, but also at the same time not enforcing their own language that might no longer speak to the second generation . . .It is biblical to be multigenerational, or for that relationship to continue—fostering this continuum is very important."

Joy and Strength from Serving the Church

Serving the church brings joy to many of us; it has been our source of strength as we navigate our lives in this new land. However, if we were to attend non-ethnic mainline church, and not our own ethnic church, the opportunities presented to us to serve the church would be very limited. And not just for the first-generation members with limited English proficiency—the same applies for the English-speaking second generation as well. Charles, a second-generation interviewee, puts it this way:

> I am more stable in this environment as I have been here for a long time. I married a Taiwanese person and I would like my kids to have an exposure to the Taiwanese community. I find that in this environment I have more opportunities to serve. I have actually gone to a [local] neighbourhood church for a few years. And this experience was a bit different because it was a big, mega church. It was less personal. There was [also] less opportunity; you really had to go and seek out if you wanted to get involved. I have been attending this church for almost forty years.

Jae Min explains how serving the church impacted his faith life and life in general:

> After arriving in Canada, I was introduced to this church by an acquaintance. I joined the church after listening to the pastor's sermon on the very first visit. I was baptized shortly thereafter.

I have been with this church for a total of seventeen years. The church has served as a source of strength and aided my efforts to adapt to a whole new life in Canada. I have stayed loyal to this church. Over the years, my faith has grown step by step through serving the church community in various capacities. I have been committed to serving my church whenever I can and I am happy to be able to do so.

Bible in Daily Life

For many Asian immigrant churches, the Bible is viewed as central to church life. So in order to lead a Bible-centered church life, we are encouraged to read the Bible daily and study together in groups across all generations, such as in cell groups. There is an especially strong emphasis placed on reading the Bible daily, so that we may learn to live as the Bible teaches us. Ideally, this practice becomes integrated into our faith. Jin Hee says, "Over the years I have seen many members of my church working hard to live their life according to the lessons from the Bible, which in turn motivated my personal journey of living out my faith to please God and his people. For example, I have strived to stand in solidarity with the weak and underprivileged members of our local community. This has become an integral part of my faith life."

In Asian immigrant churches, the stems of faith not only pass on the important Christian values and traditions from generation to generation, but also help make sense of the world in which we live. The children and youth learn to apply their Christian faith to their own life outside the church walls. And the stems of faith can be strengthened if they are allowed to address difficult questions at the church. Jin Hee stresses the important role of stems of faith for the children and youth growing up in our Asian immigrant churches, saying: "Sharing stems of faith within family and church community is becoming ever more important in this fast-paced world, otherwise how would children know and accept the word of God as the right standards of life"? Thus far, Asian immigrant churches have been able to guide children and youth's faith life beyond the limits of church walls through participating in a number of joint mission initiatives, such as the Evangel Hall Mission (cooking a hot meal for those in need), Out of the Cold (opening church doors to the people on the street and providing basic necessities including meal and shelter), Love Toronto (providing professional services to the underprivileged by a Korean local church), Yonge Street Mission (working to respond to immediate needs), local indigenous mission, and missions overseas.

Power of Language

Whether or not the second-generation members speak the ethnic language makes a huge difference. This is because the power of language is incredibly profound, as told by the following stories from the Bible: The Tower of Babel story in which one universal language was diversified to prevent us from challenging God, and the story of the Pentecost in which people from every nation at the Pentecost heard them speaking in one's own language by the Holy Spirit. Thus, language has tremendous power bringing and binding people together. These are the stories from the Bible we often refer to and reflect on time and time again, which strike a chord with Asian immigrant churches. Likewise, Brian adamantly insists on the importance of the language itself for Asian immigrant churches, saying: "The whole question is about language. Never even mind the ethnicity part—what language you are running your church services in makes a big difference. You might think: Well God is trying to send all these things, does not matter what language. But at the end of the day, you are still speaking a language. You are still singing Psalms in a language. That matters to people." Having real-time translations of the worship service is just not the same as being able to worship in one's own language. Ping agrees, saying: "In multiple services, the younger generation they can't understand Taiwanese at all, I mean they can talk about regular conversation, but when we talk about listening to the sermon, they couldn't understand it, even sometimes we translate it. But they don't like translation, they feel they don't learn anything from it." Some people find it difficult to stay awake even with real-time translations of the worship service at their disposal.

Having a language barrier at the church would become a cause of a lot of undue problems, conflicts, and misunderstandings, most of which could be avoided with seamless communication between congregations. This tells us that our language is more than a mode of communication at the worship service; it is vital in bringing about a cultural understanding at the church. Any language, regardless of origin, is developed for and by the people of a certain culture, thus it is a key element that brings about understanding between people—in this case, between congregations. As such, the second-generation or 1.5-generation members who are able to speak both languages often act as bridge builders at the church; their role is to help connect different congregations under the same roof. For example, Melia observes that:

> So I think it's kind of a rare case where second generation children can understand both languages. Because a lot of times that

language, Chinese, would be the one that would be deteriorating as a skill, but I find that it's been helpful to know Cantonese because it allows me to understand the Chinese congregation a lot more in terms of why they might not really understand like what are the kids doing. Just being like the bridge between the two.

This chapter briefly discussed the benefits and opportunities people of faith have from accommodating two or three different language congregations under one roof. There will always be challenges in whatever we do, especially if we want to make changes to our church's current system. Our Asian immigrant churches in Canada continue to deal with many challenges arising from having two or more congregations under one roof. However, we have been able to remain hopeful in faith. Next we will take a look into some of these challenges, and why we still retain our hope in faith.

Reflection and Discussion Questions

1. Which of the stories presented in this chapter do you most identify with? What are the commonalities with your own story?
2. What does your Asian Canadian immigrant church mean for you today?
3. Why is having faith significant to you today? What role does faith play in your life?
4. What benefits and opportunities do you see from having separate services in two or three languages in your church?

5

People of Faith (II)

Nam Soon Song

For we walk by faith, not by sight.
(2 Cor 5:7, NRSV)

Accommodations

THE VAST MAJORITY OF lay and clergies interviewed agree that the main strength or benefit of having separate services in two or three languages lies in the accommodation of cultures, generations, and languages at the church. More than twenty interviewees indicate that this accommodation is of utmost importance, as it brings different generations of family members together to worship at the same church, albeit in separate rooms. The added benefit of this kind of family-oriented environment is that family units and family ethos are strengthened. The latter is an observation made by nine interviewees during their interviews.

Although the language barrier prevents different generations of family members from worshiping in the same service, most family units still prefer to stay together in the same church. According to both the lay and clergy interviewees, one of the major benefits in having multiple worship services under the same roof is the ability to accommodate different generations, cultures, and languages at the church. Liu notes, "Each congregation—the TM (Taiwanese ministry) and EM (English ministry)—can grow on its own. Congregants can choose to worship in their own language or the language of their preference. In short, congregants can worship in the language they are most comfortable with."

Most interviewees express their excitement about how the ethnic immigrant ministry as they have experienced it might evolve to meet the needs of the second- and third-generation congregants. In particular, the ethnic immigrant churches can help address certain ethno-cultural needs of second- and third-generation members raised in culturally hybrid or bi-cultural environments. Min Woo confirms how the current arrangement of having separate services in two or three languages seeks to meet these specific needs:

> The Korean immigrant church can meet their language needs, associated ethnic sentiments, and cultural character. Although the English-speaking second generation were born in Canada and educated in the Canadian school system, they were raised in a Korean household by Korean-speaking parents. They have certain ethno-culturally specific needs that cannot be met in an English-speaking mainline church.

It is indeed possible to house multiple congregations of the ethnic immigrant church under the same roof by accommodating different languages, cultures, and generations therein. Interestingly, however, most common challenges faced by the ethnic immigrant churches arise from these very language, cultural, and generational differences. In other words, when there are two or three congregations sharing the same roof, their apparent differences in language, culture, and generation become a barrier to seamless communication, making it difficult to be one unified church and leading to possible conflicts and even church splits. So what we see as our strength can also become our weakness, or a source of challenges.

Challenges

While every church grapples with challenges and difficulties arising from generational differences, which caused the bulk of the younger generation to leave the church, not many churches are dealing with them at the same extent and severity of ethnic immigrant churches. The language barrier between the congregations is further compounded by the cultural and generational barriers, rendering the reconciliation process more difficult. For example, the cultures of the ethnic-language-speaking first generation and English-speaking second generation can be quite different, even if they share the same ethnicity. It is simply unrealistic to expect the people from the same ethnic background to get along without any issues or barriers. Our interaction in close quarters under the same roof is just more complicated due to the differences mentioned above. Fa notes, "Due to their different thinking and values systems, they would constantly give one another 'shocks.' Such 'shocks' would stretch out their cultural acceptance of one another, or in other words, widen their comfort zone." It is important to realize that the multiple congregations in ethnic immigrant churches may share the same ethnicity, but often operate and think differently given their distinct cultural environments in which they grew up. Put simply, the second-generation congregants grew up in an English-speaking cultural environment vastly different from that of the first-generation congregants in terms of language, norms, values, customs, and traditions. Kate, a second-generation interviewee, claims, "Now we're second generation um, you can't expect us to have that same thing because we grew up in a different culture and a different world and a different time." This suggests that our ethnicity is less important than the culture we are embedded in, how we are raised, and what values we have when dealing with issues and barriers at our ethnic immigrant church.

Communication Challenge

The communication challenges are inherent to these language, cultural, and generational barriers. Facilitating seamless communication is the most pressing challenge for all ethnic immigrant churches with multiple congregations to date. For example, the ethnic immigrant churches often face difficulties in holding joint worship services, meetings, ministry programs, and activities due to the communication challenges and associated logistic problems. Although some of our churches have one joint session or board comprised of members from all language groups, the majority of members in such positions find it difficult to work together as a team in the absence of seamless communication. Sometimes, miscommunication between members of different language groups leads to long-standing misunderstandings at the church. To summarize, the communication challenges resulting from language barriers at the ethnic immigrant church refer to not only communication difficulties between language groups, but also a general lack of communication or poor communication overall. This is a cause for concern, because such communication challenges often result in a sense of disconnect, misunderstandings, or feuds between congregations sharing the same roof.

As Sui Hui says, communication is a challenge for the whole church: "Communication is always a challenge, not just day-to-day talks, but in the church as a whole." The communication styles also vary by language groups at the church. The apparent differences in styles of communication have made Kate express her concerns as follows: "I think how Mandarin people . . . communicate is very different from how Cantonese or English people do. It could come off as more aggressive than it is and maybe they don't mean it to be so." Moreover, communication challenges unintentionally exclude people from meetings and joint services at the ethnic immigrant church. Melia raises a relevant example of exclusion at her church: "People might get excluded just because of language, not intentionally, but I guess we forget sometimes that [in] running meetings if we don't have a proper translator, some people get excluded because they don't understand the content of the meeting." Similarly, Chen Yi notes: "It is difficult because we have different languages. For instance, we have been trying to arrange some family worship in English, [but] because the parents do not understand English, they don't come and there is no participation." Such communication challenges between different language groups at the church can also make people feel uncomfortable, as Ji Yang puts it: "It can be a barrier because I don't speak Mandarin, or I can understand English but not too much, then that can become a barrier between two congregations. It is quite difficult, or you know you will not feel too comfortable in communication in one of those languages." And as a result of the language barrier between congregations, the ethnic-language congregation is often in the dark about what the English congregation is up to, and vice versa. Liu puts it this way: "If you are worshiping in the English congregation, you don't even know what is going on in the Taiwanese congregation. The language barrier, coupled with the cultural barrier, doesn't help either. This all makes things more challenging for our church." The language-related hurdles often separate the English congregation from the ethnic-language congregation into their own ministry sphere; each congregation ends up doing their own activities apart from the others. Ji Yang observes this phenomenon as "two separate areas, two separate worlds. We lost communication!"

Aside from the language barrier, the cultural differences between congregations create further communication challenges, which can develop into cultural shocks and mutual misunderstandings. If left unresolved, each congregation can end up in completely different directions from one another. Ji Yang says, "We should note that the 'cultural differences' that feed into communication barriers are multifaceted: While the first generation members espouse mainly 'Asian culture,' even the traditional ones, the second-generation members, identify with a hybrid of Western [Canadian] and Asian culture." Not surprisingly, these different ways of thinking and communication reflective of our "cultures" have often resulted in misunderstandings between the congregations, hampering not just efforts of communication, but also cooperative ministry. We rarely have a chance to communicate with members of other congregation(s) at our church, especially if we have completely separate worship and fellowship schedules.

We might not come face-to-face with each other even after years of attending the same church.

As Jane notes, the cultural differences between congregations have become a major barrier to good communications: "I always find our communications are an issue in our church." She continues, "I think the challenge is to keep the communication going, so that there is a deeper insight and understanding. Sometimes, this constant relaying of information between the EM and CM becomes quite challenging." Susan voices her frustration at the lack of communication resulting from both the linguistic and cultural barriers at her church:

> There is a lot of lack of communication between the two sides and therefore like there's a lot of frustration with both sides that happens a lot of times because people just don't communicate and because there's like this language barrier but also a culture barrier of like, for us, it's like a mentality of "oh that's so Korean" and for them it's like "oh, they're so young, or they're so EM." In terms of like a congregant member, they're over there so I don't think about them. Like I literally come in, worship, hang out with friends, fellowship and then go to eat, and I don't, most of the time I'm not thinking of that side.

Robert echoes her sentiments: "If there were more communications between each section (the Korean ministry [KM] and English ministry [EM]) we wouldn't be having as big of a problem as we do now. There are a lot of people leaving church precisely [due to the lack of communication], which really shouldn't be the case."

The growing cultural gap between generations makes for an even greater communication challenge at the ethnic immigrant church. Brian expresses it as follows: "The culture . . . this is kind of getting into the ethnicity, but I think ethnicity may be less important than the culture you are embedded in . . . you still have a generational gap. That renders our current challenges more difficult. Older people have older ways of doing things; younger people may want to do things in a different way." Furthermore, each congregation's unique culture brings different issues and interests to the table, which explains in part their focus on different priorities and diverging needs. Ba Men articulates this as follows:

> There are some struggles in coordination and communication. As for Mandarin and English, other than the differences in language, the topic is an issue: the Mandarin group likes to talk about what happened in their mother country, including politics, which touch their feelings. But the younger generation

wants to focus on what they face in social media, how to deal with drugs, school life, how to deal with parents and teachers etc. The focus is different and their patience is also different. The English (sermon) topic they like to be finished in fifteen minutes, while the Mandarin people want it longer, up to one hour, and this is a big difference. The older ones want a longer sermon also; they feel they learn more, but not the younger generation.

In addition to each congregation's different preferences for the length of sermon, the choosing of hymns poses a challenges at the joint service of the ethnic immigrant church, as the preferences differ once again from congregation to congregation. For instance, the English-speaking second-generation congregants usually prefer to sing more contemporary hymns, use a variety of instruments including bass amps and drums, and dance on stage while singing, whereas the ethnic-language-speaking first-generation congregants would likely reject these ideas based on their discomfort, claiming that it is "[T]oo noisy! This is not singing to the Lord." Shirley, a second-generation interviewee, says the following about the typical first generation's reaction to the nontraditional worship style: "I don't understand where they're coming from because I definitely grew up in the environment where we would worship with guitars, drums, and everything. And sometimes I feel like they're looking down on the English service, they feel like we're belittling our faith in a sense, just because we're steering away from the traditional way of worshiping." The ethnic-language-speaking first-generation's discomfort and rejection of the nontraditional way of worship may even be perceived as the discomfort and rejection of the English-speaking second generation in general, making it more difficult to facilitate good communication and collaboration between the congregations.

Segregation between Languages Groups

Most of us attending the ethnic immigrant church with multiple congregations yearn to coexist harmoniously, and present a united front as one church. However, there is an ongoing sense of disconnect between generations and language groups in such settings. It is problematic for the two or three different congregations to maintain an intrinsic longing to become one unified church. Both the clergy and lay express their concern regarding the segregation of congregations at ethnic immigrant churches, which is not a good witness overall and especially for children growing up in this kind of church environment. Our children are sometimes exposed to the feud between the ethnic-language ministry and English ministry at the church, including confrontations and arguments between adult members.

Moses, a second-generation pastor serving the English ministry, refers to the continued resentment amongst the English-speaking second generation toward the ethnic-language-speaking first generation at his church: "Some English-speaking second generation members are dissatisfied with the current arrangement, as evident in their negative mindset. As the minority of this church, they feel that they are being treated as second-class citizens . . . They claim that the church is KM-centered—run by the first-generation KM adults, for the first-generation KM adults." This deep feeling of resentment leads some English-speaking congregants into questioning whether they should remain at their ethnic immigrant church. So Young, a first-generation interviewee, has an empathy towards the English-speaking congregants; she feels that they are justified in their feelings of resentment and frustration over being excluded on a regular basis at the church. Thus far, we have discussed the language barrier, ethnic-centric way the church is being run, and English-speaking members feeling left out.

Jia Xing refers to the isolation of different language congregations, and a resulting sense of dissonance or reduced harmony: "We may be more isolated because when people are not speaking the same language . . . there is a distance when you worship separately. Again, it is the problem of communication; the harmony is reduced between two different generations." Seok Ho adds that "having two separate groups under one roof weakens the notion of one unified community." Sui Hui openly laments the reality of this prolonged sense of disconnect at the Asian immigrant churches: "Somehow it's an upstairs-downstairs-church, upstairs you do your things, downstairs we do our things." This tells us that there is a popular mindset of "us and them" in ethnic immigrant churches. Susan confirms the existence of this mindset, saying: "[With having] two separate services, I think there's [something] very like an 'us and them' mentality." Ji Yang echoes her sentiments: "They are doing their own and we are doing our own." In the end, the different language congregations sharing the same roof may look like completely separate entities. So Young concludes, "I think the biggest challenge is the generational disconnect. Although being under the same roof is better than the complete independence of EM, there is a lack of common ground between the EM and KM. Sometimes it feels like there are two separate entities under one roof."

Shirley describes a divide between the different language congregations belonging to the same ethnic immigrant church:

So there's sort of like a divide where we feel like we can't bother them and we can't really interact with them in a sense and we're not really there together. We're not sharing the same space at the same time either, so even though we're under the same church, I don't know them. I would see them and say, 'oh, hi, hi' and then pass them. We have nothing to do with each other, because we don't do the same things.

It appears that almost every Asian immigrant church with multiple congregations is grappling with the issue of "unity." This is because having more than one congregation under the same roof weakens the notion of unified church community. Gerry raises his concerns about this, saying: "We are still one church with one unified board. We are still one leadership trying to move our church towards maturity, although we may approach it differently."

Lian echoes his point:

> It is quite easy for our church to become a three-head-chariot, if we all run in different directions. That is why we seek unity, and that should not be lost from sight. If we don't work together for unity, you just do yours and we do ours. Even if we have the same goal in mind, we would end up pursuing it separately. The way we do it somehow is a bit different from how they do it upstairs. There is even competition between two or three congregations, although it might be friendly competition. Therefore, cooperation is one of the major challenges. Just being able to work together as one church community is difficult, if not impossible.

Kate uses the word "segregation" for describing the current arrangement of having multiple ministers at her ethnic immigrant church: One for serving each of the ethnic-language ministry, and one for the English ministry. She says, "I have no idea what the Mandarin congregation is doing, or the Cantonese congregation . . . I guess my focus is on the English ministry. Pastors are able to focus on their own ministries, but that in a way segregates us. I have no idea what the Mandarin deacons are doing . . . and so that causes more independence—we're doing our own thing." Similarly, Gerry expresses his concern, saying: "If you are worshipping in the English congregation, you don't even know what is going on in the Taiwanese congregation."

Hence, to ease the degree of segregation, the ethnic immigrant churches often encourage different language congregations to interact during the fellowship hour. More often than not, however, we stay with our own groups. A case in point: A number of our churches serve lunch for all congregants after service. At lunch time, the EM (i.e., English ministry) members tend to stay with fellow EM members and the same goes for the TM (i.e., Taiwanese ministry) members, CM (i.e., Chinese ministry) members, and so on. It is quite difficult to overcome generational differences during the fellowship hour, given that the ethnic-language-speaking first-generation members grew up under the Confucius hierarchical structure. Min Woo, a minister serving the ethnic-language ministry, is also aware of this challenge, saying: "There are some challenges arising from the generational differences at my church . . . This leads to further KM-EM segregation, causing each side to be closed-off, immobilized and disconnected." While sharing the same roof, each language congregation fails to see what other language congregation(s) might need. As Ashley puts it:

> One of the major challenges is simply remembering each other, especially in terms of planning and coordination. The KM is significantly larger. When they plan for church-wide programs and activities, they sometimes fail to consider the needs of EM. But at the same time, the KM expects full participation and co-operation from the EM. As such, some church-wide programs and activities are rendered irrelevant to our contexts and sensibilities. Even as some members of our EM congregation seek to participate in such programs and activities, they wouldn't be able to make sense of it all.

The different language congregations sharing the same roof do not work together for planning and running programs for a whole church. In other words, member representatives from all sides do not take part from the beginning of any planning processes at the church, to ensure fairness in decisions for all parties involved and equitable distribution of resources. Smith, a pastor serving the English ministry at his ethnic immigrant church, hopes to develop a working relationship between the KM (i.e., Korean ministry) and EM (i.e., English ministry):

> One of the things I am looking forward to is developing a working relationship between the KM and EM. The KM is so much bigger than us. If we would ever want to do something different, why don't we start from seeing each other more? As of now, everything is so segmented. Every member belongs to a category and his/her designated space—even the small children have their own space in the building.

Smith makes a valid point—if we have to start from somewhere, why not start from seeing each other more, face-to-face?

Another EM pastor describes the current relationship between different language congregations at his church as follows: "I think aside from occasional conflict of communication, we get along very well. This is because we maintain a healthy distant relationship, for the lack of better words. We say to each other: 'We love you, we respect you doing your own thing, you will love us albeit at a healthy distance and respect us doing our own thing.' You can say that we are very Canadian in that way." With respect to this phenomenon, Ming Dao expresses his reservation as such:

> The challenge is we don't have time to really understand each other, how you are going to bring back the connection, that's the most challenging. Unless you really have the fellowship together . . . we really translate in the way the English-speaking know what we explain to them, in this way we can always stick together. Otherwise, the second generation will leave, they will separate, [and] they will go to other places.

But there is still hope for bringing different language congregations together at the Asian immigrant churches, as demonstrated by the success of one church's joint summer retreat. Before holding the joint summer retreat, this particular church observed limited interaction between the EM and KM members, with most members staying with their own group and refusing to connect with those from the other side. For the very first time in church history, this church decided to host a joint summer retreat for the EM and KM. During the actual summer retreat itself, both congregants had a really fun time mingling, connecting, and engaging with one another. An attendee of the joint summer retreat recalls: "In all fairness it was a fun retreat, and I actually would have preferred it that way than going on our separate ways as usual. It really did make other things better, like places we would eat and sleep, because such things would be taken care of by the KM. And the educational department would take care of the EM. The problem was just the lack of communication, which was the same as always."

In most of our Asian immigrant churches in Canada, there is no intercommunication system for all leadership levels. While a few churches hold joint session meetings that bring together elders or board members across different congregations, the power dynamics at play, coupled with the language barrier, can make working together extremely difficult. It is common to find ethnic-centric agenda at the table, as the members from ethnic-language ministry have dominated the board both historically and financially. Aside from the language barrier, many board members from different language congregants find it difficult to collaborate together on a regular basis due to the different styles of planning, organization and management of church-related projects. This is why collaboration between different language groups at the church occurs very rarely, if at all. In rare instances of collaboration, one group often ends up planning and running the entire project while the other group—most likely the English-speaking—just follows along and assists. What usually happens at the end of such collaborations is that the English-speaking members do not see the meaning of continuing the collaboration in the future, because they feel like they played no meaningful role in it. They would want to be treated as partners, not bystanders.

The ethnic-language-speaking members, on the other hand, complain that the English-speaking members were of no help to them. Both sides only see the faults in each other, because in many such instances of failed collaboration they do not step in each other's shoes. As Biming says, "Theologically and namely we are one church here; practically we have two bodies, that is, two congregations. Each congregation operates pretty much on her own." It is like having two or three different churches operate under the same roof. The failed joint collaborations have had a negative impact on the spirituality of the church, leading some to misconstrue the spiritual vision of the ethnic immigrant church in question.

Leadership Challenge

Another key challenge for our ethnic immigrant churches comes from the leadership—or lack thereof—amongst both the laity and clergy. It is challenging to find—from a small pool of qualified candidates—a suitable pastor who is equipped with a sound theological understanding and good grasp of the ethnic language to meet the needs of our churches. It is even more difficult for a senior or lead pastor and associate pastors to form working partnerships, due to the hierarchical power structure of East Asian culture. Ministers serving the same Asian immigrant churches may thus experience an early burnout from the double (or triple) burden and workload.

Kate describes her concerns for the ethnic immigrant church leadership as follows: "There are so many challenges from leadership all the way down to even just lay people, and so I think leadership-wise there definitely is a mess in terms of [what] you're dealing with. So at the senior pastoral level it's as with the Mandarin, according to all the different pastors, it's sometimes very silo'ed ministries." Several laity interviewees and a few pastors express their concerns about segregated or isolated ministry leading to one-of-a-kind "ghettoized" community at the church. Charles, a laity interviewee, adds the following with respect to his pastor's leadership: "I know that our pastor is very biblical in his teaching and preaching. It is hard if you are a non-Christian to even understand him, because he is very black and white." Brian recalls a different kind of leadership challenge arising from specific language needs at his church: "It is much harder to find leadership or suitable pastors. It is because we must have a [bilingual] pastor who speaks both Taiwanese and English. It is very rare to find a candidate who satisfies this condition." While the young Taiwanese members of his church can speak either English or Mandarin, the older Taiwanese members are not fluent in these languages. Instead, they are fluent in the traditional Taiwanese dialect. At this time, most Taiwanese churches are unable to locate leaders who can speak all three languages fluently. Ideally, they would like to hire multiple ministers—one for Taiwanese ministry, one for English ministry and even one for Mandarin ministry—to care for their two or three congregations separately. Unfortunately, the Taiwanese churches are not in the position to exercise this option due to their ongoing financial struggles.

Abraham recalls a different kind of challenge arising from the imbalanced leadership between the ethnic-language ministry and English ministry: "One of the major challenges of ministering to the EM congregation is that the church is structured in a way to favour leadership on the CM side. Right now, most of the board members and deacons are from the Chinese congregation. As a lead pastor of EM, I am essentially on my own." Liu refers to the challenges associated with hierarchical power structures within church politics: "You are not really equipped to navigate a system shaped by a specific culture. It's tough. I think this is where all the pastoral burnout comes from. Everyone I talk to—the people in the EM—are great. It is the other stuff, the hierarchical politics and associated drama within the church that causes burnout in the ministry."

Space Challenge

A number of our Asian immigrant churches face issues of space availability, such that all worship services, events, church schools, Bible study, and parking are prearranged and coordinated. Many interviewees are thankful to be able to do so, even as they experience scheduling conflicts given the limited rooms and resources available at the church. The scheduling conflicts can often be resolved with efficient communication between all parties involved—between the ethnic-language congregants and English congregants in particular. Since most of our ethnic immigrant churches offer many services and activities in two or three languages, there is not enough church space to accommodate them all without a scheduling conflict. We usually have several activities going on at the same time, and very tight schedules around which to plan each activity. We can easily notice this from our worship times for the ethnic-language ministry and English ministry. One church is very thankful for the recent surge of children joining the church, as Chen Yi indicates: "We now face a problem recently, we don't know why we suddenly have a lot of little children coming, praise the Lord, but we are in shortage of rooms for children's Sunday schools." The parking spaces, along with extra rooms, are in constant demand with the growing number of young families and small children joining this church.

Lack of Ownership of English Congregants

Another challenge faced by our ethnic immigrant churches comes from the passive or inactive English-speaking second-generation congregants, who lack a sense of ownership of the church, especially given the rapidly aging demographics of Cantonese, Taiwanese, and Korean congregations. The decrease in the rate of immigration from these home countries (i.e., Taiwan, Cantonese-speaking parts of China, and Korea), coupled with the aging members of the ethnic congregations, is contributing to the declining membership of a number of Asian immigrant churches in the GTA. Despite some positive projections, the overall English-speaking membership of such churches has yet to grow. And the second generation's sense of church ownership is not quite there, at least from the perspective of first-generation congregants. Then what is preventing the English-speaking second-generation congregants from claiming ownership of their ethnic immigrant church? According to interviewees from the EM side, they feel as though they are considered insignificant and secondary to those in the ethnic-language ministry. Jae Min articulates it, saying, "In many immigrant churches, the EM is of secondary importance to the KM. The EM is not as active as the KM at my church, so the EM is not able to carry out major mission projects or relief efforts at this time. I hope the church can raise the EM up so that it can join forces with the KM in different mission initiatives and relief efforts."

Moses, a second-generation pastor serving the English ministry, expresses the same concern: "While it is necessary for the second-generation EM members to take ownership of their own church, their sense of ownership—or lack thereof—is not an end in itself. Having a sense of church ownership would just help the EM congregation stay committed to this church." One EM pastor is concerned about the EM congregants' devotion to their church—or lack thereof: "In general, the first-generation KM members are proactive, strong-willed, and highly devoted. I don't know if this is something unique about our second-generation EM members, but they are generally more laid back than their first-generation counterparts in the KM. The EM is not as devoted as the KM." Another EM pastor suggests that, "There is also one fundamental difference between the first-generation KM members and second-generation EM members: Whereas the former is church-centered, the latter is family-centered. Unlike that of the first generation, the second generation values family and family life above all else. This is partly why they are not as devoted to the church as their parents."

Hope in Faith

Hope for One Unified Church

Although sometimes the expectation brings disappointment, and our strength turns into a weakness under the current church model, our ethnic immigrant church with two or three separate congregations gives us hope for making progress towards one unified church. While the language barrier inevitably separates different generations attending the same church into two or more groups, all of us are Chinese, Korean, or Taiwanese Canadians at the core. We come from a similar family unit and background. Regardless of the language barrier, members of each family unit are united by certain family traditions and values. So why should the church family be any different? We do not think the language preference matters much; the language itself is just a tool for communication and should not be used to cause conflict between generations. There are more important things—things that matter—holding us together as a unified church family. The church should focus on sharing God's message, and whether you heard the message in Korean or English is not relevant to your individual ability to live by it. By having them in the same church, albeit in a service in a different language, the first-generation adults are hoping to instil in their children the love of God and value of consulting the word of God in challenging situations. In the long run, the first generation adults would like to help them realize that following God's directions will lead to permanent solutions. In other words, the first generation can serve as the next generation's guide for leading a faith-centered lifestyle. Jin Hee is a vocal advocate for her church's current arrangement of having two separate services in different languages under the same roof:

> I think it is important to treat the current arrangement as a mutual learning opportunity—a chance to experience things we would not otherwise be exposed to. Likewise if first-generation adults do not know anything about the Canadian culture,

how can they be of any help to second-generation children's struggles to take root in Canada? I have come to realize that my Christian faith is an integral part of my life—the two cannot be separated. The Korean-speaking first-generation members and English-speaking second-generation members are equally indispensable to my church community, and should stay together under the same roof.

Opportunity for Mutual Learning

So Young describes the differences between the English-speaking members and Korean-speaking members at her church when it comes to volunteering around the church, living a Christian life, and serving mission initiatives. She believes that these differences can turn into opportunities for mutual learning, as she says:

> Perhaps these differences are due to generational gaps or cultural differences . . . but it really does not matter why such differences exist or who is right and wrong. What matters is that they are different and there is something unique and worth learning from both the EM and KM . . . the English service offers something unique and different from the Korean service . . . When we acknowledge the differences, we will be able to improve our faith life by maximizing on each other's strengths. We have something to learn from each other.

Hope for Future Leaders

Having multiple languages spoken at the church can be considered advantageous, given that many parents today prefer to teach their children more than one language. While some ethnic-language-speaking youth and young adults are on the verge of leaving their church behind, we pray that they stay and become the next generation of leaders for our ethnic immigrant churches. Chen Yi puts it this way:

> We hope we would have younger generations growing up to pastor in the Chinese language, maybe twenty years later, which will be great! It is good to get those who are not interested in learning Chinese to be exposed to the language. So the language challenge becomes an opportunity then. We are glad to see some Chinese-speaking young people turning into future

leaders of the church, they may even go back to China to preach the gospel, which will be great!

Ruth, a second-generation interviewee, is appreciative of what the first generation has done for her church. She hopes that the English-speaking second-generation congregants would step up and begin taking responsibility for the whole church, saying:

> I think they've done a lot. They've given us this church, they continue to provide financially for this building and for our program . . . they support us. Whenever we need anything, or we have an idea of wanting to do anything, I've never had any instance where they've stopped us. They do enough . . . I think it's time for our generation to step up and start taking responsibility more.

Desire for Joint Worship Services

Both the ethnic-language-speaking first generation and English-speaking second generation love their ethnic immigrant churches, so much so that many are willing to make sacrifices for the sake of the church. For example, some conflicts can arise from the differences in worship styles and preferences from time to time. Despite these differences that are time-consuming to reconcile, and logistic challenges of providing real-time translations, the vast majority of members in different-language congregations prefer to have a joint worship service on special occasions. Members from all sides have demonstrated a willing to work with each other, in order to make the necessary compromises. Biming puts it this way: "It is relatively tolerable for all to have combined services occasionally. The English group likes playing drums and band music. Yet in combined services, they would pick some traditional hymns so that all can enjoy. All of us strive to reduce conflict of preferences."

Being Missional Churches

At this point, it is important to clarify that the Asian immigrant churches are not locked in on ourselves. We are not self-serving as to care only about ourselves or our fellow Asian immigrant churches. Particularly, in order to overcome both the inter- and intra-segregation of our ministry, our ministers and lay work to step outside our comfort zones and get involved with more activities and services for the broader local community. Over the years, the Asian immigrant churches have made significant contributions to both the overseas missions and local mission initiatives in Canada. Ga Eun asserts that:

> My church is quite unique in that our pastor is very inclusive and we are asked to not alienate ourselves from the broader local community. He emphasizes living in harmony amongst others and not just amongst members of our church. We are asked to broaden our horizons and look beyond the limits of our church, in order to be informed and involved with the matters of our broader local community.

Many of us are involved with a variety of local missions in a discreet manner, including the summer programs for the underprivileged children and youth, street cafes handing out food and drinks to the local homeless, and the targeted youth programs sponsored by a church in the Jane and Finch area, one of the most underprivileged areas in Toronto. We do it all in the name of God's love. As members of Asian immigrant churches, we believe that God loves all equally, not just Asian people, and that God wants us to spread the good news to all people. In believing that our actions can potentially change someone's life, we hope to reach out to more communities and stakeholders in the future, including the local politicians, policymakers, and donors in our area. Some of our churches have already helped shape local policy decisions, such as the ones made by the Education Committee in city hall. Many of our churches, both ethnic and English language congregations together, are also actively involved with the Out of the Cold programs (i.e., opening the church doors to the people on the street and providing basic necessities including a meal and shelter), the local food bank and Evangel Halls program (i.e., cooking a hot meal for those in need), Yonge Street Mission, Joy Women & Children's Mission Society of Canada, Visiting Senior Homes, and Love Toronto (providing professional services to the underprivileged by a local church), summer camp, and the Mission for Indigenous Peoples. A number of Asian immigrant churches are also involved with several global mission initiatives and outreach programs overseas. In general, the ethnic-language-speaking first-generation is more committed to making regular donations and going to high-needs areas for serving those in need. Some of these places include the First Nations reserves, Cambodia, Kenya, Nicaragua, South Africa, and Mexico. One ethnic immigrant church is currently involved with thirty-four independent or group mission projects both locally and globally. In some instances, this church sends out its own members to address specific needs.

So Young stresses the importance of continuing outreach mission initiatives for the community:

> First we have a number of ongoing mission initiatives serving both the Korean community and broader local community. What we do under the name of our church is also in the name of God; I only wish to glorify God through the work we do in the church. In serving those in need as a group under our church name, we will be helping to spread the good news to the non-churched.

There is a small number of people from diverse backgrounds attending the English service at our Asian immigrant churches. They are from all over the world—the Philippines, Egypt, Italy, India and so on. Some of them have formerly held other religions, such as Islam and Buddhism. And some of them were introduced to the church by their Asian spouses, upon entering interracial marriages.

Some of our Asian immigrant churches are in the position to help out other smaller ethnic-specific churches in the area, choosing to share the church spaces with them rather than charging a fee. We are able to open up our worship space to other ethnic groups by seeing a "bigger picture" of where our church would like to be headed in the future, despite the added financial burden of doing so. Jae Min describes it this way: "My church had opened up to Arabic-speaking members and has seen a steady growth of membership. Its mission initially started from Syrian mission initiatives. We first spread the good news to the Muslim Syrian refugees in our care." Other Asian immigrant churches in a similar position have opened their doors to the Vietnamese congregation, Laotian congregation, Portuguese congregation, and more. In doing so, we are reminded of our old days of renting worship spaces from other churches. In addition to sharing the worship space, sometimes we have the fellowship together after service. This is our way of giving back that fulfills the goals of our missions, which supports the smaller ethnic ministries in our community until they can set out on their own.

Being Rooted in God's Word

Some members of the English-speaking second generation emphasize the importance of being rooted in God's word, the Scriptures, since we live in a confusing world of half-truths and grey areas. For those who are unfamiliar with Christ and his teachings, the right answers seem unattainable and out of sight. Melia is quite concerned about the confusing world in which we live, but maintains hope that "[t]here's just a lot of confusion and I think if we're not really rooted in his word, then just getting back to basics, right, like, uh bible studies, knowing what his word says. Just preaching the word and teaching people how to read his word." Jia Yu, a first-generation interviewee, prefers to sing old hymns with whole verses, because they tell the entire story. According to Jia Yu, the new hymns tend to repeat the same verse over and over, so the real story behind the hymns never reaches its intended audience. She says: "Why not to sing the old ones as well, I don't know. Because it is the story, it tells us just what have happened." Other first-generation congregants might agree with Jia Yu, since the old hymns are considered classics that touch our hearts time and time again, and tend to be more spiritual than their modern counterparts. Susan, a second-generation interviewee, would like to see the culture of discipleship continue to grow and expand. For example, in college ministry, the older students are engaged in one-on-one or one-on-two discipleship training with younger students. In a similar manner, young parents can be paired up with college students or young adults for discipleship training at the church.

One Asian immigrant church with three-thousand-strong membership in the north of GTA is hoping to grow into a church of more than thirty thousand members by reaching out to the broader community of believers. The church has influenced the surrounding communities in a positive way, as it helped to make a difference at the local community level. For example, this church has become known as a place to seek immediate help and shelter in the events of emergency such as home invasion, domestic violence, and child neglect.

Hope for the Next Generation of Leaders on the Rise

Jae Min believes that the Asian immigrant churches need to adopt new approaches to attract the second generation and to accommodate people from diverse background, saying: "In order to attract second generation members, the church must raise the EM up. I hope to see the revitalization of EM once again at my church . . . The church is in the process of adopting new approaches like multicultural worship service, multiple English services on a Sunday."

Some ethnic-language-speaking congregants would like to step down from running the church, particularly those attending the Taiwanese immigrant church, as most of them are already well into their seventies. They indicate their desire to hand over the reins to the younger generation of the church. Hence they pray that the younger, English-speaking congregants would step up soon to claim their rightful roles as leaders and keepers of the church. But the question remains: Would the younger, English-speaking congregants lead the TM (i.e., Taiwanese ministry) well, just like their Taiwanese predecessors? They would do a decent job leading the EM (i.e., English ministry) at the church, but can we expect them to do the same for the TM?

Even if it takes a long time, the Asian immigrant churches with two or three congregations would like to work amongst themselves to develop a high level of spiritual maturity at the church. This is necessary for us to accept the differences between different language congregations, and those of others from outside our comfort zones. We have witnessed how faithful God has been to us as we face numerous challenges arising from the language, cultural, and generational differences. And as the people of faith, we still harbor hope for the continuation of his work through us to build the kingdom of God in this world.

Reflection and Discussion Questions

1. What challenges does your church continue to face under the current arrangement?
2. What makes you hopeful about your church's future?
3. What opportunities do you see for your own church? Are there any potential areas of growth or improvement for your church?

6

People of *Jeong* (*Qing*)

Nam Soon Song

> Ruth said, "Do not press me to leave you
> or to turn back from following you!
> Where you go, I will go;
> where you lodge, I will lodge;
> your people shall be my people,
> and your God my God." (Ruth 1:16, NRSV)

WE ARE THE PEOPLE of jeong. Our Asian Canadian immigrant church is the body of Christ comprised of people of *jeong*. What this means is that our churches display characteristics of *jeong* both within and beyond our walls. We consider *jeong* (Korean phonetic), and its equivalent *qing*, or 情 (Chinese and Taiwanese phonetic), to be one of the most difficult words to translate for a full, proper definition, let alone find a word that would serve as its English equivalent. The Chinese character 情 is composed with meanings of "heart" and "beautiful," which means "beautiful heart." Thus, the word *jeong* embodies a unique array of East Asian culture-specific emotions—that of connectedness, and togetherness, leading to a sense of closeness or belongingness. It is an associated feeling of compassion, affection, attachment, solidarity, loyalty, and relationality. It is a mutually shared feeling of tenderness and humility that arises from our relationships with another person. It can even arise from our relationships towards an entity or object. *Jeong* comes from and grows in individual relationships as well as in communal relations in a collective sense. Hence there can be *jeong* between people, *jeong* with our church, *jeong* with our nation; it is a reference to collective emotions felt by an individual person, by the general public, by the nation as a whole, as well as between individual persons and groups. As

Son says, we are bonded by *jeong*. In *jeong* the concept of "we" or "we-ness" can be expanded. In other words, the boundary of "we-ness" is broadened as *jeong* grows wider and deeper, effectively blurring the personal boundaries and allowing people to "perceive themselves as one unit rather than as separate individuals."[1] As Son continues, *jeong* is also known to be irrational and distant from the calculating aspect in relationships.[2] *Jeong* is unconditional. From the Bible we find a story of *jeong* relationship between Ruth and Naomi. Ruth's determination to follow and live with Naomi came not from duty or responsibility, but from *jeong*, which made her move to a strange land. Ruth's jeongful relationship with Naomi helped her overcome fear of unknown people in an unknown world.

Jeong can function both positively and negatively in individual relations and in the community. For example, people in *jeong*-based relationships have a tendency to care deeply about one another and stay committed to the community to which they belong. As Chung and Cho say, by *jeong* people are bonded and strive for a common goal with collective efforts, even with great sacrifice.[3] Sometimes, however, people in *jeong*-based relationships can fall into the trap of being neglectful or ignorant of the law, reason, logic, and relevant principles to advance group priorities, in favor of those in the "we" or "insiders." Then they would often end up discriminating against "them" or "outsiders" who are not part of their group founded on jeong relationships.

With this understanding of *jeong*, we would like to share stories from our Asian immigrant churches and find out exactly what happens at the church with *jeong* (*qing*). Given that *jeong* itself is quite difficult to describe, others—those outside our church—would certainly be puzzled, and may question our behaviours and attitudes influenced by *jeong*. This is even apparent when Susan, a second-generation interviewee, explains her reason for staying in her ethnic immigrant church: "I think even if I were to switch churches, like if I were to switch churches when you get married or whatever, I think I would still choose a Korean church, just because like there's something, I don't know what it is. I can't really put my finger on it, but there's something familiar and core to me that I want to keep." Indeed, *jeong* is something we cannot quite put our finger on—yet it is still familiar and core to us. Susan's special bonds to her ethnic immigrant church have been formed out of *jeong* and will deepen in time through *jeong*.

---

1. Son, "Jeong as the Paradigmatic Embodiment," 737.
2. Son, "Jeong as the Paradigmatic Embodiment," 739.
3. Chung and Cho, "Significance of 'Jeong' in Korean,"

The Church as Psychological Home

For many first-generation worshipers, the Asian immigrant church has served as a spiritual home, as well as a psychological home that helps fulfill their cultural, social, and emotional needs. At the church, we are encouraged to share everything about our life including the difficulties, challenges, joys, opportunities, sorrows, and happiness; we can do so in our own ethnic language or in English. This mutual sharing of experiences is one of the reasons why we choose to come to an ethnic-specific church over others, even from far away. Chen Cheng, a first-generation interviewee, puts it this way: "The advantage is we can listen to Taiwanese without having to listen to English all the time, that is why I said I feel at home." This at-home feeling resonates with not just the first-generation worshippers, but also the second-generation worshipers. Brian, a second-generation interviewee, observes, "We have a lot of long-term members. They have been around for a long time. It is kind of like: This is our home, and this is what we do."

Ann, another second-generation interviewee, describes how the church makes her feel at home: "Until I was five or six and then I came back for school, so I had to relearn English and it was really hard, like the first few years I wasn't comfortable in school so for me, church was a sanctuary, a safe place to be in where I can talk to adults and the kids and it was really like homey." And she insists that "at church it's easier to connect with people just because well like you're the same ethnicity there's already a sense of closeness I feel, it's easier to connect to people of the same ethnic culture because you have the same ethnic values more or less and like I don't know I feel like it's more understandable." It is not just about the language we speak at the church, it is also about the culture therein; when we can connect to the people at our church culturally, we are bound to feel right at home. Naturally, our Asian immigrant church has become the most preferred place to socialize for many worshipers. We have limited options from which to choose, and currently there is no other safe, culturally familiar and comfortable place for socialization.

Ping, first-generation minister, confirms this phenomenon: "They have nowhere to go, they come here and feel very comfortable. They know there is a place to talk with people in Taiwanese. The disadvantage is sometimes it is hard to spread the (good) news to them, all they think about is social." Also, second-generation minister Andy confirms the church as home for the second generation:

> First of all, I am serving my church because of a call to go back. Personally speaking, one of the most challenging aspects for

me is doing ministry in a dominant Korean first generational context. It has been difficult for me because in many regards I do think in a Westernized cultural mindset. The main reason why I went back to serve in that context is because there are always going to be English-speaking folks who will find comfort in that type of ethnic environment. They feel at home at church. And they need a minister like myself who can identify with and represent their feelings.

From our interviews, it became evident that both the first- and second-generation laity choose to stay with the ethnic immigrant church often because of *jeong*, particularly for a sense of home found within their own ethnic community; likewise the members of clergy frequently return to the English ministry for the second- and third-generation Asian Canadians due to *jeong*—in their case, for a feeling of connectedness and compassion.

The Family Church and the Church Family

For Asian Canadian immigrant churches, family is at the center of all the gatherings at the church. Twenty lay interviewees independently underscore the importance of having the entire family worship at the same church, albeit in separate rooms. They suggest that facilitating family togetherness is one of the major strengths of having multiple worship services under the same roof. And according to nine lay interviewees, while families may worship in separate rooms based on language preferences, the family-like ethos is strengthened just by attending the same church. When asked about the reason(s) for attending their current church, seventeen lay interviewees bring up their own ethnic community, culture, and sense of identity as the primary reasons for choosing an ethnic specific church over others, whereas sixteen lay interviewees refer to their friends and family members as the primary reasons for attending an ethnic specific church. Likewise, four lay interviewees suggest that their ethnic specific church is like a family to them, which is the main motivation for continuing attendance. As mentioned previously, being able to worship in the same church building, albeit in separate rooms, is important to the majority of lay interviewees. According to twelve lay interviewees, having the family together at the same church brings much joy. The following words and themes were frequently discussed in relation to the church during our interviews with the lay interviewees: family, family-like, and family-like ethos. We see that family plays a central role in our churches, helping to build *jeong*-based relationships while fostering connectedness amongst members.

Jin Hee puts it this way:

> I think staying together as a family becomes rather difficult as children grow up. I do not have extended family here, so keeping in touch with my children is even more important. I do not see my married daughter as much as before, because she has her own growing family. It is always nice to see her face around church and have a chance to catch up at least once a week. This is our routine and nothing out of the ordinary, but I am grateful for these shared moments. Plus, I still have at least one thing in common with my daughter—our church. I have noticed that not many immigrant families stay in the same church after children move away for school or work. So I count myself lucky.

Jae Min affirms that having both the English- and Korean-language services at the church is essential in bringing families closer together, because family members with different language preferences can still remain in the same church. In attending the same church, the bond shared between family members can be strengthened. Likewise Moses, who is currently serving as an EM (i.e., English ministry) pastor, suggests that having separate services in two or three languages at the same church is an important intergenerational bonding opportunity: "They get to see their grandparents regularly at the church, which is an intergenerational bonding opportunity. Although family members may worship separately based on language preferences, the family ties are retained through their memberships in the same church. The children and youth grow up in a multigenerational and multicultural church setting, which help them become open-minded and inclusive individuals." Young Ho concurs: "The children are able to stay in the same building with their parents even after they crossover to the EM. That is to say, the Korean parents and their English-speaking adult children are able to attend the same church and stay together as a family. They may worship separately based on language preferences, but the family ties and connections are preserved at the church." In fact, many worshipers share family ties at the ethnic-specific churches, which is an added bonus for the church's intergenerational approach for planning and services. To summarize, having family ties or relations at the ethnic-specific church helps bring different generations of family members closer together. It can also bring the different language groups together and tightness that goes along with it as well.

Stuart, a second-generation interviewee, echoes, "Well my parents go to the same church as me at the moment. I love worshiping with my parents. It is a very family-oriented thing. The other second-generation [members] have some of their parents in the church as well. My church is very much family-oriented. That is what I like. And it just happens to be a Taiwanese church." The Asian immigrant church is an important place of gathering for families like Stuart's—it serves as more than a place of worship.

While we may not all be biologically related—some of us do not have any family members attending the same Asian immigrant church—we feel like a family and often function like one. Ji Yang describes her church functioning as a family in the following way: "We are very close to each other, we are just like a family. It's a family style of church, every time when you have a problem, we just prayed for each other, we talked a lot, and we would get into intense conversations. We have cell groups as well, so that's why we are very close." We feel that the church itself becomes our family or, at the very least, "family-like." Simon claims to be comfortable at his Asian immigrant church due to this "family-like" feeling: "I'm just sort of comfortable with the church, it is more comfortable with people that are almost like family that have gone through the same experience to uh, worship together like that." Likewise Kate, a second-generation interviewee, claims that her church is like one big family:

> I think it's like we're a family. I think that's what a lot of people like to say, that we're a huge family but knowing that we're all together, worshiping in one same building and so one thing we're trying to work towards is family worship. And so, what usually happens, is there's a family, there's parents, and there's children. The parents go to the adult congregation and the children can choose between the youth service or the English congregation. So even if separated by different services, they're still able to worship together in one church in a sense. Yes, they might be going to different services, but one building, one church.

Stuart, another second-generation interviewee, echoes Kate's sentiments: "I know everybody—not just my family but also I grew up knowing everybody in the church. My parents' friends are like my friends; they are almost like my [own] parents. They saw me grew up. I saw them grow older. And I grew up with their kids and we have seen [each other] getting married and growing our families with our own kids. So we are all one big family." Such tight-knit closeness of the Asian immigrant church—like that of a family—can make us feel at ease coming to church. We fit right in at the church. We also do not hesitate to call each other brothers and sisters due to this "family-like" closeness. Shirley, a second-generation interviewee, notes that it is easier to become like a family with other members at a Chinese immigrant church than other ethnic immigrant churches:

> Uh. I think the advantages of being in a multigenerational church is, we're from the same roots. We're all Chinese in a sense. We do have groups but predominantly, mostly it's Chinese people. And being in a group of Chinese people, you sort of, it's easier to understand what somebody is going through. If someone tells you there's something going on in the family, then you'll understand why this is happening in the family because you've been through it or you've heard of it. So it's easier to connect and it's a lot easier to become a family with one another because it's sort of, I don't know what it is, but it's something, personally I feel more connected to Chinese people or Asian people rather than Caucasian people. It's easier for me to communicate with them. Because we're just interested in the same things.

Brad, an EM (i.e., English ministry) pastor interviewee, claims that the arrangement of having two or three services under the same roof helps retain "family-like" connectedness at the Asian immigrant church. He notes that such arrangement can be mutually beneficial: "The younger generation in particular benefits from the financial contributions and wisdom of the older generation in other language groups." Ashley, another EM pastor interviewee, agrees with Brad, confirming all the different ways in which the English congregation is supported by the ethnic-language congregation at her church: "Having two separate session might be easier at first, but we might lose our appreciation for certain things like prayers, church space and support and take them for granted. We don't realize how much the prayers of the people are mutually supportive." As Ashley observes, the English congregation often receives financial support, in addition to spiritual guidance, from the ethnic-language congregation sharing the same roof. Ashley also believes that having the ethnic-language congregation and English congregation together in the same building can be mutually beneficial:

> I think one of the main advantages is mutual support—the KM (i.e., Korean ministry) has strengths in certain areas that we as EM (i.e., English ministry) can look to and vice versa. We are seeing this is in session, while we were open to hearing advice from the KM side, we wanted to be proactive in sharing our thoughts and ideas with the KM. There is a mutual boost of the ministries. I have been blessed through this process.

Moses agrees with Ashley, saying how blessed the second-generation members are in his English congregation: "It is a blessing for the second generation. Specifically, the second-generation children are blessed to be growing up in a church with such active prayer life. They are often the beneficiaries of faith-centered, prayerful lifestyle of their first-generation parents."

Just as in most Asian families, the Asian immigrant churches consider sharing a meal together as a group, one of the most important rituals. As such, most Asian immigrant churches arrange to have a communal meal after the Sunday service. This creates an opportunity for table theology, where people can get better acquainted with one another and have fellowship. Charles, a second-generation interviewee, puts it this way: "Eating is a very big thing, right? Especially in the Taiwanese culture, I think this goes back to the thirties or forties when food was very scarce. Our common greeting is: Have you eaten yet? This is when you see somebody you know." The same type of greeting seems to be common all over East Asia. When we have a communal meal at our church, we are sharing more than food—we are said to be sharing *jeong*. The food may disappear from the table, but *jeong* remains. And *jeong* grows with every communal meal we have at our church.

The ethnic community in general is invested in getting together to eat as a group; the Chinese, Taiwanese, and Korean ethnic community in particular treat meal-sharing as an important cultural ritual. It is only natural that we are passionate about sharing food at our church, not just on Sunday, but whenever occasion arises. This is a unique aspect of our churches that sets us apart from other churches. To be more specific: Most other non-ethnic, mainline churches provide simple refreshments after the Sunday service. Likewise, unlike that of the Chinese, Taiwanese, and Korean immigrant churches, most ethnic immigrant churches do not arrange to have a full communal meal after the Sunday service. In the Bible, we see many examples where people gathered together to have a communal meal. And such examples of communal meal-sharing emerge even after the resurrection of Jesus. In that regard, our East Asian culture seems to resemble the culture of old Israel.

With the arrangement of having separate services in two or three languages, we are able to accommodate interracial or multicultural marriage couples that prefer to attend the same church as a family. Many such couples adjust well at our Asian immigrant churches, and become part of the church family. Jun Soo, an ethnic-language pastor interviewee, explains: "We have several interracial couples; they prefer to attend our church together as a family, rather than going to separate churches on Sunday. These couples can choose worship services based on their language preferences at my church." Min Woo, another ethnic-language pastor interviewee, explains how the ethnic immigrant churches meet the specific needs of interracial or multicultural families: "The Korean immigrant church can meet their language needs, and associated ethnic sentiments and cultural characters." Gerry, a

Taiwanese EM (i.e., English ministry) pastor, says the following about accommodating interracial or multicultural marriage couples: "We have a few members who are not ethnic Taiwanese but married to a Taiwanese spouse. When a Taiwanese spouse wishes to attend a Taiwanese service, the English-speaking spouse of course does not understand Taiwanese. We can accommodate their needs." Our Asian immigrant churches can accommodate the language preferences of both spouses in interracial or multicultural marriages, hence these couples are able to attend one church as a family. And through *jeong*, these couples experience the solidarity and connectedness with other members attending the same Asian immigrant church.

The Church as a Social Hub

In addition to serving as our psychological home, the Asian immigrant church serves as a place for caring for and helping one another, bringing solidarity and bonding together in a foreign land. It is a social hub. It is a place where we can ask questions and receive appropriate assistance in our own ethnic language. At the church, we can help each other in times of need, thereby fostering solidarity and cooperation amongst members of the congregation. We are encouraged to help out in many different ways, whether it is counseling, searching for jobs together, offering helpful tips, or praying for one another. In general, the ethnic immigrant churches have been helping the new immigrants in their transition process, from navigating the school system to securing new jobs in Canada. Ga Eun shares her story as follows: "Speaking personally as a Korean immigrant this arrangement (having two services under the same roof) helps foster a community of sort—as immigrants we face similar hardships as we navigate our life in Canada. We can share our stories and pray for each other. We can be a source of comfort for one another. We can share tips, news, and even tackle challenges together."

Jae Min shares the following story, which reflects his personal experiences:

> Seeking help from English-based local community centers or churches is difficult because many newcomers arrive with limited English skills. I was able to gain useful information from people I met at church, which in turn helped my family get started on our new life in Canada. For example, I did not really know the kind of business out there for new immigrants like myself. I was connected with the right people at church, which helped me set up my business. Forging connections

with people in the know through church has helped me a great deal; I think it was so much better than starting out on my own. I cannot imagine what my life would be like if I hadn't made those important connections at church, but I am sure that there would have been more hurdles. Who knows where my family would be if we hadn't made the decision to attend church as soon as we landed in Canada? I think the immigrant church helps address the gap in services for immigrants, as most people come to church hoping to receive support and assistance to get them settled in Canada.

Ann, a second-generation interviewee, describes the kind of help and support system she can expect from her Asian immigrant church:

> For the second generation because we go through so many of the similar things together we can help each other out like I know for us like because there's this generation gap and different cultures growing up, our values are a bit different from our parents, so sometimes that conflicts and it's really hard at home. But, we have youth groups on Friday and there's junior high groups or like um small groups on Fridays, and we would come together and talk about it and it's really relatable because we all have similar going on like little problems with our families because of different values growing up and it's nice to be able to come and be able to talk to the kids and feel connected and find a solution together, but also some of the adults in the Chinese congregation are also second generation, so talking to them really helps because they went through it and they can give us a better perspective on our parents while relating to us.

The Church for Building Long-Lasting Relationships

When the English-speaking second-generation members grow up together at the same ethnic immigrant church, they build long-term friendships over time, which helps them stay committed to their church. Melia, a second-generation interviewee, puts it this way: "I've always grown up in the Chinese community and so it's been a very natural process to be um in a Chinese church. Even though like, yes, I'm second generation, but I think I grew up with lots of friends that are also like second generation, um, like their parents were immigrants and we both speak English and Cantonese, or English and a Chinese dialect." Simon, another second-generation interviewee, concurs: "For me, personally, it's just long relationships with the people here. I've grown up with a lot of them for a long [time], for pretty much my whole life, so that's sort of the main tie. Just long relationships I have with them."

Connecting to Our Roots

The Asian immigrant church has also functioned as a keeper of ethnic culture, and thus has helped connect its members to their roots. This is one of the reasons why sometimes our churches are deemed "boxed-in" or "locked-in." Nevertheless, the Asian immigrant church's ability to make connections between the members of congregation and their roots is an important asset, as Jia Xing says: "The advantage (of attending ethnic church) is that heritage has the connection, no matter what language we speak or what generation we are, we have to consider the heritage connection, which is important to me. I think without the heritage's connection, I don't need to be here." Jia Xing further emphasizes the importance of making cultural connection to her Asian immigrant church, saying: "Even I can go to English service and understand their language, but the culture and the mentality are different, so I don't feel the passion, it is hard to feel the warmth out there. It is much easier to talk and joke in our own language." Jia Xing claims that the "heritage" connection between herself and the church is the primary motivation for continuing attendance, which makes her feel the warmth, or jeong. Sui Hui concurs: "Culturally, we all come from the same background, so we share the same ideas and communicate better. We find it easier to become close friends with one another."

The value of connecting to our cultural roots is recognized by both the first generation and second generation. Stuart, a second-generation interviewee, hopes that his third-generation children would have a chance to learn about their cultural origin and become more familiar with their cultural roots:

> The advantage is that you get the [Taiwanese] culture. You get that kind of Taiwanese background, the culture, and the food that comes with it. In a Caucasian church or another church, you would not get those kinds of experiences: All the little sayings, mannerisms, and the [cultural] stuff I grew up with. So I am comfortable with them. These are things my kids will see and learn about: [They get to be exposed to my] Taiwanese background. If my kids grow up in a Caucasian church, they wouldn't be exposed to this [cultural aspect] of the way we worship, the way we have fellowship and eat lunch together after service and even the way we do activities together. If my kids

were raised elsewhere, they would not have a chance to familiarize themselves with even the way we do certain things within the worship, such as praising in both Taiwanese and English and providing translations in our services.

Jasmin, another second-generation interviewee, thinks that "[t]o go to, to start to go to another church would be sort of pulling up roots." Deborah agrees with Jasmin, saying:

> We've tried the Anglo church. We live far away actually. It's a good drive for us to get here. There is a certain understanding of each other's position, we have very like upbringings. Even when we talk about our parents, there's a better understanding because we have grown up in the same atmosphere with the same rules, general rules. Everyone's different but just and there's a little connection there that brings us back to where we're from.

Deborah affirms that she feels rooted at her Korean immigrant church. She hopes that her children would learn more about their cultural roots in the future, saying:

> I just want my kids to, we don't have anyone Korean in our neighbourhood. We don't know anyone else Korean except through church. Yeah, so, um, and I'm very proud of our culture too. Like I don't want my kids to forget it. I put a lot of effort into learning the language and I want to teach my children the language as well. So uh, I think it's, I don't want us to forget our culture. I think it's important to love it, but still be able to open up to who we are.

Ruth also asserts her love for the Korean heritage that is closely tied to her membership at the Korean immigrant church: "I was born and raised in Canada. I have a very, like strong Korean . . . a love for my Korean heritage, but it's definitely tied into church, 'cause that's the only place where I get my cultural influence from really."

As Ruth points out, the ethnic immigrant church is one of the few places where the second-generation members can connect to their roots. Ji Hun, an ethnic-language pastor, describes how the English-speaking second-generation members can benefit from connecting to their roots in terms of their identity formation:

> I don't think a whole new identity can be established from one generation to the next . . . Being raised in a Korean home by Korean parents, the second-generation children are exposed to the Korean culture and its elements to a certain extent. They end

up with a mixed identity. As we go from one generation to the subsequent generation, the Korean immigrant churches can help make sense of this mixed identity from combined cultural experiences—the good, the bad, what to accept, and what to discard.

Challenges Arising from *Jeong*

One of the most difficult challenges that comes out of *jeong* is that the ethnic-language-speaking first-generation members continue to treat English-speaking members as children, even as the vast majority of English-speaking members become working professionals ranging in age from twenty to eighty years. This parent-child dynamic at the Asian immigrant church is influenced by Confucianism, which demands respect and loyalty upwards, and care and protection downwards. Aside from Confucianism, *jeong* plays a role in this dynamic, inducing a state of tension that can lead to conflicts between different language groups at the church. Melia addresses this dynamic, which is inadequate in the long run as the different-language ministries seek to work together under the same roof: "When we are working together, sometimes it's like we feel like it's very parental, so the Chinese congregation are the parents and the English congregation are the children . . . somehow, we've always been viewed as the younger, but when we do ministry together, how do we put aside the parent-child relationship to be like coworkers in Christ"? Susan puts it this way:

> Yeah . . . I think in a lot of times, like, advice from KM comes from a, like a very good intentioned place . . . a lot of times. Not all the time, though. Of like, we want to do things for you. But it's like still like very—we are the providers for you or we are above you so we do this for you. But a lot of times, it's like, "you don't know what we want, or you don't know what we need, but you just do these things for us." And I've learned in the past couple of years, like, they do things, but they don't tell us it's for us, so that we don't know that they've done these things so they've put all this effort into things.

Susan continues to express her frustration with this parent-child dynamic, saying: "If I were to like put it succinctly, um—don't look at us like we're kids . . . I know in Korean culture respect is a huge thing, particularly according to age, um . . . I think a lot of times for us, at least, it's misunderstood and perceived as demeaning." As an English-speaking second-generation member of her church, Deborah has had similar experiences to that of Susan. Deborah wishes to be viewed as equals—to be consulted and treated as adults from ethnic-language-speaking first-generation members of her church. She says, "I expect that they treat us as, you know, we're adults now. Sometimes I find older Korean generations don't tend to acknowledge the growth of their children and older children. And so yeah, there's an expectation of a certain bit of respect as a person. Not like, you know, you guys are old enough, you know, after a certain age, you have to let them take over I guess." Kate, a second-generation member who teaches at her local high school, agrees that the members of the English congregation no longer wish to be labeled as kids.

Although *jeong* is reciprocal, it has a tendency to flow down from the top, as in from parents to children. Once *jeong* has flown downward from parents to children, the roles become fixed. So no matter how old the parents get, the parents will always be parents, and the children will always be children. Likewise, *jeong* tends to flow from the older ethnic-language-speaking members to younger English-speaking members; this is one of the reasons why the former treats the latter as children in need of care, provision, and guidance. As noted above, the ethnic-language congregation often makes church-related decisions on behalf of the English congregation, without first checking on them. Shifting the current parent-child dynamic towards a working partnership would be met with much resistance, mostly from the ethnic-language congregation. This relationship hinders the second generation in developing leadership in the church, as Jane says, "there is this very Asian-specific dynamic of hierarchy of power. We cannot undermine that or underscore that, because it is there. So it is difficult for young people to speak up and voice their opinions, especially if they have parents serving in leadership roles at the church."

Another related challenge arising from *jeong* is misunderstandings between different-language congregations marked by cultural differences. Melia says, "I think sometimes we misunderstand each other, if we're like, um, coming from two different cultures. Our second generation and first generation, sometimes it is hard to understand each other, because for example, we might not understand, 'why is this first generation, maybe the way they view money, for example, is very different from the way we view money'. And like, why the strongholds of different cultures exist, right"?

At times, attending a family-oriented Asian ethnic church can hinder one's spiritual growth, given the associated culture of saving face and shame. Most Asian parents tend to hide their own issues from the children, making it far more difficult for these children to open up and raise concerns or questions to their parents, even faith-related ones. Shirley reflects on this culture of shame prevalent in many Asian immigrant churches:

> Spiritually I think a lot less open to sharing what's going in my personal life, because I think my culture has shaped me to be very personal and keeping my problems to myself . . . We don't want to give shame to the family name. When my parents emphasize that I feel like it's necessary for me to hide my sin, hide like every single dirty little secret I have in me, so that really prevents me growing spiritually, because if I'm hiding from myself and I can't bring myself to face the fact that I'm dealing with these sins, how am I going to bring that to God? How am I going to like pour it out and be vulnerable to Jesus if I'm hiding it from myself, hiding it from my closest dearest friends around me? So I think that part aspect of the culture has impacted a lot of the younger generations' faith in a sense because even the older generation they don't tell you what they're dealing with. They don't tell you what their struggles are so naturally we will not share what we are going through. We have to strain it out of somebody, like please tell me what you're going through. Other than that, we will not initiate it.

Not only does family-focused church hinder spiritual growth because of private life, but the reversed order of relationship in the church also hinders spiritual growth of Asian Canadian church members. Second-generation minister Jane shares her concern: "Placing our relationship with Jesus first before relationships with family, friends, or careers. Our relationship with Jesus must be the first and foremost priority over anything else, even our cultural ethnic identity. Our identity has to be centered on Christ. Christ has to be the foundation." Also, another second-generation minister, Ashley, shares the same concern: "Sometimes I wonder if we are more Asians than we are Christians in our churches. I would say this is something that we would need to be thoughtfully engaging continually about the kingdom culture within our given 'Asian-ness' . . . I don't think we should throw out the fact that we are Koreans. I also think that this needs to be redeemed and transformed in the likeness of kingdom culture in its best form." Another second-generation minister, Andy, echoes:

> I think for ethnic churches you would need to be very careful about why it is that you come together in the first place. At times you could say it is for Christ, but at other times it could be for cultural promotion. And some people may become comfortable with that notion. When you do not promote a missional community-minded church, the cultural elements may take over and become the main reason why people come to church at all.

Our family relations are heavily dependent on the church life. For example, when family members live far away from one another, coming to the church is one of the only ways of checking in on a regular basis. These family members may worship separately based on language preferences, but they gather together for fellowship or family meal after the service. Having the family together in the same church building, albeit in separate worship services, is a source of great joy for many of us attending the Asian immigrant church. Hence, the vast majority of those interviewed express their desire to worship together as long as possible, space permitting.

Overall, this arrangement of having multiple worship services simultaneously is highly beneficial for the Asian immigrant church. In the long run, however, this arrangement becomes problematic for some English congregations lacking the opportunity to worship at the main sanctuary. Due to space limitations, the main sanctuary is usually reserved for use by the ethnic-language congregation. Ben, an EM (i.e., English ministry) pastor, regrets not having the opportunity to worship at the main sanctuary in his entire thirty-six-year ministry career:

> Currently, the EM (i.e., English ministry) worships in the gymnasium and the CM (i.e., Chinese ministry) worships in the Sanctuary. The services take place at the same time on Sunday. I was hoping to use the Sanctuary as the place of worship for the EM. We tried to negotiate and settle on different worship times: Perhaps the CM would go earlier and the EM would go later. The families however want to come to church together. As a result, we were not able to move the EM to the Sanctuary. It was a bit disappointing that we could not work something out.

Another challenge that comes from *jeong* is having "no private life in the church." Leaving our private life aside, in favour of public life, is a characteristic of *jeong*. As previously discussed, there are various activities and services for the members of Asian immigrant church during the week. These provide plenty of opportunities for chitchat among members, especially among parents who end up comparing their children's achievements. Some first-generation parents ask sensitive personal questions without thinking twice, because doing so is acceptable in our *jeong* culture. The English-speaking second-generation members raised in an individualistic Canadian culture have great difficulty in understanding such behaviors. Ann, a second-generation interviewee, shares her experience in that regard: "So it's like they exchange notes and compare kids but then whenever they see us, you know they love you because they're so proud of you but then at the same time, they always ask you like 'how's your marks? What are you doing?' and you're like, I'm still trying to figure it out, I really don't know."

Hope in *Jeong*

Despite the numerous challenges that arise from *jeong*, we remain hopeful about the place of *jeong* in the future of our Asian immigrant church. But if we fail to put ourselves in each other's shoes, we would never understand the perspective of the other generation at the church. And there would be no hope of bringing us—the older ethnic-language-speaking generation and younger English-speaking generation—together in harmony. When we try to see others in terms of Christ's teachings, the two or three congregations divided along generational, cultural, and language lines will be able to see eye to eye. And any such efforts would require patience and humility from the different-language congregations involved. Melia puts it this way:

> I think we need a lot of humility in that. When we're kind of like still holding on to our culture roots, uh instead of together trying to hold onto what Christ is teaching us about how we should view those things. So I think uh culture brings in with a lot of baggage or burdens that might, that both sides might not be able to identify with readily, because they haven't experienced that breakthrough yet.

One of the weaknesses of our church with the people of *jeong* is that we face more difficulties when trying to reach out to those "outside" our inner circles, at least in the beginning. Thus, there is a need for us to be more purposeful and intentional with our approaches. But once we bring people into our inner circle, we build lasting *jeong*-based relationships. In that regard, Deborah and several other interviewees from both the first generation and second generation hope that their congregations would become more open and inclusive. In other words, they would like to see more openness at the Asian immigrant churches, in hopes of creating a warm, inviting atmosphere for the newcomers, and for those who crossed the cultural, ethnic, and generational boundaries. Deborah says the following about openness and inclusivity at her church: "I think we could being more open . . . Because although we all have cliques, everybody has their own group they're closer to—usually it's by children's age because we get together a lot more or we're more comfortable, um, so sometimes we might not recognize someone that new—so it makes us more purposeful I think." Robert and Ga Eun agree that we need to be more open and welcoming of newcomers from the broader local community, especially those who are ethnically and culturally different:

> We need to be more open. If a stranger comes to the church during service, and you look at them like "Why are you here?" then this is not a church. It is just a gathering. It is a meeting of signed up members. A church should be a place where people are open with God's hands, and they should accept whoever walks through the door. But they do not accept the communities around here [because] they do not see themselves as a part of the [local] community.

Deborah expresses hope that her Korean immigrant church will no longer experience church splits in the future. She is still deeply traumatized by the experience of repeated church splits in the past. The people of *jeong* can be more emotional than rational, particularly during times of conflict. Deborah remains cautiously hopeful, despite her wounds from the past church splits: "A lot of us have seen our families and churches break up. It's heartbreaking because it's community then too. I pray that God keeps us in good, like people can leave, we have had friends that go to other churches and we still meet together and we have a loving fellowship in our own way. I hope and pray that our church won't break up."

So Young, a first-generation interviewee, hopes for a more caring and supportive church community. She would like to see the different cliques at her church—called *chon* or cell groups—mingling together:

> In such times, some of us wish that church members would help us through the ordeals. Yes, God is the one holding us together but I believe that the support of church members can also help. My current church is very respectful of privacy and personal decisions pertaining to faith and church attendance. This could be a good thing, but what about instances where we could potentially save someone's faith by showing our support? I came to this church about eleven years ago. To this day, I am only friendly with those in my own age group at my church, because I only ever get to communicate with this specific group of people on a deeper level . . . I do not get to know anyone outside of my circle. This has also exacerbated the generational gap within the church. The strengths of older members are not passed on to the young members of the church as a result of this physical and emotional disconnect. And younger members do not get a chance to contribute and assist older members of the church. I think church should provide more avenues through which to

connect all members of the church. I have felt that I really need to get out and get to know new people at my church.

Sometimes the people of *jeong* show an active interest in other people and their business, which can make them appear too intrusive, and untrusting. In particular, the ethnic-language-speaking first-generation members have a tendency to interfere in the English-speaking younger generation's business, leading to overdependence and resentment in the EM (i.e., English ministry). It appears that the first generation seeks to exercise almost complete control over all matters related to the church. Such behaviors and attitudes can be easily misconstrued by the younger generation, even if they come from *jeong*. Kate, a second-generation interviewee, expresses her hope that the first generation would begin trusting them more and "let go of the control." And she wishes that the first-generation members at her Chinese ethnic church would open up to those other than the Chinese. She says:

> The first generation being able to trust us and being able to um, maybe, just let go of that control and being able to know that this is the direction that we want to go towards 'cause it's new. I think being a lot of the Cantonese and Mandarin side perhaps they love like Chinese people, that's all they think about. But God is great, it's more than just the Chinese people, I think it's great that you want to minister towards them but I think there are just so many other people that need the gospel. So I think that's why, that's where that idea came from it's like, well, if that's the case, then maybe, will the leadership trust us and being able to you know, like, we want to try something new and so like uh maybe like whether it means teaching or evangelizing in a different way that they're not used to I think that's a huge thing, being able to trust us. Or try something new or be bold or take risks for God and so perhaps the first generation have—I'm not sure, okay, I don't want to say they've lost it, but they're scared. I think they don't—and maybe that boils down to they don't trust us and being able to take risks for God, so . . .

Chen Cheng echoes Kate's sentiments, saying: "When the old people are in power, they like to be in control." Chen Cheng continues the observation: "However, when young congregants come out, then the old congregants should've gone. Yes, they (young congregants) have to take over sooner or later anyway, but they are doing well even though our English service is recently stable with about thirty people, something like that, but with good future." Deborah would like to strive for a working partnership between the KM (i.e., Korean ministry) and EM (English ministry) instead of continuing the parent-child dynamic at her church. She insists that the older generation at her Korean ethnic church needs to let go of the Confucius mannerisms or the traditional Korean way as much as possible, saying: "Always a kid, yeah. If they're older you just have to listen whether it's right for us or not."

Sui Hui describes the negative characteristics distinct to the people of *jeong*, hoping to see a change for the better at her church. First, she would like to see fewer disagreements and more forgiveness among church members. The people of *jeong* can be quite stubborn, sensitive to criticisms and easily upset by opposing arguments. They often prefer to do things in their own way, backed by *jeong*-based relationships in their inner circles. She thinks that we should not be "so stubborn, always I am right and you are wrong. In God's living, everyone may be different, not always you're wrong or I'm right. We can always communicate in our church, don't be so sensitive and so easy to be upset with others: I don't like you because you're not on my side, or you disagree. Forgive, we are all broken."

Melia hopes for an enhanced support system for the youth and family ministries at her church, given the generation gap. She observes that in Cantonese churches, the congregation size is getting smaller due to a reduced number of immigrants and aging first-generation members. Melia has the following diagnosis for the rapidly aging Cantonese churches: "There's a missing gap of families, like families with small children, or even families who have um, who have like teenagers. We have an age gap in our church. And for a healthy church we need like the different generations to be there. So I think we need to maybe provide more support to youth and family ministries."

So Young wants to help categorize the emerging group of singles in their thirties at her church:

> I have come to realize that there is a whole new group of people that the church failed to categorize. The church categorizes members as youth, High-C, young adults, and adults, which probably used this categorization for the past 100 years. But we have a whole new generation of people now, the thirty something singles who are considered too old to be young adults. Without a category in the church, we will be seeing more and more people falling through the cracks of the failed church system.

As discussed in detail in this chapter, *jeong* fosters family-like closeness, solidarity, togetherness, affection, compassion, and care amongst members of Asian immigrant churches. From our interviews we heard good stories, heartfelt stories, sad stories, heartbreaking stories, and challenging stories of our church, all of which were influenced, to varying degrees, by *jeong*. Because of *jeong*, we stay at our churches although we experience challenges and hurts from our cultural generational and language differences. Because of the same *jeong*, we return and return to our ethnic churches from feelings of connectedness, solidarity, and something we cannot explain exactly. These are our own stories as God's people and as the people of *jeong*, which remind us of where we are now and where we should be headed.

Reflection and Discussion Questions

1. Reflect on or discuss the story of Ruth in the Old Testament in terms of *jeong* (*qing*) relationship.
2. What do you think are the benefits and challenges or issues that arise from the *jeong* (*qing*) culture, considering the selected excerpts of interviews in this chapter?
3. How would you share the *jeong* culture with both the ethnic- and English-language congregants, particularly to help them understand generational dynamics of the whole church influenced by *jeong*?

Part III

Future Story

7

Future Story

Nam Soon Song

> There was a great multitude that no one could count, from every nation, from all tribes and peoples and languages, standing before the throne and before the Lamb. (Rev 7:9, NRSV)

How do we want to shape the future of the Asian immigrant churches in Canada? What would our future hold? In which direction is God leading these ethnic specific churches? Would the church signposts in the future contain the ethnic-language versions of the church names, as they do now? Would we still identify as immigrants or children of immigrants? What do the lay and clergies from both the English- and ethnic-language ministries envisage for the future of our church, twenty-five years from now? None of us can predict the future in certainty—we do not know what story will unfold in the coming years. We are uneasy about the prospect of losing our church, the one and only "home" as we have known it in Canada. What we do know for certain is that the bulk of the first-generation members attending ethnic-specific churches will be gone within the next twenty-five years, and so the current English-speaking second-generation members will be left in charge of our churches alongside some younger ethnic-language-speaking members. How might our churches be different from today, if at all? What would our churches look like? It is interesting to realize that with the changing church demographics in mind, the clergy and lay members attending Asian Canadian immigrant churches (ACIC) envisage a similar fate for their respective churches in twenty-five years.

The Same Current Church: No Change

Of note is that a very small number of those interviewed predict the current arrangement of having both the English- and ethnic-language service will continue into the future. Overall, only a few interviewees paint a very optimistic picture of our churches in twenty-five years, saying that the church will be "smaller in size but [with] more devout members," "more vibrant," and "growing [in membership] by evangelizing broad areas." Ba Men is especially optimistic about his church's future: "We truly want to serve for the Lord, we have now only four thousand people, but we could grow to ten thousand or a hundred thousand, by drawing people from Markham or North York and surrounding areas by letting people know that we have a mission." One EM (i.e., English ministry) pastor shares a similar vision for the future of Asian Canadian immigrant churches (ACIC), but hopes to see ACIC having a greater impact on the society at large:

> I think visually what I see happening is with all things being the same in terms of immigration and such, the bigger churches will become even bigger and stronger. Smaller churches will remain small and continue to struggle. What I would like to see more of are—I don't want to just talk about simplistic trends or relationships—people who have been influenced by their ethnic culture using what God has given them to make an impact in our society at large.

One ethnic-ministry pastor predicts that the future of ACIC will be plagued with the same problems and concerns, thus holding our churches at a standstill: "In ten to twenty years they will be in the same place as we are right now. They will be wrestling through the same issues: aging, senior founding congregation, and very highly diminished Cantonese-English congregation. Many of them would probably have a Mandarin congregation as well." Another ethnic-ministry pastor makes a similar prediction, recalling the problems and concerns in the early days of his ministry career, which are similar to those facing his church today:

> When I was a young University student, they said that the second generation in the EM (i.e., English ministry) would take over the church, and the first-generation churches will no longer exist. That is not how things turned out. The second-generation EM congregations are still being supported by the first-generation KM (i.e., Korean ministry) congregations. If there are new immigrants from Korea, the first-generation Korean churches will survive and continue to do well. I believe that there is a

potential for growth amongst Korean immigrant churches, and more are thriving, not just surviving. But the smaller Korean immigrant churches may draw a completely different picture based on their realities.

Evidently, our current ministry context is reflected in our visions and predictions for the future of ACIC. Of note is the stark contrast between interviewees from the bigger, flourishing ACIC and interviewees from the smaller, struggling ACIC: The former tends to be more optimistic about the future outcomes of ethnic immigrant churches in general than the latter. The former is also more likely to be satisfied with and wish to continue "business as usual" at their church. But most pastors and lay interviewees belong to the latter, meaning they do not foresee the continuation of "business as usual" at their respective ACIC. For example, according to popular predictions, only a handful of ACIC would choose to retain their ethnic-language signposts outside the church.

The English Dominant Church

The vast majority of interviewees predict an English-dominant or English-led church as the most probable scenario for their respective ACIC in the coming years, given the declining immigration rate and aging of ethnic-language-speaking first-generation members. Unless we gain more younger ethnic-language-speaking first-generation members, the EM (i.e., English ministry) will become our leading ministry in twenty-five years. And this would serve as a reflection of evolving demands and needs at our ACIC. In other words, both the church dynamic and composition will be opposite to what they are now, with the much smaller ethnic-language congregations taking a backseat. Interestingly enough, a number of lay interviewees think that the ACIC should become predominantly English-speaking in the future, in order to remain viable and relevant. Jin Hee, a Korean-speaking first-generation member, predicts that the bulk of the older first-generation Korean members would no longer be at her church in twenty-five years, because many of them would have already passed away by that point in time. Thus, she thinks that her Korean immigrant church would eventually offer one bilingual service for all congregants, combining "small [group of] ethnic-language congregants and large [group of] English-speaking congregants." She hopes that "with one bilingual service . . . the church will be involved deeply with the local community which will in turn help children of the future." Here, Jin Hee is referring to the third-, fourth-, and fifth-generation Korean Canadians as the "children of the future."

Moses, a second-generation pastor interviewee currently serving the EM (i.e., English ministry) at his Korean immigrant church, makes a similar prediction: "In twenty-five years the Korean Canadians will be the minority of the church, especially given the immigration trends . . . The English language will be the main, dominant language used at the church in twenty-five years, with a small subset of members using the Korean language." So Young concurs with Moses, saying: "With less Korean speaking members, there will be an inevitable decline in the KM (i.e., Korean ministry). Meaning the English service members will eventually form the 'dominant' group of the church." Jae Min is in agreement with both Moses and So Young: "Today as mentioned we have about five hundred members worshiping in the three Korean services. The second-generation members worship in a smaller worship hall. I think this will be reversed twenty-five years later." Chen Cheng predicts a similar fate for the Taiwanese immigrant church to which she belongs: "English ministry will be the major and most Taiwanese congregations will be gone." Sui Hui, a first-generation member, thinks that the future of her church is rather unclear: "I know it is very 'grey' picture, we pray for God's guidance [and for now] at least we still have a group of Cantonese-speaking brothers and sisters . . . [Without] the Cantonese-speaking, the chance [of future survival] is very slim." Sui-hui continues with her observation, saying: "We [the] Cantonese-speaking from Hong Kong are getting smaller and smaller. The immigration stopped years ago, so the older Chinese-speaking people will [be] eventually going to Heavenly home. Our second-generation [members] speak English mostly, not many can speak Chinese. [Only a few will survive and as] for the greater church I can see that, it is going to die off." Fa is an ethnic-language minister who thinks that the ethnic-specific churches will not cease to exist, because the English-speaking congregation will take over and run the church:

> Twenty-five years from now, my dream is to let the "real" Canadians run our church. Twenty-five years later we will be a multi-ethnic, mutually respectful church with significant Chinese presence. We will still have the different languages. I can project what is to happen for all Asian immigrant churches, be they Japanese, Korean, Filipino, or Vietnamese. I do not think they will give up the ethnic language, nevertheless. In twenty-five years our major congregation will be the English group. Mandarin and Cantonese will serve as supplementary roles.

Moses, an EM pastor, shares a similar vision to that of Fa:

> The EM will become the leading ministry, because having the KM alone leading the church will not be enough by that time. It will

probably not retain its unique ethnic color and become an inclusive place of worship for people of different ethnic backgrounds. In twenty-five years the Korean Canadians will be the minority of the church, and the English language will be the main, dominant language used at the church in twenty-five years, with a small subset of members using the Korean language.

Lian is an ethnic-language pastor who is putting his faith in the younger English-speaking members coming back to his church: "It is obvious that our hope is in English congregation, we expect it will grow, even they may face bottleneck as well, but it is still our future. We thank God that our second generation are still coming back to this church, what worries us is the inevitable decline of Cantonese group." Likewise, Seok Ho thinks that at his Korean immigrant church "the EM will become the dominant group and the KM will be the minority group" in twenty-five years. Thus he emphasizes the importance of bringing two or more generations together at the church, each with varying needs, language preferences, and cultures:

> While some members of EM may not identify as Koreans, from the outside they look Korean and can easily blend in with the rest of KM members. I think it is important for the church to consolidate different cultures—specifically the Korean culture and Canadian culture—and make it one of our strengths. As of now, the church is segregated by two different cultures and this segregation is not ideal in the long run.

Min Woo foresees the continuation of ACIC for the next twenty-five years and beyond, but under the leadership of EM (i.e., English ministry):

> In twenty-five years, there will be a generational shift with a relatively larger presence of the second- and third-generation EM members at the church. They will be the leaders of this church. I think that in twenty-five years' time, this church will still be an ethnic Korean church. The EM pastor will be the senior pastor and the EM will be the leading congregation of the church. The KM will be a much smaller congregation at that time.

Like Min Woo, most ethnic-language ministry pastors project that the EM will become the dominant ministry in twenty-five years, with the ethnic-language ministry gradually stepping aside to make way for the new EM leadership. According to their projections, the ethnic-language congregation will be the minority and become much smaller than what it is now—in time, they would be relegated to minor roles in church-related events and decision-making processes. Such projections render many ethnic-language speaking first generation members uneasy; they question whether their ethnic-language ministry will continue to receive the proper support and resources under the new EM leadership at the church. They do not have much hope—or plan—at this time, because all the signals seem to point to a "grey picture" as noted above by Sui Hui. Sooner or later, our church signposts would be altered to display the names and service times in English first, followed by the ethnic-language translations in smaller letters, if at all. Our signposts will become the most prominent reminder that the English language and English-speaking members are taking over to become the dominant majority of the church. With more members choosing the English service over the ethnic-language service, some ACIC might consider offering one worship service in English with real-time translations. Alternatively, a bilingual/trilingual pastor might be able to offer a separate ethnic-language worship service at a different time.

No More Ethnic-language Congregation; English-speaking Congregation Only

Approximately half of interviewees from the ethnic-language ministry think that the ethnic congregations of ACIC will cease to exist in twenty-five years, given the fewer number of new immigrants and advanced ages of ethnic-language-speaking members. Brad, an EM (i.e., English ministry) pastor interviewee, predicts that the smaller ethnic-specific churches will cease to exist—only the sizable ones with predominantly English-speaking congregations would survive. He says:

> In twenty-five years, a lot of the smaller churches would be gone. The select few that have focused on the un-churched and willing to make those changes without compromising their beliefs will flourish . . . The church will survive as long as there is a godly minister who is English-speaking and willing to minister to the community, regardless of ethnicity and cultural background. It has to be in English though, because the next generation will use English as the main language.

Some interviewees think that the ethnic-language ministry will be phased out of the ACIC completely, which would leave the English-speaking congregations in sole charge of their respective ACIC. Luis is an ethnic-language pastor who thinks as such; he foresees that only the English-speaking congregation will remain at his church: "If we do not initiate Mandarin ministry, the TM (i.e., Taiwanese ministry) will end in ten years.

The church will be left with only the EM. The EM will be comprised mostly of English-speaking Taiwanese people." Jia Yu makes a similar prediction, saying: "[Our church] probably will become all English-speaking, because we are so close to the university, that I [think] we will [see] lots of young people . . . all English speaking, probably in twenty-five years." With all the young people in close vicinity to the church, Jia Yu hopes to see growth in the youth and young adult membership in the English congregation. But how might her church encourage English-speaking youth and young adults in the neighbourhood to come out and join the church? First, the current English congregation needs to be revitalized under the support and guidance of the church, or the church board in particular. Second, the EM leadership needs to be empowered to take on more responsibilities at the church. Even if the church signposts are altered to drop the ethnic identifiers from our names and services, we would still retain a hint of our ethnic heritage and culture at our church. The question is: How can we use this to our advantage to encourage membership growth and retention at our ACIC?

Growth of Mandarin-speaking Congregations

There has been a consistent influx of Mandarin-speaking Chinese immigrants to Canada in recent years. Considering this relatively large influx of immigrants from mainland China, both the Chinese and Taiwanese immigrant churches envisage the growth in their respective Mandarin-speaking congregations. What this means is that the Cantonese Chinese and Taiwanese members will have to accommodate the incoming Mandarin-speaking Chinese members at their ethnic-specific churches. Ji Yang makes the following observation: "Mandarin-speaking could become bigger and bigger, more and more, but Cantonese-speaking churches, it wouldn't grow a lot in next twenty-five years." Similarly, Joan observes the growing demand for Mandarin-speaking churches: "The TM (i.e., Taiwanese ministry) side will definitely draw in more Mandarin-speaking members in the future. But I hope that the EM (i.e., English ministry) will become more multicultural, so that those who are not Taiwanese or Chinese feel more comfortable during the English-speaking service." Stuart concurs, saying, "Yes for sure. I still think there would be some sort of ethnic church; not necessarily a Taiwanese church but [a type of hybrid] Mandarin-English church. Even now there are a lot more Mandarin churches and many Taiwanese people choose to go to them, in preference to stay anonymous in those bigger Mandarin churches." Charles, an English-speaking second-generation member attending a Taiwanese immigrant church, draws a similar conclusion to that of Stuart:

"If it is still around, it is going to be a different church. The mix is going to be different. It won't be a predominantly Taiwanese church anymore. Well it serves as a draw to Taiwanese people seeking to feel more at home in an environment they are used to worship. That in itself is a bit problematic if you do not have Taiwanese people coming in."

Ben, a long-time EM (i.e., English ministry) pastor at a Cantonese-speaking Chinese church, foresees that the Chinese immigrant churches with a large presence of Mandarin-speaking members and a smaller group of Cantonese-speaking members will continue to flourish in the future. Accordingly, he thinks that there are two options for the Cantonese-speaking Chinese churches: Either open up to the new immigrants from mainland China through a Mandarin-speaking service, or open up completely to become a multicultural church. He elaborates as follows:

> In twenty-five years, many of the Chinese churches with Mandarin ministry will still be in existence. They will have a very vibrant Mandarin ministry, and a smaller Cantonese ministry until people pass on. We might be what the Mandarin-speaking Chinese churches would look like in fifty years, because we started early with the Tai Shan immigrants. Many of our Tai Shan people have already passed away or passed on. We have not replenished it with new immigrants. If this church does not open up to Mandarin-speaking new immigrants, this church will likely become a multicultural church in the future. Again, there are two choices for this church: We can either become a church for Mainland Chinese immigrants that will guarantee our survival for at least twenty-five years or become a multicultural church.

Jane also thinks that sooner or later, her church will begin offering a separate Mandarin-speaking worship service in response to the growing demands of new immigrants who speak Mandarin only. This would be one of the survival tactics employed by her church:

> With the declining Cantonese Ministry, we say that the church will cease to exist without a Mandarin Ministry. Thus, serving and expanding our ministry with the growing need right now, which is largely the Mandarin-speaking population, will be necessary, although there is contention between Cantonese population of Hong Kong and China politically, socially, and historically. This contention has to be worked out first. Again, it is about being more than Hong Kong people. It is about being more than Cantonese speakers versus Mandarin speakers.

Gerry, an EM (i.e., English ministry) pastor, predicts that the Mandarin-speaking congregation will continue to survive and thrive, but remains uncertain as to what that means for his Taiwanese congregation. He says, "I don't know if we will still have our TM (i.e., Taiwanese ministry) congregation. I would hope to see our Taiwanese culture endure. We would probably have a Mandarin congregation by then, I am uncertain whether it would be a Taiwanese-Mandarin or mainland China Mandarin congregation." To meet the growing demands, most Cantonese-speaking Chinese and Taiwanese immigrant churches are planning to offer a separate Mandarin-speaking service in the near future. Seeing as the young Taiwanese Canadians speak Mandarin and rarely Taiwanese, offering a separate Mandarin service seems imperative and logical for the struggling Taiwanese immigrant churches. In other words, developing a separate Mandarin ministry, in addition to the existing Taiwanese or Cantonese ministry, is necessary to stay on a healthy path as a church. A select few Cantonese-speaking Chinese immigrant churches are already offering three separate services in Cantonese, Mandarin, and English. Some Taiwanese immigrant churches are considering doing the same, in order to guarantee their survival into the next generation and beyond. However, even if these churches begin offering three separate services under the same roof, their signposts outside rarely display all three languages in which they offer the worship and other services. For example, the signposts outside the Taiwanese immigrant churches are usually displayed in English or Mandarin or both, not Taiwanese, because Taiwanese use the same characters as Mandarin.

Pan-Asian/Multi-Asian Church

Some of us express a desire to amalgamate for the purpose of creating a pan-Asian or multi-Asian church, given that it would be easier to bring together the different ethnic Asian groups for worship. This would be the case at least initially, because the different ethnic Asian groups in Canada have a lot of similarities in terms of physical features, cultural heritage, values, traditions, and emotional sensibilities. Thus what we have is a close bond or attachment between Asian immigrant churches, one that is established on a common ground: We can easily identify with each other. The resulting solidarity and cooperation can solidify the shared common ground, making the close bond we share with each other even stronger, in a cyclic manner. Brad thinks that the pan-Asian churches will become a reality in Canada in the near future. And these newly created pan-Asian churches will seek to meet the evolving needs and desires of ACIC, just as was the case in the States: "This is going to happen to the ethnic Asian churches, without true adaptations. It might become multi-Asian or pan-Asian, like KKP's church in LA called Evergreen Tree church." Moses shares a similar vision for the future of ACIC, saying: "Canada is generally slower to adapt than the States. This is inevitable given the longer history of immigration and larger Korean immigrant populations in the States. In the future, there would be no choice for most ethnic Korean churches but to become pan-Asian or multiethnic." If their predictions hold true, then we will see the inclusion of the word "Asian" on the church signposts outside such pan-Asian or multi-Asian churches.

A New Model of Church: Home/House/Digital Church

When we hear that the home/house church is one of the rising church models, we would wonder whether the same models can be used or modified to suit the needs of ACIC. Some of us see home/house church as an inevitable part of the future of ACIC, considering the rapidly aging first-generation members, decreasing immigration levels overall, and of course the burden on the second-generation members to keep the current church building and fund the associated costs of maintenance. One ethnic-language pastor would like to adopt the home church model in the future, which would help raise up the small groups of congregants to worship God outside the church, and without the current restrictions: "The church will be formed around small group settings in the future. When we say church, we tend to imagine the Sunday worship service. In the future, the church gatherings will take place at private homes, and through the interweb. The congregants will celebrate small groups and meaningful relationships amongst themselves. They will also be more mission-oriented. This institutionalized church will be supportive of those small churches."

Let us consider an excerpt of an interview with Sui Hui, a Cantonese-speaking first-generation member, who speaks about her reservations and concerns regarding the future of ACIC.

> Sui hui: I think it (i.e., referring to her Cantonese-speaking Chinese immigrant church) will die down!
>
> Interviewer: It will become English only?
>
> Sui hui: Not English only, eventually I don't see the building.
>
> Interviewer: The building?
>
> Sui hui: People are not going to settle down in a building. They will scatter around. Look at the university students, a lot of times

when they come back, they don't return to the church where they grew up, they either go somewhere else, or [stop attending church altogether] so eventually I don't see the church being in a building. They may be meeting in families . . .

Interviewer: Like the so-called "family church"?

Sui hui: Or even internet church, digital church, our church has started having our Sunday service available online.

Interviewer: Wow. They worship through internet at home?

Sui hui: Yes, they can watch the service at home.

Interviewer: I heard about that too. That might be a new trend?

Sui hui: I can see that the church in a building is not going to be the norm in the future. Especially if the government is going to impose a lot of restrictions on church buildings, like the property taxes or other taxes later on. People wouldn't think of buying a land and build a church on that. And the second generation they don't fix with one church. Even my daughter, not because she does not like that church, but because she didn't like the big churches, they like the small ones. I think even if we don't have a church building, it does not mean that we don't have a church. When we did not have a church building in the beginning, we were still able to preach the gospel. Now we have hundreds of thousands of dollars tied up here.

Interviewer: So in a way you find out the building becomes a burden, right? You have to look after the building, because you spent a lot of money on it.

This is an interesting interview excerpt, which is in line with the prediction that the home/house/digital church models may become popular amongst ACIC in the future. How can the ACIC prepare for the evolving needs and preferences of their congregants? What kind of leadership is required? How can the ACIC help equip the next generation of clergy and lay members to take the church beyond the limits of the church building?

Multicultural/Multiethnic Church

It is interesting to note that the vast majority of clergy and lay interviewees envision a multiethnic or multicultural church in their future. While nine out of fifteen English-speaking lay interviewees foresee that our church would eventually move in a multiethnic or multicultural direction, four out of five Korean-speaking lay interviewees make similar predictions. About half of pastor interviewees also foresee that the ACIC would become multiethnic or multicultural in the future. As such, it appears that becoming a multiethnic or multicultural church is a real possibility for our church; it brings both hope and viable vision for the continued survival of ACIC. In discussing the multiethnic or multicultural directions of the ACIC, several interviewees bring up the need for our church to be a "more welcoming church with open mind." This particular vision for the ACIC is reflective of the demographic changes in Canada, specifically within the GTA (i.e., Greater Toronto Area). But what does it mean to become a multiethnic or multicultural church? What would it entail? According to Jasmin, it means having "more colored faces, different nationalities" in ACIC. It would entail opening our church doors to all to help nurture a multiethnic or multicultural congregation, starting with inviting friends and members of local community to join our English-speaking service on Sunday. This will in turn help facilitate growth in church membership. We would have to open up to not just the diverse ethnic groups in our midst, but also to the different cultures that can arise within the ACIC moving in a multiethnic or multicultural direction. Seok Ho claims that "having a separate English service at our church can serve as an open invitation to non-Koreans or those of diverse backgrounds." Biming thinks that more opportunities would open up for his Cantonese-speaking Chinese immigrant church from choosing one or the other: Setting up the Mandarin-speaking service or becoming multicultural. He says, "Perhaps the opportunity for this church lies in expanding beyond the Chinese. I think this church has two choices: Either open a separate Mandarin service and take in the next wave of immigrants like many other ethnic Chinese churches in the GTA, or become a multicultural Canadian church and no longer be an ethnic Chinese church."

Melia envisions "a very multicultural church" that reaches beyond the ethnic Asian groups, thereby bringing together all nations through God's transforming power:

> I think it would be like multicultural. Very multicultural. I think as God, so this is kind of what I've observed. As God transforms our hearts to be more like him, we begin to see our, I guess our identity as more in Christ. And as it's more in Christ, he puts in our heart for more to open our eyes, my heart is not only for the Asian people, but it's also for all nations. And as he puts that in our hearts, um, our church will naturally become more and more multicultural.

Likewise Kate wishes to see a mosaic of people at her church, saying: "Because we live in a North American society where it's multicultural, English is the main language. I think because of that I'm hoping our English ministry will be more multicultural and not just Filipinos and Malaysian people but really seeing like a mosaic of people and so um . . . I think [it is important to move in that direction]." Susan believes that God's church is currently in the works—one that will rise up to bring different nationalities together in harmony. She recalls her experience worshiping in multiple languages with those from diverse ethnic and cultural backgrounds: "My most memorable worship is like Urbana, it's like worshiping with nineteen thousand people of different races and like in different languages too it's just like it's such a powerful reminder of like how huge God's church is and yeah that like our narrow-minded view of like church done in the Korean Christian way is like shattered to pieces."

Ruth, an English-speaking second generation, thinks that a multiethnic or multicultural church is not something out of the ordinary. It is quite natural for her generation to accept the idea of becoming a multiethnic or multicultural church, especially considering the frequency of interracial or multicultural marriages today: "It'll be more multicultural and that's just going to be, that's just natural evolution of uh generations. I mean, my generation, I'd say half of my friends married Korean, but the other half didn't, and then our children." Ruth believes that the ethnic-specific churches will become multiethnic or multicultural churches one day, as part of the church's "natural" evolutionary process. Jae Min concurs with Ruth, saying: "My church will become a multicultural church and actively involved with the local community. I believe my church will become less distinctly Korean in the future to become an integrated community church, with members from diverse backgrounds." So Young, a Korean-speaking first-generation member, anticipates the same phenomenon occurring at her Korean immigrant church. She says, "There is no guarantee that the church will have exclusively Korean members. We may have members from diverse cultural backgrounds. With less Korean-speaking members, there will be an inevitable decline in the KM (i.e., Korean ministry). Meaning the English service members will eventually form the 'dominant' group of the church." Likewise Ga Eun envisions a multicultural church where we can praise God with people from diverse ethnic and cultural backgrounds, even going as far as to say we need to start preparing better for it. She claims: "I think my church would be more multicultural considering our outreach efforts in the local community and contributions to the local mission . . . If the church is to become more multicultural, we should be more understanding and considerate of those coming from different cultures."

Brian also believes that moving in a multiethnic or multicultural direction is a part of our church's natural flow, thus he claims that we need to do more than opening up our church doors to all. He expresses a desire to celebrate the cultural diversity as a church: "Not just open but celebrate the diversity of cultures. As an example, just to make it more concrete, our church right now is located beside an ethnic Indian area known as Little India. We are also in the Beaches area, which is considered an upscale White-dominant area. This seems like a natural flow to go from a Taiwanese church to a more multicultural church." Daniel, an EM (i.e., English ministry) pastor, expresses the inevitability of becoming a fully inclusive church with people from different backgrounds, generations, and socioeconomic status. He says, "I imagine that our church will be multigenerational, or intergenerational, multi-socioeconomic, and inevitably multiethnic."

Ji Hun, a KM (i.e., Korean ministry) pastor, thinks that we will eventually lose our distinct ethnic color at our church:

> In the next twenty-five years, I think the Korean immigrant churches will lose their distinct ethnic color. This is the direction that we should be headed, to welcome all who comes through our doors. However, I think it will be difficult to get rid of our ethnic color completely. As long as racism exists in this society, there will be a need for ethnic churches . . . I think the ethnic Korean churches can open their doors to welcome more non-Koreans.

Abraham is an English-language minister who similarly envisions a multicultural church, where the English congregation is the leading congregation: "This church will become multicultural . . . the EM (i.e., English ministry) congregation will become the leading congregation of the church in twenty-five years. This is to ensure that my church develops into an openminded church serving and ministering to all people." Jane, another EM pastor, laments the deep-rooted ethnocentrism within the ACIC arising from the linguistic, political, ethno-geographical, and cultural differences among us. She hopes to overcome these differences by moving in an English-led multiethnic direction in the next twenty-five years: "Some things have to change for the church to continue. For example, they can no longer maintain this boundary of ethnocentrism. This definitely has to change. It can also be very culturally specific, in terms of Chinese-ness or Korean-ness . . . the EM needs to be more open. Still the majority of EM is Asians. There is an Asian diversity within the EM. But this diversity is limited to Asian-ness."

Hai, another ethnic-language ministry pastor, envisions a multiethnic church that seeks to serve the needs of the local community: "I hope that this church becomes an inclusive church with multiple ethnic groups. There may be multiple ethnic-language services by that time, however I hope that people from different ethnic backgrounds can come together at the church to serve the Lord. I hope that the church can serve the community in various ways."

In picturing what our church would look like in the next twenty-five years, several interviewees suggest that the ACIC would look completely different from their current demographics: Whereas the ethnic-language-speaking first-generation members are the majority now, the younger English-speaking generations will become the majority in twenty-five years. In other words, the positions would be reversed and the ethnic-language congregants would become the new minority. We foresee this reversal as inevitable, unless drastic measures are undertaken with respect to the immigration policies and trends. There is no doubt that the membership of ACIC would decrease significantly over the next twenty-five years, unless something is done quickly and effectively. Sui Hui thinks that this kind of research was much needed among the ACIC, and wishes that it had been conducted much earlier: "Maybe this [research] should have been done years ago? It is kind of too late to fix the problems, it's hard." Perhaps we are at the right time to make much needed changes at the ACIC, just when we think it is too late to do so. We are confident that the time has come for our churches to consider trying something different; we can reach an appropriate solution through a process of trial and error at our respective ACIC, which will lead to better future outcomes.

Many interviewees remain hopeful about the future of our church, especially about the English-speaking ministry. Although the vast majority of interviewees from the EM (i.e., English ministry) express a desire to move in a multiethnic or multicultural direction, they remain doubtful about making any progress in that direction as a church. One of the reasons is because they feel detached from the ethnic-language ministry, as both the English and ethnic-language ministries struggle with certain challenges that come from sharing the same roof. On a more positive note, these same challenges can be turned into opportunities for the ACIC. Of note, not a single English-speaking interviewee hinted his/her intention to leave the current church to start a new, independent church at the time of interview. Instead, they expressed their desire to tackle the challenges together with the members of ethnic-language congregation. We have come to love—or at the very least, have become deeply attached to—our ACIC whether we belong to the ethnic-language ministry or English ministry. Thus, we wish to stay together as one church, and strive for better future outcomes that serve and please the Lord. For example, we would like to help build a multiethnic congregation for our respective ACIC, broadening the kingdom of God in Canada, specifically in the GTA (i.e., Greater Toronto Area). While the ethnic-language congregants express their concerns about the fate of our churches' existence in the future, the English-speaking congregants have a more positive outlook on the future of ACIC. We expect to develop different models of church in the future, ones that are more relevant and adaptable. In general, the younger English-speaking generation has cultivated a vision of becoming a church for all and hopes to reach beyond our own ethnic Asian groups. Therefore, our ACIC will continue to work to accommodate the different-language needs, cultures, and preferences in the future.

Implications for a Better Story in the Future

Our stories of the present—where we stand—and our envisioned stories of the future—where we are headed—have been presented on behalf of the ACIC. In reflection, several common themes emerged including a passion for the church and for God, *jeong* (*qing*) for the next generation, fear about the uncertain future of the church, desire to navigate the future of ethnic-specific churches, and renewed call for well-supported English ministry for the future generation of worshippers in the church. Correspondingly, some of the more common phrases and terms that have appeared in our stories include a desire for one unified church joining two or more churches, leadership for the next generation or English ministry, and vision for multiethnic or multicultural church. In consideration of the ongoing challenges and opportunities presented at the ACIC, we need to explore the relevant educational and pastoral implications in order to build truly unified churches comprised of a single-ethnic or multiethnic congregation.

The first educational and pastoral implication, particularly to become one unified church, is concerning the importance of improving communication between different-language congregations and cultures. What do we need to improve the overall communication at our church? First, we need to work on our interpersonal communication skills, along with the intercultural sensitivity and intergenerational understanding. This is the case even in the ACIC with a single-ethnic congregation. Most ACIC, if not all, would like to strive for one unified church, yet are dealing with communication challenges that arise from the cultural, linguistic, and generational differences.

The second educational and pastoral implication is in regards to the empowerment of second-generation leadership, that is, the leadership for EM (i.e., English ministry). Developing the next generation of church leadership requires attention, time, and of course, prayer. Both the clergy and lay leaders of the first generation need to learn to establish a common ground with the second and third generations of the church. This will help us communicate better with one another, facilitate understanding about each other's cultures, and empower EM leaders to demonstrate their own leadership to the entire congregation through new opportunities and programs designed for the whole church. The ACIC need to focus especially on developing women's leadership, which is lacking among laity and clergy across all ministries.

The third and final educational and pastoral implication pertains to strategies for building a multiethnic church in the future. As mentioned previously, the vast majority of the ethnic-language-speaking and English-speaking clergy and lay interviewees would like to move in a multiethnic direction that reflects the changing Canadian society, particularly within the GTA (i.e., Greater Toronto Area). They believe that in doing so, they can follow the Biblical model of church and the Kingdom of God. This requires intentional intercultural education and practice. While many clergy and lay interviewees express an interest in becoming a multiethnic church, they are unsure about how to move beyond their own ethnic Asian groups or Asian-ness. One possibility is not framing itself as an Asian specific church. But before we change our frames to be more inclusive, the way we perceive others need to change first, otherwise how can we move beyond being an Asian-specific church for Asians only? We will also have to grapple with the following dilemma: Should we uproot ourselves of our own cultures at the ACIC for the purpose of becoming a multiethnic or multicultural church?

In the following chapters, we will explore these implications further with practical suggestions for the better future outcomes of ACIC.

Reflection and Discussion Questions

1. How do you envision your church in the next twenty-five years?
2. Which church model discussed in this chapter is most suitable for your own church and why?
3. Upon thinking about the future church, what implications can you draw in terms of your own church's future?

Part IV

For Better Stories

8

Building One United Church

In Kee Kim

> There is no longer Jew or Greek, there is no longer slave or free, there is no longer male and female; for all of you are one in Christ Jesus. (Gal 3:28, NRSV)

As we discussed previously, in our present stories, many Asian Canadian immigrant churches (ACIC) have two worship services under one roof in order to accommodate the second-generation English-speaking members. This was one of our ways to adapt to the changes taking place within our churches. Some churches have more established English-speaking congregations alongside ethnic-language congregations, each with their own, independent governing body. But the vast majority of the ACIC are still governed by the ethnic-language-speaking first-generation congregation. Hence, most ACIC are not properly equipped to do effective ministry for the second-generation English-speaking congregants. Further to this point, the minister interviewees responded as follows when asked about their relationship with other congregants from services in different-language: Eight stated they stay loosely connected with congregants from the "other" side; seven stated that their church functions as one church under a single ethnic-language senior pastor; four described running a church with completely independent congregations in terms of finance and governing system; one described the interdependency or coexistence of congregations, as in having one minister, one church, and two bodies. Interestingly enough, an English ministry pastor's view on this matter usually differed from that of the ethnic-language ministry pastor serving the same church—whereas the ethnic-language minister tends to describe their relationships as mutually independent, the English minister tends to describe their relationships as one-sided, especially when one ethnic-language senior pastor is overseeing the entire church.

The Desire and Concerns to Be One, United Church

When ACIC began offering English-language services, we assumed that there would be no objections to proceeding as one unified church, even if we worship separately based on language preferences. However, in reality, we observed something quite different from what we anticipated: Although the two or three congregations often yearn to coexist harmoniously as one unified church, there is an ongoing challenge of generational disconnect between the two or three congregations, as discussed in previous chapters. In the long run, this may result in church separation and splits. Let us consider a story that describes the reality of some ACIC now, and the likely future of most ACIC. This particular story comes from one of the oldest Chinese churches in Toronto, where the English minister is officially the senior minister.

> (Your church sign outside displays both language service times; Chinese and English. What kind of relationship do you have with the Chinese ministry [CM] or Chinese congregation at your church?)
>
> Ben: I have established a good relationship with the Chinese congregation at this church. Many members of our Chinese congregation are bilingual—they speak both Chinese and English. I speak to them in English. I still have a good relationship with the elderly, even though we may not be able to communicate as well. There are some senior members in the Chinese congregation who can converse in English, because they have been here for a long time.
>
> (What kind of relationship do you have with the CM minister? Can you describe the relationship between the EM and CM in terms of church governance?)
>
> Ben: Although theoretically I am the senior and only Presbyterian minister at the church, I see the CM minister as my colleague. My Chinese colleague is not a part of PCC . . . This is unfortunate. He still functions as a minister, and most people don't know the difference anyway.
>
> (Are there any meetings between the CM and EM?)

Ben: Although we get along well, we run our own ministries independently. So we don't actually have many meetings with both the CM and EM in attendance.

(The CM-EM relationship is not a parent-child relationship.)

Ben: No. We are two completely independent congregations in the same building. We do have one joint session, which is an occasion for the CM elders and EM elders to meet together. However, the EM elders are more dominant than the CM elders.

(In terms of numbers, how many elders are from the EM side?)

Ben: We have about six EM elders and five CM elders. So the number of elders from each side is almost the same.

(Are there any joint ministry ventures?)

Ben: I would say very little. We have one combined picnic and two or three joint services per year. Otherwise, we are pretty much independent.

(So there is no joint outreach ministry.)

Ben: No. We are almost like two separate churches sharing the same building.

Just as the case above, each of our ACIC might separate into two or three independent churches sharing the same building in the future. And as noted in previous chapters, the two or three congregations within the same church building continue to struggle with differences in language, culture, and generation. Almost all members, regardless of whether they belong to the younger English-speaking generation or older ethnic-language-speaking generation, often find it challenging to become one unified church. Members from both generations feel as though they belong to separate churches. Many interviewees raise their concerns about the apparent disconnect between the two or three congregations sharing the same roof, which is seen as a hindrance to their becoming one unified church. For example, Seok Ho is concerned about having two separate groups under one roof; he thinks this weakens the notion of one unified community. So Young, a first-generation ethnic-language-speaking worshiper, agrees with Seok Ho: "Sometimes it feels like there are two separate entities under one roof." Sui Hui and Ji Yang are also in agreement, saying: "Somehow it's an upstairs-downstairs-church, upstairs they do their things, downstairs we do our things."

Susan, an English-speaking interviewee, raises her concerns about the "us and them" mentality—specifically with "two separate services . . . there's a very like 'us and them' mentality" within the ACIC. Shirley, another English-speaking interviewee, raises similar concerns: "in a sense and we're not really there together. We're not sharing the same space at the same time either, so even though we're under the same church, I don't know them. I would see them and 'oh, hi, hi' and then pass them, we have nothing to do with, with each other." Kate, another second-generation English-speaking interviewee, expresses the same concern: "I have no idea what the Mandarin congregation is doing, we're doing our own thing." These concerns originate from their desire to build a truly unified church with those on the "other" side of the church building. Robert says, "I feel that we do have the motivations to be one church, not just KM and EM." Ultimately it is problematic for the two or three different congregations to hold intrinsic longing to become a unified church.

Several members from both the ethnic-language congregation and English-speaking congregation feel that the latter is often treated like second-class citizens. This is mostly because our ACIC are ethnic-dominant churches and are being run as such, giving priorities and delegating decision-making powers to the ethnic-language congregation. This is also reflected in our parent-child mentality or stereotype. Seok Ho describes this phenomenon as follows: "The EM has been treated like a separate entity within the church." Meaning, our ACIC are very much focused on the first generation ethnic-language-speaking members and their needs, neglecting the younger English-speaking members in the process. As a result, the English-speaking members feel lesser of themselves as a congregation, thinking that they have a lower status at the church compared to their ethnic-language counterparts. While the different language congregations may coexist under the same roof, they have yet to become equal partners in carrying out Christ's mission.

These concerns demonstrate that the most popular church models for our ACIC are the "Room for Rent" model, or "Duplex" or "Triplex" model, as per the "Asian church models as residences" in the United States.[1] With the "Room for Rent" model in ACIC, the English congregation typically starts out in a single room with mostly English-speaking children and youth, and is not expected to pay rent to the church. Under this model, the ethnic-language congregation treats members of English congregation like their children, even as they grow up and become working professionals in the mainstream Canadian society. Some churches have transitioned from the "Room for Rent" model to the "Duplex" or "Triplex" model. The basic structure of the "Duplex" model entails having the English congregation

---

1. Shin and Silzer, *Tapestry of Grace*, 8–12.

and ethnic-language congregation together, side by side. The two groups would coexist as two units under one roof with separate leaders, but under one senior leadership. The "Triplex" model can be applied to some Chinese and Taiwanese immigrant churches in Canada, which are comprised of three congregations, namely the Mandarin, Cantonese (or Taiwanese), and English. These congregations would coexist side by side as three units under one senior leadership. A few of our ACIC have already transitioned to the "Townhouse" Model, that is to say having two language congregations under two different leaderships. They would share the church building and facilities, but function as two completely independent churches.

Under such models, we cannot build one unified church. These models of church are characterized by disconnect and separation, exacerbating the concern for unity felt amongst both the ethnic-language congregation and English congregation. It is about bringing together the "upstairs and downstairs" church, in order to overcome the existing barriers between different language congregations. But how can we build a truly unified church community founded on unity, trust, and harmony between the different language congregations? Can there be an "Open Concept House" church that seeks to destroy the walls that divide us? In order to build a truly unified church, we would need to have a vision for the "Open Concept House" Model of church. An "Open Concept House" has rooms with a minimum number of doors; the focus is on the open space, which is reserved for all. In each room of the church under this model, there would be individual gatherings with separate leaders. However once congregants come out to the open space, there would be communal life under one leadership. The leaders of each room would be treated as equal partners and take turns to serve as the "one leader" for all in the open space.

The Need for One, Unified Church

If the first generation formed the ACIC by necessity, the second generation and the third generation stay with the ACIC by choice. Instead of going to the English-speaking non-Asian churches, the members of English-speaking second and third generations make the choice to come to the ACIC regularly, even after they move outside their respective ethnic enclaves. They would rather drive a long distance to their own ACIC every Sunday, instead of attending a neighboring church nearby.

Many of the second generation say that their church is like their home. A church that houses multiple generations is like a big family. Their parents' friends are like their own parents. They are like uncles and aunties. Stuart says, "My parents' friends are like my friends; they are like my own parents. They saw me grow up. I saw them grow older. And I grew up with their kids and we have seen each other getting married and growing our families with our own kids. So we are all one big family."

Thus, for many members of English-speaking second and third generations, the church is more than a religious institution; it is their home, albeit in a different sense from the ethnic-language-speaking first generation. It is their own safe place, a sanctuary for cultural solidarity. The English-speaking interviewees use one or more words from the following list to describe their ACIC: "[H]omey, food, unspoken understanding, a sense of closeness, connection, able to click, no need to explain who [we] are." Deborah, a second-generation interviewee, says "I feel rooted here." She confirms the reason why the ACIC are still needed for the younger English-speaking generations. Likewise Jasmin, another second-generation interviewee, says: "Going to another church is like pulling up roots." Susan concurs, saying: "I don't know what it is. I can't put my finger on it. But there's something familiar and core to me that I want to keep." They choose to attend ACIC not just for practical reasons, but also for a sense of "home" or "connection" to their cultural heritage. Their church is where their parents and grandparents are; their church is where their childhood friends are. Although they consider themselves Canadianized for the most part, the ACIC, along with their ethnic home life, played a major part in their upbringing. In order to become one unified church, our ACIC need to continue serving as a "home" for generations to come in a racially compartmentalized society like GTA. This would allow the ACIC to stay relevant.

Russell Jeung clearly confirms the need for unified Asian immigrant churches in his book, *Faithful Generations*. According to Jeung, most Chinese and Japanese second-, third-, fourth-, and even fifth-generation congregants in the Bay Area of California choose to drive a long distance to attend their respective ethnic-specific churches or pan-Asian/multicultural churches, passing by other non-ethnic churches.[2] Jeung claims that most Asian Americans continue to attend the churches of ethnic affiliation for worship and fellowship. Currently, the ethnic-specific churches in the States outnumber the pan-Asian/multicultural churches, even as the former is becoming hybridized. Jeung's book discusses a number of reasons why the fully acculturated Asian Americans continue to attend an ethnic-specific church or pan-Asian/multicultural church over mainline non-ethnic church. These reasons are quite similar to those given by the fully Canadianized English-speaking congregants of ACIC, which include distinct cultural

---

2. Jeung, *Faithful Generations*, 17.

bonds, similar social and family values, a sense of closeness, comfort and familiarity, connectedness, and rootedness.[3] Given the similarities, what lesson(s) can we take away from Jeung's book on the Chinese and Japanese immigrant churches in the States? Following their lead, the ACIC need to focus on helping subsequent generations integrate better with the church, and not so much on the church's future logistics.

A Case Study: Pilgrims Presbyterian Church

To help us envision the "Open Concept House" model for our ACIC, let us consider Pilgrims Presbyterian Church (N.B. not its actual name) as a case study. Specifically, let us examine how this church has successfully become a unified church with two different-language congregations: Korean and English. Pilgrims Presbyterian Church was founded in 1996 and is currently located in the suburbs of Toronto. On the church webpage, they clearly identify who they are with the following phrase: "with roots in the Korean immigrant community." What sets this church apart from other churches is its ability to bring together the Korean congregation and English-speaking congregation; they coexist under one roof and identify themselves as one unified church. It is interesting to note that the vast majority of English-speaking members at this church do not have any family ties—that is, approximately 85 percent of the English-speaking members are not the children of the first-generation Korean members. In other words, most English-speaking members at this church choose to come on their own will. These days, more third-generation English-speaking Korean Canadian members are joining the church, as well as some non-Korean members.

The second-generation English-speaking members at Pilgrims Presbyterian Church are vocally appreciative of the continued sacrifice and dedication of the first-generation Korean members toward the church. In particular, the younger generation would like to continue the legacy by learning from the first-generation Korean members' strength, love, and spirit of commitment for the church—all of which allowed them to survive through the imperial occupation, wars, and harsh realities of immigrant life. While the first-generation Korean members at this church experienced the pain of church splits in the past, they did not leave the church. Instead, they helped bring about the healing, growth, and maturity of the church congregation.

Going forward, the second-generation English-speaking members at Pilgrims would like to address any scars and wounds of the first-generation Korean members, especially those from the church splits in the past. They

3. Jeung, *Faithful Generations*, 31.

feel the need to do this, in order to confront the scars and wounds of their own incurred from their experiences living as the children of ethnic immigrants in Canada. Thus the healing and learning can take place mutually at the church; the second-generation members learn from the first generation's ways of doing ministry, and vice versa. Likewise, the first-generation members challenge the second generation to be more Christ-like in their attitudes, behaviors, and lifestyles. The second-generation members challenge the first generation to be more open-minded about ongoing social issues and church strategies.

Most, if not all, members of the first-generation Korean congregation attending Pilgrims Presbyterian Church are willing to make sacrifices, and put their own needs on hold in order to meet the second-generation English-speaking members' needs. This mature spirituality of self-sacrifice is very much needed for the unified coexistence model to be viable; the selfishness that comes from a sense of entitlement would make any existing and future unified coexistence models onerous, if not unrealistic. This means that both generations learned to cooperate with one another, and make the necessary sacrifices willingly; it took a long time to build the spiritual maturity required to do so. Members of both generations put the vision of Christ's church first, rather than the needs of their own. They exhibited this kind of selflessness for the sake of the whole church, and the future church of Christ. This comes from the theological teachings of what the church is. And the church culture and ethos based on such values take a long time to build from within. For example, let us consider the worship time at Pilgrims Presbyterian Church. The 11:00 slot on a Sunday morning is largely considered as the golden time for worship, even though Martin Luther King Jr. once claimed it to be the most divided hour in the States. While Pilgrims has its own church building, the first-generation Korean members have given up that golden hour of worship to the younger English-speaking members, having moved their own worship time to early morning. The first-generation Korean members made this sacrifice willingly to accommodate the needs and preferences of the younger English-speaking members. The English-speaking members were moved by the Korean congregation's act of self-sacrifice; this was a good message to witness for the younger English-speaking members at Pilgrims. The younger English-speaking members especially appreciate the attitude of being considerate of others' needs. This in turn earned their trust in other church-related matters, although this was not the original intention. This was just the side effect of the first-generation Korean congregation's decision to act selflessly toward the English congregation—a decision purely motivated by their spiritual and theological vision. What can we learn from this experience? When our actions reflect Christ's selflessness, we can start the healing and reconciliation process at the church, which is an important step at all ACIC.

Pilgrims is equipped with a strong pastoral team. Even though there is one senior pastor, the pastoral leadership is like a team leadership. Having a team leadership is important—the traditional hierarchical leadership of ACIC is not the best fit for the "Open Concept House" model. Each member of the pastoral team at Pilgrims brings unique gifts and talents to the table. And the team seeks to maximize the gifts and talents of each member. There is no such thing as a KM (i.e., Korean ministry) pastor or EM (i.e., English ministry) pastor at Pilgrims. All members are simply pastors of the church, and thus equally responsible for overseeing the whole church. The members of the pastoral team take into consideration the needs of both the English-speaking congregation and Korean congregation in an equitable manner. For example, the pastors take turns delivering the sermon to both the English-speaking congregation and Korean congregation on Sunday. The designated preacher delivers the same sermon twice, once in Korean for the Korean congregation and then in English for the English-speaking congregation. And over the years, the members have worked to overcome the cultural and linguistic barriers through bilingualism and bicultural accommodations. While the bilingualism and bicultural accommodations are not always necessary, they are the preferred methods to overcome the cultural and linguistic barriers at the pastoral level. As such, the diversity within the pastoral team is considered an asset for the church, and not an insurmountable barrier.

Pilgrims runs two sessions, one for each congregation. The members of each session are elected by their own congregation. The session meetings are held separately, and deal with matters that are specifically related to each congregation. Occasionally, the joint session meetings are called to deal with matters that affect both congregations. It has taken a long time for a separate session to be formed for the English-speaking congregation. Of note is that the second-generation English-speaking members were initially reluctant to be elected elders of the church, unlike the first-generation Korean members. Indeed, it has taken a long time for the English-speaking members at Pilgrims to take charge and acquire a sense of ownership of their church. After the creation of a separate English session, the church has strived to nurture a mutually respectful atmosphere. The Korean session does not interfere with the English session's decisions relating to the matters specific to the English-speaking congregation, and vice versa.

The English-speaking congregation and Korean congregation raise the funds together for church's mission projects. They are equally committed in that regard. For example, when raising funds for the first Korean nursing home for seniors, the English-speaking congregation contributed as much as the Korean congregation. Financially, the two congregations plan according to their own budgets, which are independent and separated from one another. The stipends of some of the pastoral staff are divided proportionally by the two congregations, depending on the amount of work contribution required. The two congregations also plan and execute some mission projects together, including the overseas mission and inner-city mission.

There are a few joint services throughout the year at Pilgrims, where the two congregations come together for worship. At the joint worship service, the KM (i.e., Korean ministry) and EM (i.e., English ministry) choirs also come together and sing in celebration. The focus of the joint worship service is on the celebratory aspect, and not the teaching aspect. Therefore, a short sermon would be followed by a number of special celebratory activities during and after the joint worship service, to remind all congregants that they belong to one unified church community.

One of the most important elements to having this kind of unified coexistence church model is the mutual respect between the different-language congregations, in this case the English-speaking congregation and Korean congregation. So far, both sides seem to value each other's differences and honour them. For example, the first-generation Korean congregation values the second generation English-speaking congregation's new, innovative ideas for ministry, and appreciates their heightened understanding of the mainstream Canadian society. Whereas the English-speaking congregation values the spiritual dedication and sacrifice of the first generation Korean congregation. They seem to value and appreciate each other's strengths and gifts.

An added benefit to this kind of unified coexistent church model is in gaining a deeper theological understanding of what the church should be. Pilgrims' vision has always been clearly communicated: "There is no longer Jew or Greek, there is no longer slave or free, there is no longer male and female; for all of you are one in Christ Jesus" (Gal 3:28). It takes a long time to cultivate a theological understanding of the church. But it helps to have the members of the pastoral team share a similar vision for the church's future, as in the case of Pilgrims Presbyterian Church. Our diversity in unity is our strength that can help us make the church vision into reality. The differences do not break us apart; intolerance of our differences do.

Foundations of One Unified Church

Creating a separate independent church just for the second-generation English-speaking members, as in a pan-Asian/multicultural church, is not the only option. This is a complex issue that involves not only the language and culture but also history, family, relationships, friendships, and emotional attachment. The ACIC need to develop a new model for the future church. How can two or three language ministries work together as partners to build one church beyond differences of language, culture, and generation? First, the ACIC should focus on developing effective ministry not only for survival but also for the opportunity to do a new ministry. Traditional first-generation ministry will not necessarily be the best way to do effective ministry but at the same time, traditional Western ways of doing ministry will not necessarily fulfill the needs of modern Asian Canadians. The ACIC now have the opportunity not only to reach out to their second generation, but also the general population by envisioning a fresh new way of doing ministry that is relevant, effective, and meaningful. From the case of Pilgrims Presbyterian Church and our research findings, we would like to make the following suggestions for our ACIC to help build the foundation of one unified church in the future.

1. The one-team ministry: The ACIC need to understand the team ministry, which is cooperative, and not competitive among different-language group ministries. At Pilgrims Presbyterian Church, there is no designated name of English minister or Korean minister. All members of ministry team serve the church according to their gifts and talents. Calling ministers to a certain ministry such as English ministry or Korean ministry is the starting point to be competitive, not cooperative, making them to focus on "achievements" rather than serving and caring. When the ministers are designated under specific language ministry, the congregations also see themselves divided, and are easy to separate themselves around ministers. In the Asian immigrant church context, it might not be possible to avoid the hierarchical power structure altogether. But striving for a strong ministry team as a church will help mitigate this hierarchical structural system. This would lay the first foundation to becoming one unified church under the Open Concept House model. The crucial key for the future of the ACIC (and as a matter of fact, all churches) is to focus on the development of qualified leaders who are theologically open, spiritually deep, and biblically critical. They need to be socially and politically well-informed, culturally sensitive, and emotionally strong enough not to be influenced by

social pressure. They need to be able to help people process what they experience in their lives through the lens of the Scripture. They need to understand the power of God's grace that brought the Gospel to break the boundary of Jewish culture and embrace the new people of God.

2. Two-step decision process: As discussed above, Pilgrims has two separate sessions—the English session and the Korean session. The session meetings are organized according to the matters at hand. If the matters at hand affect the entire church, a joint session meeting would be called. If not, each session has separate meetings to make decisions on its own. The popular "Duplex" and "Triplex" model churches are most concerned about the hierarchical decision-making process, which favours the ethnic-language congregation. Sometimes these churches face communication challenges during the session meeting, even with translations. The English members of session in particular are frustrated about not being able to express their opinions during the meeting, given the parent-child power dynamic of the "Duplex" and "Triplex" model churches. Before calling a session meeting, the ministers need to decide whether the matters at hand are related to the whole church, or congregation-specific. Then the ministers can decide if it is necessary to call the whole session, or smaller language-specific session meeting. This would not only be more efficient, but also relegate the decision-making powers to each congregation where appropriate. Alternatively, the ministers can call a two-step meeting: The first portion of meeting can deal with matters affecting the whole church, and the second portion can be reserved for more specific issues relevant to each congregation. Sometimes, the ACIC need to be reminded that their English ministry is not just for the children and youth anymore. A typical second-generation English-speaking congregation at the ACIC is comprised of a relatively high proportion of adult congregants between the ages of twenty to sixty-five. If the English-speaking congregation continues to be treated like children, they will not remain at the ACIC. Thus we need to start creating a church environment where the first generation and second generation can work together as equal partners. Given that the majority of leaders serving the English ministry are adult working professionals, they need to be given the proper respect and voice to represent themselves at their ACIC. Meaning, the ACIC need to change their overall attitude toward the younger English-speaking generation, from treating them as children in need of care to encouraging and inviting them to become coworkers or partners at the church.

3. Spiritual maturity with critical Bible study: Overall, the ACIC need to learn how to become more considerate of others' needs. Currently we are concerned mostly with the interests of the language group to which we belong, rather than that of the other language group at the church. We as a congregation can start caring for others' needs once we reach a certain level of spiritual maturity. But how can we nurture spiritual maturity at the ACIC? The case study above of Pilgrims Presbyterian Church illustrates that one of the best ways to nurture spiritual maturity is through critical Bible studies. For most ACIC, it is quite difficult to put the English-speaking younger generation first, due to the deeply embedded Confucianism. For example, when deciding the worship time and place for each congregation, the main sanctuary would be given to the ethnic-language congregation without question. The younger English-speaking congregation would be expected to take the gym or church basement as their place of worship. As discussed previously, Pilgrims decided to offer the "golden" time of worship to its English congregation. This church's pastoral team, as well as its Korean congregation, are at a level of spiritual maturity where they can put others' needs first before their own—in this case, the needs and preferences of the younger English-speaking congregation. This is an example of spiritual practice in everyday life.

   The ACIC's both ethnic and English ministry should not be overly focused on the social aspects of the church, such as providing fellowship, friendship, celebration of special ethnic festivals, and ethnic foods. There has to be a critical understanding of their history, their roots, and their current situations in this society through the eyes of the Scripture. The kind of spirituality we need is not emotional, sentimental, and feel-good spirituality. The kind of spirituality we need is a critical understanding of who we are, what we are called to be and to do, what our dreams and visions are. We need the kind of spirituality that critically guides us through their complex and confusing hybrid social situations. We need the kind of spirituality that not only heals our pain and struggles of living as an ethnic minority, but also uses our unique situations to develop mature and compassionate faith. We need the kind of spirituality that helps us have a strong desire to be in solidarity with the weak and the vulnerable of this society.

4. Opportunities for both congregations to be and to do ministry together: As mentioned previously, Pilgrims Presbyterian Church holds a few joint worship services throughout the year. In addition, the English-speaking congregation and Korean congregation participate

in several mission projects and church events together. One interviewee from another church described how memorable and effective the joint summer retreat was in building a unified church community. Several interviewees from both the ethnic-language and English congregations expressed their yearning to have more joint worship services with real-time translations. Although having more joint worship services would not always be convenient, they would serve as opportunities to instill a sense of one unified church community among congregants from both sides. A number of interviewees mentioned that the English-speaking congregation is often left out of the church-related activities, such as mission projects and special church events. As a result, the English-speaking members have sometimes felt undermined and isolated at the church. The ACIC should seek to include the English-speaking members as much as possible in the planning, coordination, and organization of church-related activities. Once the English-speaking members feel fully included at the church, they would be more proactive about sharing church responsibilities with the ethnic-language-speaking members. This would help the English-speaking members with their sense of ownership and belonging at their respective ACIC. Such cooperative church atmosphere would remind the English-speaking members, as well as the ethnic-language-speaking members, that "We are Together; We are One."

In summary, for two churches under one roof to be viable, there has to be a mutual understanding that we are equal partners with different gifts and callings. We need to respect each other's differences and understand that unity is possible only in diversity. We can allow each other a space to do our own things freely as the Spirit guides us. While allowing each other's individuality and uniqueness, we can create an atmosphere where every member feels respected, appreciated, and valued no matter who she/he is. We are all one in Christ. We should serve each other with love and care. We should empower each other to live out the calling uniquely given to each one of us.

One of the most important elements to make one unified church among different-language groups is communication. The empowerment of second-generation leadership is also equally important. In the following chapters, we will take a closer look at these two elements.

Reflection and Discussion Questions

1. Which model of church discussed above best describes your current church?

2. In considering the case study above of the Pilgrims Presbyterian Church, what implications can you think of for your current church in becoming one unified church?

3. How can we create a safe space where people can comfortably raise questions without the fear of feeling rejected and judged? How can we help each other speak up during meetings, regardless of age, gender, and preferred language?

4. What are some common projects that the first-generation immigrants and the second-generation Asian Canadians can do together?

9

Communicating and Bridging Relationship Gaps across Language, Generational, and Cultural Divides

A Case of Asian Canadian Immigrant Churches in Toronto

BEN C. H. KUO

> Let no evil talk come out of your mouth, but only what is useful for building up as there is need, so that your words may give grace to those who hear. (Eph 4:29, NRSV)

IN THIS CHAPTER I endeavor to adopt an analytical approach to help interpret and understand the findings of this research on Asian Canadian immigrant churches that pertain specifically to culture, communication, and relationship. It's an approach grounded in current knowledge of cross-cultural communication, intergenerational relationship, and transnational migration experience of Asian immigrant families. From such a standpoint, I will first report the findings from the interviews conducted with fifty Asian Canadian participants, including thirty laypeople and twenty clergies, from fifteen Korean, Taiwanese, and Chinese churches across Toronto, Canada. A specific focus of the analysis is placed on the themes that reflect the intersection of culture, communication, and relationship within and among Asian Canadian churches, as emerged from the interview data/transcripts. Secondly, in the chapter I will carefully consider and analyze the themes/issues emerged from the interview findings in view of our current empirical and conceptual literature on: 1) acculturation, 2) Asian traditionalism and familism, and 3) transnational immigrant experience.

Communication in the Crosscultural Context

To better situate the current chapter on intergenerational communication and intercongregational relationship within Asian Canadian immigrant churches, it is essential to first delimit what we mean by "communication" and what we know of communication across cultures.

Drs. David Masumoto and Linda Jung provide a psychological definition of communication; they describe communication as "a complex and intricate process that involves the exchange of message between interactants, both verbally and nonverbally."[1] As such, human communication system and ability is a distinctive, God-given endowment to humankind with all its complexity and intricacy.

However unique, communication between people and groups can be complicated by other critical contextual factors, such as culture, language, and migration in intercultural or crosscultural situations. In particular, Samovar et al. note that "Intercultural communication occurs whenever a person from one culture sends a message to be processed by a person from a different culture."[2] Ethnic immigrant churches represent one such crosscultural complexity. In the case of Asian immigrant churches in Canada and the United States, they are often comprised of congregation members with varying immigrant statuses, generational cohorts, degrees of acculturation levels in the host culture, and proficiency in one's heritage language (Taiwanese, Mandarin, Cantonese, Korean, etc.) versus in the language of the host society (i.e., English and French in Canada). Despite many shared cultural roots and heritages between the congregations under the same roof, members of Asian Canadian immigrant churches (e.g., Chinese Canadian immigrant church) can vary significantly in their sociodemographic background characteristics. For example, a Chinese Canadian church might simultaneously house a Cantonese-speaking congregation, a Mandarin-speaking congregation, and an English-speaking congregation. Such a composition of diverse memberships sets up an example of "intercultural" or "crosscultural" communication dynamics. Therefore, intercongregant communication and relationship within Asian immigrant churches are indeed complex processes involving bridging across language, generational, cultural, and even theological divides.

Operating from the above framework on culture and communication, it can be easily understood that while effective communication can enable us to convey our needs, wants, and wishes to others to garner resources and

---

1. Matsumoto and Juang, *Culture and Psychology*, 248.
2. Samovar et al., *Intercultural Communication*, 8.

support across cultures and cultural groups, ineffective communication or a lack of communication can give raise to misunderstanding, resentment, and even conflict. For example, Chen's study of Taiwanese immigrant churches in California found that the transition from the traditional Taiwanese/Chinese unidirectional parent-to-child communication to a more egalitarian Western reciprocal communication between first-generation parents and their second-generation children is one example of communication challenge faced by immigrant parents both at home and in the church.[3] Clearly, poor communication or miscommunication can critically undermine interpersonal relationship, social harmony, and group solidarity, including families and churches within the body of Christ. However, adopting a new pattern of communication between Asian first-generation parents and their second-generation children goes beyond simply acquiring new skills on conveying and receiving message, it involves major adaptations and adjustments of social roles, statutes, and hierarchies within Asian immigrant families[4] and by extension within Asian immigrant churches.[5] These social, cultural, and familial influences will be carefully explored and considered in greater detail, as part of the interpretation of the study's results in the discussion section later.

Purposes of the Current Chapter

In this chapter I propose that the gaps and conflicts currently exist intergenerationally between first-generation heritage congregant and the second-generation English-speaking congregant within the Asian immigrant churches in Canada can be more fully and effectively understood from a comprehensive, socially/psychologically/culturally informed lens—a perspective that is well-grounded in the current knowledge of acculturation, East Asian traditional and family values, and transnational migration family experience.

---

3. Chen, "From Filial Piety," 573–602.

4. See Kim and Ryu, "Korean Families," 349–62.

5. Chen, "From Filial Piety," 573–602; see Lee and Mock, "Asian Families," 269–89; Kim, "New Missions," 1–9.

The Nature and the Sources of Intergenerational and Intercongregational Communication Conflicts

In general, these themes represent Asian Canadian Christian participants' perceptions and understanding of the nature and the impact of intercongregational communication on their relational, spiritual, and church lives. As a whole, there is a general yet overwhelming sense of a lack or even an absence of effective communication between different generation and ethnic-language congregants within Asian Canadian churches, despite worshiping under and operating from the same roof. These themes have multifaceted and multilayered contents and implications. In particular, the themes reflect complex intersections among the language factor, generation factor, and ethnicity factor overlaid with Asian familial and social values, cultural adaptation and identity of immigrants and immigrant families, and spiritual/faith/religious practices and traditions.

Theme #1: Language Difference as Communication Barrier

An obvious issue that contributes to crosscultural communication difficulties and at times misunderstanding is not having a shared, common language medium between the parties involved. Not surprisingly, Asian Canadian participants in the current study clearly identified language problems between the heritage congregant and the English-speaking congregant as a major underlying factor that impedes intergenerational and intercongregational communication and collaboration. This is evident in Ji Yang's response, who is a Cantonese speaker and attends a church with Cantonese, Mandarin, and English congregation.

> It can be a barrier because I don't speak Mandarin, and I can [only] understand English [a bit] but not too much. That could be a barrier between two congregations. It is quite difficult! You know you will not feel too comfortable in communicating in one of those languages [that you are not familiar with].

Ji Yang further lamented:

> If [we] all have the same language [then the problem may be solved], but it is difficult because we have different languages. For instance, we have been trying to arrange some family worships in English, but the parents could not understand English, they don't go and no participation.

The issue of language barrier is significant and can have wide-ranging impacts on the various aspects of congregational life, as illustrated by Seok Ho's response: "Communication is always a challenge, not just only day to day talks, but the whole church as a whole."

In view of communication obstacle due to linguistic concerns, some participants have attempted to bridge such a gap on their own initiative. For example Chen Yi stressed the importance of first-generation Chinese-speaking congregation learning English, so as to improve the relationship with their second-generation English-speaking congregation.

> I learn [English] not only for myself. I even encourage those from China, even [if] their English is not so good, go and try English service if you want to maintain your communication with your kids twenty years from now. If not, they cannot understand you, you cannot understand them, that's it, forget it!

Theme #2: Intercongregational Differences in Sociocultural Affiliations, Identities, and Biases

Language is also closely tied to one's sense of ethnic and cultural identity and their social-political positions. The participants' interviews also point to the fact that the congregational relationship between the heritage congregant and English-speaking congregant is further complicated by group ethnic and regional differences in addition to language hindrance. This is apparent from the following quote by Ba Men, who spoke about Mandarin versus English services:

> As for Mandarin and English, other than the differences in language, the topic is an issue: Mandarin group likes to talk about what happened in their mother country, including politics which might touch their feelings. But the younger generation wants to focus on what they're facing in social media, how to deal with drugs, the school life, how to deal with parents and teachers, etc., the focus are different and their patience are also different. The English [sermon] topic they like to be finished in fifteen minutes [during the service] while the Mandarin people want it [the sermon] longer, up to one hour.

Similarly, within Korean churches, cultural and value reference points differed between Korean-speaking congregation and English-speaking congregation. Ga Eun observed that "Many first generation members are very conservative as per the traditional Korean culture with its ties to Confucianism."

Ping highlighted the distinctive cultural tendency of "face-saving" among older Taiwanese members as one obstacle to social interaction and communication in the church.

> It's part of Taiwanese culture that people like to save face, a lot of people have the "face problem." It's very hard especially [for] the older generation they feel that they don't like to change, just keep as it is.

That is, the relationship between the two congregations within Asian Canadian churches can be additionally challenged by the divergent interests, concerns, identity affiliations, and values of the respective congregants. A lack of common conversational topics and shared perspectives can obscure the effort and the desire for promoting intergroup and intercongregational relationship within the church.

Incidentally, these divergences in intergroup interests and social-cultural-political identifications between congregants within the same immigrant church can lead to further schism due to underlying misconceptions and biases between church groups. In the following quote, Shirley highlighted such unease between members of Mandarin service and members of Cantonese service in her Chinese church. Shirley asserted:

> [I] know from hearing from my parents speak because they're in the Cantonese congregation in their church and then we have a Mandarin congregation; they do not mix well at all. They have a lot of conflicts with one another because they sort of have different values in a sense, even though we're Chinese but Cantonese and Mandarin, we come from different parts of China. So everything is very different and they're always conflicting with one another, and I always hear my parents complaining about the Mandarin congregations, "Oh why are they doing this, it doesn't make any sense, they're ruining blah-blah-blah, our reputation" in a sense so it's sort of like we're all under one congregation but then there's different groups, the congregations are different groups.

The intergroup rivalry and suspicion, however, stands in opposition to the spirit of the Gospel as revealed in Melia's reflection.

> The Mandarin people are constantly coming to us [Cantonese], but we just have this resistance because we're like "we don't know what to do with you because we don't speak your language," right. But I think that's, that's something that God's trying to

tell us. It's like, how do you receive them despite, um, you're not equipped to speak perfectly, right.

Despite being in the body of the Christ in the same "church" and community, the intergroup tensions (e.g., between Mandarin versus Cantonese congregants) can be palatable. The roots of these tensions and discords can often be found in the larger sociopolitical history and context between Mandarin-speaking congregation who are most recent immigrants in Canada from mainland China, and Cantonese-speaking congregation who are mostly long-established immigrants in Canada from Hong Kong. This finding in the current study corresponds to Tse's observations of transnational Chinese churches in Vancouver.[6] Tse reported that contestations and between-group conflicts exist in the church life of Chinese Canadian churches housing immigrants from Hong Kong and those from mainland China (the People's Republic of China). In particular, the schism between these congregations often occur due not only to linguistic difference (Cantonese vs. Mandarin), but also perceived dissimilar educational backgrounds and biases between these groups.

Theme #3: Intercongregational Differences on the Role of Immigrant Churches and the Approaches to Worship and Faith Expressions

It is also apparent from the participants' responses that there exist intergenerational and intercongregational differences in the expectations and the conception of what the role of their churches should play and how expression of faith through worship should be manifested between congregants within the Asian Canadian immigrant churches. For instance, the first generation often conveys a deep sense of nostalgia for one's cultural roots and a strong sentiment for preserving cultural heritage and communal-familial unity through their churches. This perspective is clearly articulated in the following two quotes. Debora, a second-generation Korean, noted:

> I would love to see a little bit of something cultural for our children. Because they're third and fourth generations and I don't want them to lose the Korean culture. So that's more personal. I don't know if it's a church thing, it's as a parent of a Korean—I would love for them to know more, yeah.

---

6. Tse, "Making a Cantonese-Christian Family," 756–68.

Another Korean participant Ruth also stated that "A love for my Korean heritage, but it's definitely tied into church, 'cause that's the only place where I get my cultural influence from really."

A similar sentiment was expressed by first-generation Chinese participants, as Ji Yang commented:

> Culturally, if we are doing the work in the same language, then we should be able to communicate. And we hold the meetings according to our culture, like to have the festivals and Chinese New Year, we hold some parties or gatherings during those festivals. Yeah, we keep ourselves family-like, doing things according to our own culture, especially we are talking in the same language.

Taken together, these quotes point to the critical desire to see Asian Canadian immigrant churches to function as a "vessel" or "instrument" for "cultural transition" or "cultural preservation"—a common perspective upheld by many first generation immigrants and a theme repeatedly identified in the previous research of Asian American churches. However, these nostalgic expectation and wish of first-generation, heritage-language-speaking church members are often met with incongruous aspiration for the church and expression of the faith and worship style among the second-generation, English-speaking members. This following quote from Shirley poignantly speaks to this issue in the Cantonese-English Chinese church:

> [It] feel(s) like the Cantonese [congregant] is a lot more reserved [than the English congregant] and they don't understand how the English side worships. I know that some older generation Chinese um individuals, they complain about the English service and their worship because they think, "Oh my goodness, why is this necessary? You can just sing some hymns, but why is it necessary to beat some drums, like it just causes a wreck? You guys lost all meaning of worship, there's not like, you don't need to do this, you're just italicizing music and everything?" I don't understand where they're coming from because I definitely grew up in the environment where we would worship with guitars, drums, and everything . . . Sometimes I feel like they're looking down on the English service, they feel like we're belittling our faith in a sense, just because we're steering away from the traditional way of worshiping.

Ji Yang underscored a similar discord.

> During worship, or singspiration, the second generation like more singing, sometimes they danced as well, on the stage they

danced, and they used a lot of instruments, or even drums. The first-generation guys they don't feel comfortable, they would say, "too noisy! This not singing to the Lord."

The same concern was noted in Mandarin Chinese churches as highlighted by Ba Men:

> Their [Mandarin congregants' and English-speaking congregants'] patience are also different. The English [sermon] topic they like to be finished in fifteen minutes [during the service] while the Mandarin people want it [the sermon] longer, up to one hour. This is a big difference. Especially the older one wants the longer sermon, they felt they learn more, but not the younger generation.

Interestingly, Ji Yang suggested "compromise" as a solution to bridge such a divide:

> I think the only thing we could do is to compromise, compromise between the first- and second-generation cultures. Like for instance, music during worship they could replace the second generation to play the music, you know, to the more lower the tune. And on the other hand, we can persuade the first generation to accept, to appreciate what the second generation are doing.

Theme #4: Intergenerational Gaps as Barriers

It is important to note that all the preceding themes reviewed thus far, including language issues and intergroup differences in cultural identities, ministries, and worship styles, are influenced and interwoven with intergeneration factors. From an East Asian immigrant perspective, the intergenerational relationship can be viewed from a parent-child relationship within a family, which is typically characterized by a hierarchical, "top-down" relationship. Brian noted that "You still have a generational gap. That adds [to other] challenges. Older people have older ways of doing things; younger people may want to do things in a different way."

Similarly, So Young identified generation factor as a key contributor of communication problem between the different congregants:

> I think the biggest challenge is the generational disconnect. Although being under the same roof is better than complete independence of EM, there is a lack of common ground between the EM and KM. Sometimes it feels like there are two separate entities under one roof.

Shirley's expression below poignantly highlights a desperate "cry for help" resulting from feeling that second-generation youth are not being heard by the first-generation "parents" in her church.

> And we were not growing anywhere in size or spiritually, or the youth. There's no youth anymore. It's diminished, that whole side. It's just gone. It's not there either, it's cause we were not heard. No one prioritized the English side, which is why the English side was only decreasing in size because it sort of, when you go to church you expect to be fed in a sense.

Susan asserted:

> I think in a lot of times, like, advice from KM comes from a, like a very good intentioned place . . . a lot of times. Not all the time, though. Of like, we want to do things for you. But it's like still like very—we are the providers for you or we are above you so we do this for you. But a lot of times, it's like, "you don't know what we want, or you don't know what we need, but you just do these things for us." And I've learned in the past couple of years, like, they do things, but they don't tell us it's for us, so that we don't know that they've done these things so they've put all this effort into things.

Incidentally, these reactions coincide with Dae Sung Kim's observation about second-generation Korean American congregant's experiences in the United States. Kim observed: "They are typically dissatisfied with the Asian-style leadership of the church, the ethnic emphasis on church culture, and the lack of opportunity for the younger generation to realize spiritual growth."[7] Interestingly in Ann's comment below, we see that these intergeneration conflicts observed in Asian immigrant churches can mirror intergenerational conflicts occurring within Asian immigrant families.

> We go through so many of the similar things together. We can help each other out, like I know for us like. Because there's this generation gap and different cultures growing up, our values are a bit different from our parents, so sometimes that conflicts and it's really hard at home [as well].

Deborah, a second generation Korean, spoke of the effects of the hierarchal relational structure in traditional Asian family on the intercongregational interaction in Korean churches.

---

7. Kim, "New Missions," 1–9.

> They [first generation] treat us [second generation] as, you know . . . we're adults now. Sometimes I find older Korean generations don't tend to acknowledge the growth of their children and older children . . . Always a kid, yeah. If they're older you just have to listen whether it's right for us or not.

Some participants, however, took a more hopeful and reconciliatory stance and offered potential solutions to address such a perennial generational gap within Asian Canadian churches. So Young, a first-generation Korean, stated:

> Yes, first generation members need to watch over second generation members. This is because we come from different cultures. My children come from a very different place culturally and generationally. If we were living in Korea, the cultural and generational differences would not be as pronounced. But as immigrants if we do not take the time to study the cultural differences between older and younger generations, the differences become insurmountable. So my children and I may end up not understanding one another culturally and emotionally. When first-generation members observe a certain behavior pattern among second-generation members, it is easy to attribute that behavior to the language barrier or Canadian school system. But that is neither fair nor completely accurate.

The participants' responses above indicate that second-generation Asian Canadian members' desperate needs to contest and change the existing "status quo" of the relational dynamics between the two generation groups and the structural governance of the current Asian Canadian immigrant churches. In Sharon Kim's study of Korean American churches in 2010, she described this movement as "shifting boundaries" with second-generation Korean American Christians.[8] According to Kim, ethnic second-generation churches in North America are going through a period of experimentation and flux to redefine its parameters both across generations and across cultures. Conceptualizing from this perspective, many of the communication and relational difficulties observed in the present study can well reflect part of the "growing pain" in the life of Asian Canadian immigrant churches, as the churches struggle and seek out new prospects and paths for their future.

---

8. Kim, "Shifting Boundaries," 98–122.

Theme #5: Wishes, Desires, and Means to Improve Intergenerational and Intercongregational Communication and Relationship

Finally, during the latter part of the interview, participants were additionally asked to speak to what and how they would like to see changed and improved in their churches. The resulting responses were comprised of a wide spectrum of wishes, needs, and ideas. These points are summarized with highlighted keywords below and the corresponding excerpts are included to illustrate the participants' positions.

First of all, ensuring *openness*, *transparency*, and *honesty* between congregants was suggested.

Ann contended that "I think more transparency or better communication skills."

Stuart also noted:

> We need more open and honest communication; so members of church are able to say that they just want to change because the old ways are not working anymore. But first everyone needs to realize that tweaking and updating the worship does not mean that it is not good. Having an honest communication channel and implementing upgrades just mean that the church is open to change for the better. I feel that some members feel too criticized at times and take it too much to heart.

Secondly, promoting *equality*, *equity*, and *mutual respect* within the church family was sorely needed. As noted by Seok Ho,

> Members of the EM want the full recognition from the rest of the church. They do not want to be treated as second-class citizens at the church or be regarded as rule-breakers by older church members. In other words, they want equal treatment but are often viewed as rebellious children in need of discipline by some older church members. Members of KM want to be treated with respect regardless of age group and status within the church. Some young KM members have been criticized for their lack of respect toward older members in the past.

Similarly, So Young contended:

> As I mentioned before, the church is [currently] very adult-centric whether [it be] planning for church-wide events or coordinating worship service. I want High-C members, English service members, and all youth members to feel heard and

equally valued at the church, regardless of age and count. I want them to be in equal standing with the rest of the so-called "dominant" group [i.e., Korean speaking adults] at the church.

To achieve a greater reciprocal understanding between and among congregants, some participants noted the need to challenge the existing hierarchy and the "top-down" relationship pattern of traditional Asian families, which inadvertently permeates in Asian immigrant churches. This is evident in Shirley's response, as she described the English-speaking youth pastor felt pressure from the Cantonese-speaking senior pastor of her church:

> I do know that in a Chinese church setting, [what] I hear from my youth pastor is that there is a lot of pressure from the senior pastors going down to the younger pastors . . . but there's a lot of stress. And again, this hierarchy, the head is almost always from the Cantonese side and they are first generation or immigrants, they weren't born here.

Thirdly, the need to establish and enhance *trust* and *humility* was also stressed by several participants.

Kate suggested:

> I think for them [first generation] being able to trust us [second generation]. I think that is a huge part where sometimes the older generation don't trust the younger generation . . . the first generation being able to trust us and being able to um, maybe, just let go of that control and being able to know that this is the direction that we want to go towards 'cause it's new.

On the other hand, Shirley advocated for a greater trust through openness: "To be more open and vulnerable with us at least, but definitely, that expectation has not been met. Um, yeah."

Whereas, Sui hui noted the importance of humility: "Cut down on the disagreements, or the forgiveness, don't be so stubborn, always I am right and you are."

Discussion

Based on the participants' interview results, the present study's findings highlight the prevalence of critical differences and communication and relational gaps between the heritage congregation and the English-speaking congregation in contemporary Asian Canadian immigrant churches. As such, at the first glance, at the surface, these Asian Canadian churches with multiple congregants appear to be a big ethnic "family"; a deeper level of analysis, however, suggests otherwise. As revealed in the participants' responses in this research, at multiple levels the heritage congregant and the English-speaking congregant coexist but operate as two "culturally divergent" congregational entities within the same church building. As one participant Ji Yang claimed: "They [the two congregations] are thinking differently, put it in a [simple] way, they are culturally different." In fact, this observation finds support in the tenet posited by Dae Sung Kim about Korean American churches.[9] Kim suggests that first-generation Korean immigrant churches should view their ministry to their second-generation congregation as a "crosscultural mission" despite the superficial similarities between them. To more fully comprehend and accurately interpret the intergenerational and intercongregational differences and gaps with respect to communication patterns and social and interpersonal relationships within Asian Canadian immigrant churches as reported by the participants of the current study, the interpretation of the study's findings calls for a broad social-psychological-cultural analysis. To this end, in the following I will offer three frameworks to help understand and conceptualize the five observed themes shared by the participants: acculturation, Asian traditionalism and familism, and transnational migrant experience.

Acculturation

Crosscultural researchers and immigrant researchers such as Kuo have long attested that intergenerational differences and conflicts between immigrant parents and their children often stem from varying degrees of their "acculturation" to the host society.[10] Specifically, Dr. John Berry, a prominent scholar on migration and cultural change, noted that "acculturation" is a concept that describes the process and the experience associated with migrant newcomers' cultural adaptation in their resettled, host society.[11] In essence, varying degrees and strategies associated with acculturation among immigrants dictate how they identify with their heritage culture and society (e.g., Taiwanese/Chinese/Korean home culture) versus how they identify with their host society (Canada). Accumulative research has shown that intergenerational conflicts among immigrant families, including Asian family, are linked to acculturation difference between their foreign-born, first-generation immigrant parents and their native-born, second-generation children of

---

9. Kim, "New Missions," 6.
10. Kuo, "Coping, Acculturation," 16–33.
11. Berry, "Immigration, Acculturation," 5–68.

immigrants. As in Canada or the United States, children of immigrants are typically more "acculturated" (or "Westernized") towards their Canadian or American norms than their immigrant parents. Lee and Mock assert: "Conflicts may be caused not only by different degrees of acculturation, but also by religious, philosophical, or political differences."[12]

In fact, we observed clear evidence of communication difficulties and conflicts within Asian Canadian immigrant churches due to intergenerational acculturation differences. For instance, language barriers between members of the heritage service and those in the English-speaking service. In the present study, the participants' responses suggest that first-generation congregants struggle with limited proficiency in English to be able to fully understand and converse with second-generation English-speaking congregants and vice versa. Additionally, we observe the impact of acculturation on the differential preferences of worship styles between the heritage congregant and the English-speaking congregant, which might lead to further intercongregational disagreement and discord. The former prefers and finds comfort in more subtle and traditional service and worship approaches, whereas the latter is dissatisfied with the long-established approaches to service and styles to workshop. English-speaking congregants often prefer more outwardly expressive worship style, with contemporary music and more open expression of faith. Hence, these differences can be partly attributed to divergence in their cultural and acculturation experiences between immigrant parents and their children in Canada.

Considering the intercongregational communication difficulties and discords and from the framework of acculturation, it can be said that many of these differences in preference and behavior patterns between the first-generation heritage congregants and the second-generation English-speaking congregants reflect a natural and expected consequence of the larger process of cultural adjustment and adaptation experienced by immigrants and immigrant families. Some have referred to such a conflict as part of migrants' "acculturative stress."[13] These characteristics exhibited within Asian Canadian immigrant church parallels what Chung observed: "In such cases, parents and children may reside under the same roof but live in different worlds with little connection and mutual understanding. Lack of fluency in a common language exacerbates the situation, leaving families few bridges to span the ever-widening gulf."[14]

---

12. See Lee and Mock, "Asian Families," 276.
13. Kuo, "Coping, Acculturation," 16–33.
14. Chung, "Gender, Ethnicity, and Acculturation," 377.

The implication of viewing these intergenerational and intercongregational communication and relationship tensions within Asian Canadian immigrant churches from the acculturation perspective is that both congregants should been encouraged to see these differences as an often "normative" experience for immigrants and immigrant families, despite the distress and the discomfort that come with these differences. Such a perspective will help reduce the misconception and mischaracterization between members of the two congregations and bring about a greater empathic understanding of each other.

Asian Traditionalism and Familism

Immigrant churches often provide "a home away from home" for immigrants, particularly newcomers. In such a capacity, immigrant churches often serve to both perpetuate and challenge traditional values. This points to the interconnectedness of family and church for ethnic immigrants. Relatedly, the participants' interview responses on the intercongregant communication challenges further reflect that Asian traditional values, norms, and worldviews are implicitly operating and affecting the congregational life of Asian Canadian immigrant churches.

Moreover, the centrality of family and *familism* has a pervasive and persisting effects on Asian individuals and families. Asian familism represents the value system that believes in family as a united entity striving to preserve harmony, cooperation, and respect and obedience from children to parents. One such example is the Confucian idea of "filial piety." In essence filial piety promotes obedience, obligations, respect, duty, and honor by the children to their parents as an ultimate social goal and personal aspiration. Similarly, in a traditional Asian family, it has also been observed that the role of a father is to be a disciplinarian, and the role of a mother is to be nurturing and supportive to her children. Even though Asian Canadian immigrant families have undergone some changes to their traditional values and familism, the enduring effects of beliefs and practices continue to shape the communication and relationship dynamics among Asian Canadian families as well as churches.

As illustrated in the previous section, the second-generation participants in the current study, most of whom mainly speak English, talked about feeling dismissed and alienated by the heritage congregation. These feelings exist especially given the fact that the leadership of the heritage congregation is comprised of the "adult" or "parent" generation. Korean participant, Seok Ho, asserted: "they [second generation] want equal treatment but are often viewed as rebellious children in need of discipline." Another participant, Susan, related the message she received from a first-generation congregant: "We are the providers for you or we are above you so we do this for you." These "top-down," hierarchical, first-generation-driven leadership styles and structures continue to pervade among many Asian Canadian immigrant churches, as reported by the participants of the study. It is, therefore, imperative for the leaders of first-generation congregants and of second-generation congregants within Asian Canadian churches to engage in a critical self-reflection and dialogue about these traditional, culture-conditioned Asian values and role expectations. An open, honest, and informed evaluation and discussion is needed between the congregants to strike a balance between maintaining and preserving aspects of cultural strengths from one's heritage culture and venturing into new and productive ways of change. Such a bold attempt would likely go a long way in improving not only communication but also mutual understanding and relationship between the congregations across their various dividing lines.

Transnational Immigrant Experiences

Additionally, the identified differences in communication patterns, preferences, and relationship expectations between the members of the heritage service, who are typically the "immigrant parent" generation, and those of the English-speaking service, who are typically the "children of immigrants" generation, can be conceptualized from the sociology and the psychology of the transnational immigrant family. It has been observed that within Asian immigrant families, first-generation parents often feel that they must be the keeper of their culture of origin, which include collectivistic traditions, values, and practices of Asian heritage, both at home and within the immigrant churches. This often stands in contrast to the increasing influences Asian children of immigrant experience in and from the mainstream, predominantly individualistic white society, including socialization through schools, workplaces, and peers. In particular, first-generation parents often reflect a more "other-focused," collectivistic attitudes (i.e., deference, cooperation, obedience, and modesty), whereas second-generation children reflect a more "self-focused," individualistic attitudes (independence, self-expression, self-sufficiency, and confident).

In the current study, we see a common reaction among first-generation participants but also some second-generation participants who sentimentalize and maintain the traditional role of Asian Canadian churches as a conduit of enculturation (i.e., learning about one's home/heritage culture). For instance, one participant, Debora, recounted:

> I would love to see a little bit of something cultural for our children [in the church]. Because they're third and fourth generations and I don't want them to lose the Korean culture. So that's more personal . . . it's as a parent of a Korean—I would love for them [children] to know more [Korean culture], yeah.

However, the intergenerational cultural conflicts between congregations can sometimes stem from the view of English-speaking, second-generation youth and young people that the role and function of their churches should serve purely as a place of worship and spiritual learning, as opposed to an institution of cultural preservation and social connection. The challenge for Asian immigrant children is that even though they realize their obligations to their parents, family, and heritage culture, they expect and demand greater equality and respect from their parents and focus less on the demand for obedience. The end result is what we often see in a form of an impasse playing out not only within the immigrant family but also in intergenerational and intercongregational immigrant churches.

In short, the intercongregant communication and relationship difficulties in Asian Canadian immigrant churches should be analyzed and understood from the deep-seated social and psychological experiences of Asian immigrant individuals and family, including their perceptions of the roles and functions of churches between the first generation and the second generation. Furthermore, the impacts of contextual and cultural socializations along the dimensions of collectivism and individualism on the two generations should be considered. In particular, both congregants should be helped to better understand their own and each other's sociocultural views, perspectives, and positions from collectivistic versus individualistic value orientations.

Practical Implications from the Current Chapter

In view of the findings of the current research project as described in this chapter, I will offer four suggestions for the consideration of Asian Canadian immigrant churches and readers of this chapter. These suggestions are meant to offer potential tools for Asian Canadian immigrant churches to contemplate ways for their churches to enhance communication, to cross cultural divides, and to build and repair relationships between generations and congregants.

First, members of intergenerational and intercongregant immigrant churches are strongly encouraged and urged to learn *how to listen*. The art and skills of listening are often not something people are born with naturally, and yet it is the foundation of constructive communication. As noted previously, open communication is often difficult and uncommon within traditional Asian families and churches. Within the field of counseling and psychotherapy, "empathic listening" is the quintessential skill that a counselor/therapist/helper must possess in order to fully and deeply understand their clients' experiences and emotions. Empathic listening invites the conversants to listen to not only *what the other person says* (contents), but also equally important *how the other person says it* (the speaker's nonverbal expressions, emotions, underlying meanings, etc.). Empathic listening and communication is also characterized by genuine curiosity, openness, and nonjudgmental attitude. These basic skills and manners of conveying, sharing, and listening should be regularly discussed, cultivated, and reinforced within the body of Christ within and between members and churches, to help increase mutual understanding.

Second, as a springboard to facilitate and engage more constructive communication and relationship-building between generations and congregants, Asian Canadian immigrant churches may consider using the findings and the information generated from this current research project, *Asian Canadian Churches of Today for Tomorrow*, as the basis for forging new and critical conversations—that is, for the churches to use the results and the knowledge that has emerged from the current study and been reported in this chapter and the book, to help reflect, examine, and dialogue about the experience and quality associated with their intergenerational communication and relationship within their congregations. In particular, churches would benefit from considering the state of their congregation, their issues, circumstances, relationships, and future from a broad social-psychological-cultural perspective, as propositioned in this chapter, in addition to a faith-based and spiritually-informed framework. Discussion and understanding from the common experiences encountered by Asian immigrants, families, and communities, including acculturation, Asian families and traditionalism, and transnational immigrant experiences discussed in this chapter would be especially relevant and informative.

Third, given that intergenerational gaps exist mainly between first- and second-generation congregants within Asian Canadian immigrant churches, the churches may benefit greatly from having a "cultural broker" in aiding and mediating such intergenerational and intercongregational relationships. Ideal cultural brokers are those who understand the lived experiences and the worldviews of both generations. For example,

1.5-generation immigrants may fulfill such a role within immigrant churches. By definition, the 1.5 generation is considered the "in-between generation" between the first- and the second-generation immigrants. Most of this generation are well-versed in their heritage language as well as English; they are familiar with the "cultural ways" of Asian traditionalism but are, at the same time, highly acculturated in the "Canada ways" and/or the "American ways." Hence, immigrant churches may solicit the assistance and the perspective of trusted members of the 1.5 generation as the cultural and relational bridge between generations. These bicultural individuals can potentially be an effective "go-between" or mediator between the first- and the second-generation congregation members in resolving conflicts and building positive relationship.

Finally, as a recommendation for the future, Asian immigrant churches in Canada and the United States may take cues from Dae Sung Kim's recent proposition. The idea of bridging the two congregations is for the first-generation church leadership to apply missiological principles in planting churches with the second-generation members. Kim asserted: "Rather, the churches should invite second-generation Korean Americans to the kingdom of God in ways appropriate to them, just as overseas mission proceeds in planting indigenous churches."[15] In other words, Kim recommends that immigrant church should view and consider the ministry to and of the second generation from the perspective of crosscultural mission and as a church-planting process. Under this provision, a second-generation church should be supported to strive towards the principles of self-governance, self-support, and self-propagation. This model of ministry will empower and encourage ownership and independence of second-generation congregants and remove paternalism that exists in traditional Asian immigrant churches. Kim envisions that such a model of Asian immigrant churches would promote a new paradigm shift for the future of these churches:

> No longer would they [first generation] think primarily in terms of teaching and transferring their faith and cultural practices to the second generation; rather, they would study how they could become an incarnational mission community that exercise patience, takes initiative, and identifies with the culture of the second generation.[16]

---

15. Kim, "New Missions," 6.
16. Kim, "New Missions," 6.

Conclusion

This chapter reports and summarizes the results of fifty participant interviews conducted in Korean, Taiwanese, and Chinese Canadian churches, with multiple generation congregants, in the Greater Toronto Area. Distinctively, the chapter adopts a social-psychological-cultural lens in analyzing and conceptualizing the issues pertaining to culture, communication, and relationship within Asian Canadian immigrant churches. The results suggest that intercongregant communication challenges and relational conflicts stem from five key themes. The intergenerational and intercongregational conflicts and difficulties within Asian Canadian immigrant churches reflect characteristics of crosscultural communication, acculturation of immigrants and immigrant families, East Asian traditionalism, familism, collectivism, social hierarchy, and the relational dynamics within transnational immigrant families and communities. In concluding this chapter, I would like to draw readers' attention to the complexity of intergenerational communication and relationship issues between congregants in Asian Canadian immigrant churches. The paradoxical feelings and attitudes, both positive and negative, associated with Asian Canadian immigrant churches for its members are profound, nuanced, and, at times, conflicting. In the following quote, Susan's heartfelt description of her relationship with her Korean church summarizes up such a sentiment poignantly and vividly.

> I actually grew up in British Columbia till grade four and we went to predominately white church . . . When I went to university, I explored a bunch of churches there. I explored multicultural churches, white churches, Korean churches. At the core of it, I think maybe it's the way that my parents raised me. I'm still very Korean. And I crave something about Korean culture that is very familiar. Like it's familiar, and I love—it's ironic because sometimes I criticize Korean culture for being very formal and like you have to een-sa or like say hello to elders in a very specific way or use a very specific type of speech. But there's something very familiar in that like even though you're een-sa'ing to people like they've seen you grow up and it's kind of like family . . . But like there's something very communal about eating and like because we put it at such importance like there's a lot of bonding that goes around eating. So yeah, like. I think even if I were to switch churches, I think I would still choose a Korean church just 'cause like there's something, I don't know what it is. I can't really put my finger on it, but there's something familiar and core to me that I want to keep [through remaining in a Korean Church].

In closing, it is hoped that the findings and recommendations of this chapter may encourage effective communication, improve relationship, and enhance growth and harmony within and between heritage first-generation congregant/church and English-speaking second-generation congregant/church, and inspire Asian Canadian immigrant churches to envisage new hopes and visions into the future.

Reflection and Discussion Questions

1. Considering the distinctive social, psychological, and cultural characteristics of Asian Canadian immigrant churches as revealed in this chapter, please identify, discuss, and compare how communication and relationship challenges faced by Asian Canadian immigrant churches may be different from: a) nonimmigrant churches; and b) non-Asian immigrant churches.

2. Think about an Asian Canadian immigrant church with multiple congregations that you are a part of or that you know of. Discuss in what specific ways might the influences of acculturation, Asian traditionalism and familism, and transnational immigration, the three key cultural factors reviewed in this chapter, might have shaped or impacted the congregational life and the ministry of this church, particularly with respect to communication and relationship between and among congregants. Explain your observations and give specific examples to illustrate.

3. In view of the current chapter, what other additional issues do you see as critical in affecting intergenerational and intercongregational communication and relationship within contemporary Asian Canadian immigrant churches? What other ideas and suggestions might you have that could help bridge the gaps across the language, generational, and cultural divides for Asian immigrant churches in Canada?

4. Discuss your thoughts and reactions about Dae Sung Kim's recommendation that immigrant churches should view and consider the ministry to and of the second generation from the perspective of crosscultural mission and as a church-planting process?

10

Empowering Second-Generation Leadership

Dong-Ha Kim

> One generation shall laud your works to another, and shall declare your mighty acts. (Ps 145:4, NRSV)

THE PURPOSE OF THIS chapter is to help the constituent communities of the ACIC, first to address some of the key challenges on leadership issues that have surfaced from the research interviews, and then to envision together a future where such leadership issues may work to the benefit of the ACIC, in however limited ways. It's not surprising that other Asian immigrant researchers also echoed similar concerns arising from their own respective projects. Nancy Sugikaw and Sydney Park, two scholars in this field, sympathize with such audiences in that "younger readers . . . find themselves struggling for autonomy and empowerment in the midst of a hierarchical ethnic culture that often values age over vision, experience over passion, and tradition over innovation."[1] Far from being a conclusive statement on the scope of this research, it nonetheless highlights some of the important underlining issues beneath the challenges and opportunities for Asian Canadian immigrant churches (ACIC) within the Greater Toronto Area (GTA); namely, *cultural differences that have led to many misunderstandings and conflicts.*[2] Moreover, Sugikaw and Park's observations highlight areas of challenge that are most impactful in the health of the ACIC within the GTA. On that note, this chapter explores concerns about leadership brought forth by data from interviews with the ethnic first generation and the second-and-beyond generation of both the lay congregants and their respective ministers/pastors.

---

1. See Sugikaw and Park, "Formation of Servants," 121.
2. Shin and Silzer, *Tapestry of Grace*, 1.

Leadership Concerns

Participants of this research were engaged for the purpose of exploring not just the challenges facing ACIC, but also the opportunities for growth (concrete and aspirational), especially around "leadership," that would be beneficial to congregations within and beyond the ACIC. On this note, both the ethnic first- and the second-and-beyond-generation ACIC interviewees openly expressed numerous concerns and insights regarding their circumstance within their respective churches. Most relevant and central to the discussion in this chapter are the principles of "leadership" that may bridge the complexities of the Asian Canadian Immigrant Churches and possibly help propel it into a growing future.

The impetus behind the urgency of the ACIC to grapple with "leadership" was most aptly expressed by Min Woo,[3] a first-generation Korean minister, who notes, "One of the key priorities is building leadership and giving rise to the next generation of leaders, including the lay leaders and ministers. The church should focus on raising the next generation of ministers first and foremost."

Resulting data from our interviews concerning the "challenges and aspirations" around "leadership" are categorized under the following themes:

- Intergenerational challenge
- Hierarchical relationship between ethnic senior ministers and English-speaking ministers
- Lack of succession plan/leadership training

These concerns, as many are all too willing to point out, have contributed negatively towards creating an unfortunate ethos of misunderstanding and conflict within and amongst the ACIC in the GTA. At the same time, our interviewees, from both the ethnic first-generation and the second-and-beyond-generation members, have expressed an earnest desire to remedy the same areas of challenges that the ACIC may grow to the benefit of the current and upcoming generations.

Intergenerational Challenges

One of the most common issues raised during our interviews with the second-and-beyond-generation ACIC members had to do with "perceived

---

3. As with identities of other interviewees used throughout this chapter, an alias has been used to honor the privacy of our participants.

lack of respect" from the ethnic first-generation congregation. Moreover, this perception is identified by both the laity and the leadership of the second-and-beyond-generation ACIC members. Moses, an English-speaking minister/pastor, poignantly stated, "Given that there are fewer English ministry (EM) members serving in positions of influence at the church, the EM congregation sometimes feels that they have no say in important church matters." Interviews of the lay second-and-beyond-generation members, sadly, echo this opinion. Ruth, a second-and-beyond-generation interviewee, reflects, "A lot of times we see eye to eye, but we don't see eye to eye. It will be the first generation's decisions that are carried forward."

It does seem that the representative voices of the laity are frustrated over being denied meaningful participation at the table of leadership within each of the respective ACIC. In some ways, no issue could be greater than the perception that the opinion(s) of the second-and-beyond generations are ignored or dismissed by the ethnic first-generation members. The seriousness of this practice is highlighted by the fact that amongst most ACIC interviewed for this research, laity or ordained ministers, it is not uncommon to see the so-called second-and-beyond-generation members encroaching late-forties or fifties in age. Additionally, many of the second-and-beyond generations, especially those involved in secular careers, are successful and contributing members of the Canadian society in his/her respective professions. Where the ethnic first-generation members have struggled the most in their new home in GTA—being influential members of this society—the second-and-beyond generations are now successfully doing just that. Understandably, the latter generations are frustrated from the lack of their inclusion at the table of decision-making amongst the ACIC. We shall see later that this weakness may just be the means through which ACIC may move forward towards being and becoming relevant gathering not just for the second-and-beyond-generation members, but for the greater society in which they are part of.

Clash of Culture

Data from the interviews have shed some interesting facts around the places of birth amongst the participants. Amongst the ethnic first-generation congregants of the ACIC, in both the "lay persons" and "ordained ministers" categories, those born outside of Canada far exceeded those born in Canada. When the same set of questions were applied to the English ministry congregants—lay and ordained—however, something rather interesting surfaced. Given that the English congregations are typically made up of second-and-beyond generations, those who are considered "lay persons," were by majority born in Canada. For ministers in the English ministry, however, those born outside of Canada exceeded those born in Canada.[4] There are limited conclusions that we may draw from such limited data. What such data suggest, however, is that there may be cultural implications amongst the various generation of the ACIC.

Data from the interviews, for instance, provided a rather interesting breakdown of "gender," especially amongst the "lay persons" and "ordained ministers." Out of the three ACIC communities (Chinese, Korean, and Taiwanese), twenty ministers were interviewed. While the representative number of ministers from each respective ethnic community were not equal, we ensured that the ratio of ethnic and English ministers interviewed within each community was equal. Moreover, with regards to the gender of interviewees, we were able to ensure an even fifty-fifty ratio of "female" to "male" participants amongst the lay persons. Amongst the "ordained ministers," we ended up with a group whose breakdown of gender ratio was skewed, i.e., 90 percent were males as compared to 10 percent females. Jane, a female minister from the Chinese English ministry, identified such disparity of gender representation amongst the ministry leadership as an alarming issue that clearly impacts any attempts to foster constructive growth within any of the ACIC:

> I believe I am either the first or the second woman minister . . . There is another woman minister serving in one of the Chinese churches in Mississauga. She has served as a children's minister for a long time, around twenty to thirty years. She was ordained just two years ago. This was hard to process.

Needless to say, and despite the advances made in recent years concerning female leadership within the ACIC, the resulting data of gender representation amongst "ordained minsters" is dismal at best. Presence of female-ordained ministers amongst the ethnic first-generation congregations within the three communities interviewed, with no exceptions, is virtually nonexistent. Jane's circumstance of being part of a small handful of female ministers within an English ministry of an ACIC, i.e., second-and-beyond-generation Chinese congregation, if anything, speaks to the unfortunate and lingering gender biases towards male leadership.

Further, to interview results on issues of culture, other identifiable issues of the ACIC that have surfaced include areas such as "identity issues" and "language barriers." Ethnic first-generation members of the ACIC

---

4. Based on research data.

tend to reflect a traditional way of life while the children, the second-and-beyond generation, embrace the culture and language of their birthplace for the most part.[5] What's not so general seems to be the existence of an identity dilemma (Canadian or ethnic) faced by many second-and-beyond generation ACIC members who were either born in Canada or who immigrated at a young age. For many members of ACIC in this category, with fluency in English language and cultural exposure, there really aren't any precedent reasons for them to remain in their respective ethnic churches. There are plenty of "other churches" where the primary language spoken during service of worship and governance (session, board of governors, etc.) is the familiar English language.

When asked as to why they choose to remain in the ethnic churches, realizing full well that language barriers and other cultural clashes are inevitable, many of the responses referred to familiarity in culture as a main reason. Melia, a second-and-beyond generation interviewee from the English ministry of a Chinese congregation, noted as to why she continues to remain within her church despite the struggles she faces in communicating with the ethnic first-generation church members, "I think my upbringing has probably had an influence."

Still another second-and-beyond-generation interviewee commented as to her reason for remaining within the multi-generational Chinese church,

> I found my place there because [of] a lot of other people. [Basically, e]veryone in the fellowship were all [from the] second generation, [and] from Chinese families. We were able to sort of click [together] because we were all from the same background. So, we understand each [other] in a sense. So [having] growing up with them, we sort of had the same values; we went through the same things. We see the same things and we sort of want to see the same changes, which is why I stayed there. So, all throughout the years I stayed there, because I found community there, because I was able to find an identity in that group.

For the second-and-beyond-generation ACIC members like this young woman remaining with the church that houses multi-generations, elements like familiarity of relationships, food, and even snippets of familiar language are all referred to positively and in one form or another by the interviewees. At the same time, the interviewees were aware that these very things that attracted them back to the "ethnic churches" in the first place

---

5. Choi and Lee, *Hiring an English Ministry*, 228.

remain at the crux of challenges that keep them from full and meaningful participation in decision-making.

In short, it's an interesting mix of "needs" and "disdain," this cultural component, like language, that both attracts and keeps away the younger generation of ACIC from becoming and being effective members. Won Sik, a first-generation Korean minister, was frank and open about the dynamics of communication as fueled by language barriers between the two congregations of the same church as follows: "Due to the language barrier, it is difficult for me to reach out and connect with the English-speaking young people."

Echoing this minister's sentiment on the challenges of the language, and perhaps the cultural barrier in general, Susan, an English-speaking second-generation member of a Korean congregation, expressed her frustration as such:

> There is a lot of lack of communication between the two sides and therefore like there's a lot of frustration with both sides that happens a lot of times because people just don't communicate and because there's like this language barrier but also a culture barrier.

Hierarchical Relationship between Ethnic First-Generation Leadership and English-Speaking Second- or Third-Generation Leadership

Considering the interview data, we were also privy to glimpses of challenges around the relationship between ethnic first-generation leadership and English-speaking second-and-beyond generation leadership. Abraham, an ordained minister of the English-speaking Taiwanese congregation, expressed this struggle as follows: "As a lead EM pastor, I find the current direction of the church too restrictive and limiting for the growth of EM congregation. I cannot speak for the CM congregation, but I would think that they find the current arrangement to their advantage."

This uncomfortable situation in the relationship between the ethnic first-generation ministry and that of the second-and-beyond generation ministry alludes to something that is quite prevalent amongst the ACIC, namely, the hierarchical culture under which many of the ethnic first- generation leadership functions. In the case of Korean Canadian immigrant churches, for instance, leadership dynamics between the first generation and the second-and-beyond generation are often, and if only subtly, characterized by a demand of respect for authority.[6] Suffice to say, this cultural conflict is an important area that any ACIC committed to empowering the second-and-beyond generation in areas of "leadership" must address.

Lack of Succession Plan/Discipleship Training

Concerning the complex, intertwined lives of the multiple generations within the many ACIC, it can also be said that, in general, ACIC are characterized by leadership style wherein "the minister has decided that [she/he] want(s) to establish or build something that [she/he] believe(s) will solve a problem," a very much top-down style of communication within the respective congregation(s).[7] It would seem a rather biased perspective to just present the views of the second-and-beyond generation. On that note, Hai, a first-generation lay associate-minister from a Taiwanese congregation, echoed the sentiment by summarizing this tendency within the congregation where he served:

> The [first-generation minister] thinks that they know what is best for the English ministry (EM), and even fails to consider the differences in viewpoints and priorities. The leadership's [first-generation minister's] decision-making process is often poorly communicated to the EM, which might lead to misunderstanding tension between the two congregations.

Not surprisingly, the second- and third-generation members of ACICs, ordained ministers or otherwise, are overwhelmingly of the view that, as opposed to fostering an environment of encouragement and cooperation, the "top-down" form of leadership emanating from many of the ethnic first-generation ministers/pastors appears to have a damaging effect on the overall well-being of the ACIC. Moses, a rather frustrated, but not necessarily out-of-line English ministry pastor from a Korean congregation, blurted out:

> Some English-speaking second-generation members are dissatisfied with the current arrangement, as evident in their negative mindset. As the minority of this church, they feel they are being treated as second-class citizens.

These may not be the exact words echoed across the second- and third-generation English ministries; they do, nonetheless, convey the widespread

---

6. Choi and Lee, *Hiring an English Ministry Pastor*, 224.
7. Beckman and Gallagher, *Discipleship Focused Youth Ministry*, 70.

ethos of concern amongst this group of ACIC. Specifically, and as alluded to earlier, this has led to a widespread perception of lack of respect by the ethnic first-generation congregation towards the English ministry members, comprised largely by the second- and third-generation members. More importantly, the ACIC are at risk of underutilizing and/or overlooking the wealth of skills amongst the second- and third-generation members to adequately and fairly voice their stance at intercultural and ecclesial gatherings.

Endeavors to address and represent the voices of the second- and third-generation members of ACIC, as a result, is just that, an outcry to be heard in earnest by the ethnic first-generation members. On the part of the second-and-beyond-generation members, this lack of communication in the forms of dialogue, being heard, being mentored, and becoming contributing members of the ACIC remains a major source of frustration at the time of the research interviews.

Significant portion of those interviewed had indicated that, despite the communication and logistical challenges, they and their young families were still drawn to the ACIC, largely because of the allure of cultural familiarities. This is not to say, however, that ACIC are merely looked upon as "familiar cultural centers" housed within the ACIC. Nor does it imply that the second- and third-generation persons and families are content with the organization and leadership of their ethnic churches as is.

Interviews with the second- and third-generation members of ACIC have struck a theological nerve in some ways, resulting in calls for deeper rootedness and growth in fundamentals of the Christian faith, i.e., spirituality that could be demonstrated by the ethnic first-generation members of the same churches. Nancy Sugikaw and Sydney Park, in their contributions to an anthology of scholarship exploring the "Asian North American congregations," illustrates one young lady who was "discouraged and frustrated, complaining frequently about the church's lack of cultural relevance and spiritual depth."[8] That is, apart from cultural familiarity, family and friends connections, many of the current ACIC are unable to meet the foundational "spiritual longing" of the second- and third-generation members of the English-speaking ministry. On this note, one of the traits of the leadership that many of the second- and third-generation identify as being important points is just this, the ability of the leadership to provide spiritual leadership/guidance to the English-speaking ministry.

This deep, spiritual longing on the part of the younger generation of ACIC and the failure of the ethnic ACIC provided as such, was most aptly expressed by Min Woo, a first-generation Korean minister, who advised,

---

8. See Sugikaw and Park, "Formation of Servants," 120.

"the older generation must focus less on the proper Christian appearance; rather, they should focus on communicating and passing on the core values of Christianity to the next generation." Collectively, the multi-generation members of the ACIC seemingly conveyed to the researchers an ethos that "[t]he Church [to them] does not exist fundamentally to meet needs; in its being, the Church, like Christ, exits to glorify the Father."[9] Second and third generations of the ACIC appear much more "faith-focused" than originally thought by many of the researchers.

Apart from the commonalities of challenges voiced by those who were interviewed, the researchers observed a unified (ethnic first-, second-, and third-generation) acknowledgement of the need for solid leadership within the ACIC. That is, the ethnic first generation congregation of ACIC must first demonstrate credible leadership for all other generations worshiping under the same roof, albeit at different times of worship service. Andy, an English-speaking pastor from the second- and third-generation ministry of a Korean congregation sounded off: "Unless there is a very strong leadership in the church, coupled with a concrete plan for where the church is headed, the reins will never be transferred over to the second generation or English ministry."

Second- and third-generation members of the ACIC have echoed this sentiment by expressing the need for the leadership to have "vision" for their respective ACIC. This was passionately express by Kate, a second- and third-generation person from a Chinese English congregation: "But a bigger challenge would be finding a vision or . . . having a direction or future."

Leadership Illumined by Findings

The myriad of responses from those interviewed amongst the Taiwanese, Korean, and Chinese Immigrant Churches across the GTA awarded us with a wealth of information regarding the state of their churches that, as outlined earlier, house multi generation of worship services under the same roof. It became clear for the researchers that cultural differences, complicated by language and other factors, have led to many misunderstandings and conflicts between the ethnic first generation and second- and third-generation congregations housed under the same roof.[10] Shin and Silzer, in their intercultural study of Asian American life and ministry, further reiterate our interview data that

9. See Kunst's "Toward a Psychologically Liberating Pastoral Theology," as cited in Swinton and Mowat, *Practical Theology and Qualitative Research*, 231.

10. Shin and Silzer, *Tapestry of Grace*, 1.

the clash of Asian and [Canadian] cultures within the [Asian-Canadian Immigrant Churches] can easily create an environment of suspicion, distrust, and anger between the first-generation and the second- and succeeding generations.[11]

In short, what became clear to us was that cultural clash/barrier is a result of several factors, all intertwined in the delicate lives of the ethnic first-generation and the second- and third-generation members of the ACIC.

An important theme of this chapter pertains to the ramification of "cultural clash" on leadership, or lack thereof, amongst the ACIC. What we gathered in our interviews were stories of frustration, shame, guilt, bitterness, anger, and desperation of multi generation of Asian Canadians, all who are aware that *status quo* is not an option for the Asian Canadian Immigrant Churches at this crucial point in time.

Summarily, the collective data gathered from this research interviews tell a story of the ACIC in that, as oppose to fostering an environment of encouragement and cooperation, such form of leadership emanating from many of the first generation minsters/pastors appears to have a damaging, a discouraging effect on the overall wellbeing.

There is, without a doubt, a widespread perception amongst the second- and third-generation members of the ACIC interviewed that the English-ministry congregations, typically comprised of second- and third-generation members, are not respected by the ethnic first-generation members, in particular by those in the leadership. Ruth, a second- and third-generation member from the English ministry of a Korean congregations affirmed, "a lot of times we see eye to eye, but when we don't see eye to eye, it will be the first generation's decisions that are carried forward." This observation was noted in an important preceding research on intergenerational, intercultural immigrant church and highlights an issue also seen here by the researchers, that "[first-generation ethnic church leaders] who were brought up in Asian cultural backgrounds are trained in traditional philosophies of ministry and tend to postulate a focused view of leadership practice primarily defined by power and authority."[12] It's about cultural differences in the most fundamental form, and lies at the foundation of the ACIC today, impacting most especially the efficacy of "leadership" at all levels. This last point is perhaps what's most disturbing to the interview participants from the three Asian Canadian immigrant church communities. In all manner of speaking, and through the identified

---

11. Shin and Silzer, *Tapestry of Grace*, 1.
12. Wong et al., *Listening to Their Voices*, 258.

challenges faced by the ACIC across the GTA today, "[its collective] future depends on the courageous leadership of church leaders."[13]

Beyond the identification of the importance of "leadership" within the ACIC, those interviewed, especially the second- and third-generation members, beckoned for an environment of "trust" within the ACIC. If a new vision for the ACIC is to take place, there needs to take place a form of solid trust-building, or "an intentional fostering of a climate of open communication where people take time to listen to each other."[14]

It became clear to the researchers that interviews with the second- and third-generation members of the ACIC have struck a theological nerve in some ways, a call for rootedness in the fundamentals of the Christian faith. Sugikaw and Park's observation of one young lady who was "discouraged and frustrated, complaining frequently about the church's lack of cultural relevance and spiritual depth,"[15] might as well have been our own encounter for all intended purpose! Suffice to say, apart from providing cultural familiarity, family and friend connections, many of the current ACIC are simply not meeting the core "spiritual longing" of the second- and third-generation members of the English-speaking ministry within the engaged communities (Taiwanese, Korean, and Chinese).

Hopeful Future Built upon "Bridgebuilders"[16]

Through much of this research project, one theme has stood out above the rest, "culture." To the extent that ethnic first-generation congregations, especially the leadership, has been and continues to be impacted by the culture of the "old country," and that the second- and third-generation members have been exposed to the same growing up in their respective households, culture continues to be an influential factor within the ACIC, albeit to varying extents.

Mari Firkatian, in a study concerning "cultural education-cultural sustainability with regards to Armenians residing in Bulgaria," identified culture as "still vibrant but changing, adapting to new life conditions."[17] More importantly, Firkatian suggests that the key towards moving toward as an intergenerational community lies in "focus[ing] on adaptability and

---

13. Hammett, *Spiritual Leadership*, 11.

14. Everist and Nessan, *Transforming Leadership*, 2.

15. See Sugikaw and Park, "Formation of Servants," 120.

16. See Kunst's "Toward a Psychologically Liberating Pastoral Theology," as cited in Swinton and Mowat, *Practical Theology and Qualitative Research*, 231.

17. See Firkatian, "Retaining Ethnic Identity," 183.

a willingness to embrace change as a valuable commodity rather than insisting on time-honored methods of cultural sustenance."[18] With regards to the vitality of the ACIC, voices like Moses, a minster from the English ministry of a Taiwanese congregation, have called out for the current ACIC to "focus on passing the baton, in order to build up the next generation." This, of course, is easier said than done. But approached through the advice of Firkatian, i.e., "as a measure of adaptability," this endeavor to "pass the baton" within the ACIC possesses immense potential and benefits for all generations.

In light of the constructive and hopeful responses from both the ethnic first-generation and the second- and third-generation members, we would echo the recommendation arrived at by the authors of a study aimed at Canadian-born Chinese Christians, that "immigrant church leadership can open doors for [second- and third-generation members] to be recognized as emergent critical partner in ministry—not only for [that] generation and the immigrant church, but also for the Kingdom."[19]

This recommendation raises a rather important and hopeful vision for the ACIC as they discern their collective future—that is, for the second- and third-generation congregants to become effectively engaging members of the ACIC and the greater community of this society, both of which they are integral members. This hopeful vision was shared by Young Ho, a Korean first-generation minister:

> The second-generation members should receive the support, education, and resources necessary to raise themselves up as the next generation of Christian leaders. They would need to be educated and raised as the leaders of the immigrant church and beyond, to serve both the community and broader world in which they belong. This is the only way for the immigrant church to survive into the third and fourth generations.

This statement, coupled with the prayerful yearning of the second and third generation, points towards a hopeful future in the eyes of the researchers. By all accounts, the lackluster participation of the second and third generations, as evidenced in our widespread research interviews, stands out as the crucial piece for the ACIC to work on immediately. Regardless of the ethnicity, most of the ACIC are missing out on the second- and third-generation members on stepping up to take over leadership in ministry within their respective congregations and ecclesial communities—as lay or ordained leaders, and perhaps the greater communities. Enoch Wong et al. refers to

18. See Firkatian, "Retaining Ethnic Identity," 183.
19. Wong et al., *Listening to Their Voices*, 264.

this new and upcoming church leaders as the "emergent critical partners."[20] So, having identified the many concerns raised, especially by the second- and third-generation members of ACIC, we will focus on the best course of action-oriented discourse for the ACIC to start writing, for the next chapter of their history in Canada, especially the Greater Toronto Area.

Filling the vacuum of "spiritual" yearning and a sense of direction for the second- and third-generation ACIC, without a doubt, requires a special category of church leadership. One practical implication of the challenges that has been readily shared by the participants of this research is the need for a special type of leadership which Jennifer L. Kunst identifies "bridgebuilders."[21] These are leaders who are able to bridge the gap created by social, cultural, and political forces of the environment that the ACIC members, of all generations, find themselves to be in today. Importance of such leadership is highlighted by Kunst, who explains, "[o]ne of the roles of the English ministry (EM) pastor is maintaining unity between the first-generation members and their children, the EM congregation. [The EM pastor] reduces the 'cultural gap' by becoming the 'bridge builder' between two cultures."[22]

Interviews have shown that, for the most part, ministers of the ACIC, regardless of the generations, are acutely aware of the need for "bridgebuilders" within their congregations if they are to effectively and constructively move into the future. Gerry, a minister from the English ministry of a Taiwanese congregation, explains:

> I think there is a need for ethnic Taiwanese churches or ethnic Chinese church to have English ministers who can navigate the difficulties of working with a structure of leadership that is very hierarchical by design . . . I am willing to work within this to grow the English-speaking congregation.

By way of "bridgebuilders," then, the ministers of ACIC have in mind English-speaking ministers who are familiar with the North American culture, though not necessarily born here, and were trained at respective seminaries as such. Abraham, a minister from a Taiwanese English ministry clarifies, "I think if the senior pastor is one-point-five generation [not second generation][23] and has some English ministry experience under

---

20. Wong et al., *Listening to Their Voices*, 264.

21. See Kunst's "Toward a Psychologically Liberating Pastoral Theology," as cited in Swinton and Mowat, *Practical Theology and Qualitative Research*, 231.

22. See Kunst's "Toward a Psychologically Liberating Pastoral Theology," as cited in Swinton and Mowat, *Practical Theology and Qualitative Research*, 231.

23. The 1.5 generation is a reference to those Asian Canadian immigrant children

his/her belt, he/she can serve as a bridge between different congregations in the [same] church." It would be a bonus if such "bridgebuilders" are also equipped to speak the ethnic language fluently enough to span both cultures. On this note, it is not unheard of for such "bridgebuilder" minister to eventually oversee both ethnic first-generation and second- and third-generation congregations.

Helping to inspire and train "bridgebuilder" ministers within the ACIC is clearly not an end-in-itself for both generations interviewed. Liu, a first generation minister of a Taiwanese congregation advises that short of having a circumstance wherein "the Ethnic pastor and English ministry pastor function as equals," it would be prudent, and there is certainly a need, for ACIC congregations to support "bridgebuilders" within their leadership portfolio. Brad, an English ministry Pastor from a Chinese congregation emphasized this practical need as follows: "I believe there is a potential if the church is willing to be led, to hand over the authority to the EM, and further invest in the EM."

The key word here is "investing" in the future of the ACIC by taking interim steps such as equipping and empowering current leaders of the English ministry to effectively function as "bridgebuilder" congregational leaders.

Putting into place a concrete succession plan within the ACIC, however, require firm commitment on the part of the ethnic first-generation ministry. Jim Beckman and Eric Gallagher, in their delightful book on "discipleship focused youth ministry," share an age-old wisdom: "If you want to build a ship don't drum up people to collect and don't assign them tasks and work, but rather teach them to long for the endless immensity of the sea."[24]

Translated into actual ministry practice, this wisdom, for Beckman and Gallagher, undergirds the fact that "the most effective way you can grow and sustain a ministry that exists even when you are gone . . . is to equip and empower others to do it."[25] Beckman and Gallagher refer to this mode of encouragement within the church as "discipleship training." In fairness, despite the lack of reference to such descriptive terms, ethnic first-generation ministers like Hai, who serves at a Taiwanese congregation, were certainly cognizant of its need for their respective congregations:

> I think that we need to encourage the young English ministry (EM) leaders to take on more responsibilities at the church, or at

who were born in their respective ethnic countries and have immigrated to Canada as children. Technically, youths in their teens could be considered a 1.5 generation.

24. Beckman and Gallagher, *Discipleship Focused Youth Ministry*, 70; quote by Antoine de Saint-Exupéry.

25. Beckman and Gallagher, *Discipleship Focused Youth Ministry*, 71.

least have the work alongside [first-generation ethnic ministry] leaders to prepare the next generation of leaders for this church.

Fa, a first-generation minister of a Chinese congregation, also added:

> The current leaders need to set a model for an open, tolerant, respectful system. We got to give more opportunities for the young Canadians in church, so that they can grow to become future leaders of this church. We must pass on our experience and allow the young people to make mistakes.

Those leaders who adapt this approach, or are at least cognizant of its need, we would argue, are seeing the benefits of being flexible, not only towards the cultural differences between the multiple generations but also towards empowering the next generations through gracious accountability—which leads to greater trust and relationship.[26] Given that we have also observed a strong basis, or hunger to become upcoming and accepted partners within the ACIC on the part of the second and third generations, we are hopeful to share some constructive wisdom to help move the current ACIC into the future.

To foster leadership amongst the second and third generations of the ACIC, as noted by myriad of representative generations of the ACIC, what's clear is that simple implementations of "discipleship training"—a common methodology of ecclesial leadership training found amongst churches—isn't enough! Such approach, as prevalent it has been throughout the ACIC, does not appear to have taken traction in concrete terms. Instead, we'd like to build upon the foundations of discipleship training by proposing what we'd identify as "collaborative empowerment" that would entail both the ethnic first-generation members and the second- and third-generation members of the ACIC.

Foundational rubrics of the "collaborative empowerment" approach would entail deliberate and empowering partnership of the second- and third-generation members, lay or ordained, to work alongside the ethnic first-generation ministers in decision-making processes, i.e., the governance or polity of the church locally and within the wider church body. It's easy enough for the current ethnic first-generation church leadership, like Young Ho from a Korean congregation, to say that "the second-generation members should receive the support, education and resources necessary to raise themselves up as the next generation of Christians leaders [within the ACIC]."

To take this statement beyond rhetoric, the practical implication may entail active participation of the second- and third-generation members, lay

---

26. Beckman and Gallagher, *Discipleship Focused Youth Ministry*, 72.

and ordained, within the local governance (session and board) and other levels of church government. More importantly, encouraging church meetings to take place with allowances for the second- and third-generation members to speak in a mix of ethnic/English, as to his/her comfort level, and all the while conducting official presbytery church business meetings, would go a long way towards fostering any leadership training and growth! Other than some preliminary endeavor to think outside the traditional norm, we feel that there is no credible reason as to why this intentionality could not work amongst ACIC. In the least, this encouraging show of support seems to address the cumulative challenges of communication as brought forth by the intergenerational and cultural barriers that are currently and deeply embedded amongst the ACIC, especially regarding leadership.

Through this research, we have clearly heard from the ethnic first-generation members who seem to be at their wit's end, but who also recognize the urgency of the situation to "pass on the baton" to the next-generation members that are children no more but those that could be visionary and impactful leaders—lay or ordained—of the Asian Canadian immigrant churches in the Greater Toronto Area. Those ACIC that are fortunate to have in their inventory of second- and third-generation leadership, the "bridgebuilders," no doubt the task of *passing on the baton* could see a quicker transition period. Where it is not the case, and a large contingent of ACIC fall into this category, intentional and immediate attention to accommodating the manner in which the second- and third-generation leaders, lay or ordained, may engage and be engaged in church governance, we argue, would be crucial and hopeful for the ACIC to transition in a healthy manner!

On that note, this chapter has covered one key area from the myriad of constructive, hopeful, and emerging conversations—leadership opportunities for the second- and third-generation to engage and own, in order that the Asian Canadian immigrant churches can one day become "trusting, life-giving relationships with God and with one another so that together we might serve in transformative ways in a world hungering for God's unconditional love."[27]

Reflection and Discussion Questions

1. This chapter discusses the need for active and equal participation of second- and third-generation members of the English ministry in church governance (i.e., areas of leadership at the session and board

27. Everist and Nessan, *Transforming Leadership*, 2.

meetings) as a potentially fruitful way of bridging the current isolation of two congregations under the same roof, i.e., ethnic first-generation ministry and the second- and third-generation English ministry. How do you see this "constructive relationship" taking place in your respective church(es)?

2. How else might your congregation foster engagement and growth in "leadership," especially amongst the second- and third-generation members?

3. How might insights gained from this research, especially in areas of intergenerational leadership, benefit other areas of the ACIC congregational life?

11

Moving towards a Multicultural Church

Nam Soon Song

From one ancestor he made all nations to inhabit the whole earth, and he allotted the times of their existence and the boundaries of the places where they would live. (Acts 17:26, NRSV)

Why a Multicultural Church?

WE BEGIN THIS CHAPTER by introducing selected excerpts from our interviews with Brian, who is a member of English ministry (EM), and Ben, who has been serving his church as the first ethnic EM minister. Brian has been attending his Taiwanese immigrant church all his life; he was baptized at this very church and became a member at the age of sixteen. He continued to attend this church during his university years at another city, and still commutes over a hundred kilometers to the church every Sunday from the city where he currently resides. He now serves as an elder of this church; he considers this church to be his home church.

> Brian: Why am I still at this church today? . . . I guess the first reason is [due to the long] history and lots of connections here. The second reason is I am still committed as an elder. I am involved in a leadership [role at the church]. I guess because we have just recently moved to another city (i.e., Waterloo), so we are still having some continuity in our worship. But I think eventually in the next couple of years, we will probably have to stop going to this church and start finding a local church in our new city (i.e., Waterloo).
>
> (Do you mean a local church, such as an English-speaking, Caucasian, or any church?)

Brian: We are open. That is a good question. There is no Taiwanese church in our new city (i.e., Waterloo). I wouldn't say that I am necessarily interested in finding a Taiwanese church, but I am hoping to [try out] maybe a different kind of [ethnic church].

(Okay. So ethnicity is still important to some extent in choosing church.)

Brian: I would say less important.

(Okay. But is it still important? How important is ethnicity in choosing church? Or are you just uncomfortable with the non-ethnic mainline churches? Have you been to mainline churches in your life?)

Brian: Yes.

(Okay. So were you comfortable with the mainline churches?)

Brian: Yes.

(So ethnicity would not play an important role in choosing church.)

Brian: I think I would not be so comfortable going to an all-white church. But if it is a multicultural church, I think that might be the best fit for me.

(I see. Okay.)

Brian: I do not think I would want to or prefer to go to an all-Taiwanese church, even if there is one in my new city (i.e., Waterloo). This is interesting, right?

(Yes, very interesting. So, you may not choose a Taiwanese church, even if there is one in your new city (i.e., Waterloo)?)

Brian: That is right.

(I see. You are looking for a more multicultural church?)

Brian: That is my current thinking.

(Okay. I see. Is there any reason why? You have been to a Taiwanese church all your life.)

Brian: Right. Ethnicity is a factor but it is not a straight yes or no factor. It is a complex factor.

Brian explains his theological belief in striving to become a multicultural church on earth, just like how it would be in heaven:

> You should be building your church within your community and be committed to that. I think it would be more biblical to do it that way . . . theologically in heaven I am not sure if there would be different parts of heaven for different types of people. I think everyone would be worshiping together in one multicultural setting. So, if we want to reflect that here on Earth, maybe we should all be striving to become multicultural.

He believes that the ethnic makeup of the local community should be directly reflected in our congregational composition, especially in a multicultural city like Toronto.

Ben has been an English ministry (EM) minister for over thirty-five years at the same Chinese immigrant church in Toronto. Established 109 years ago, it is not only the oldest Chinese immigrant church in Toronto, but also one of the oldest Asian immigrant churches in Canada. He says, "If I ever took another church, I would look for a multicultural church." He firmly believes that the future church will eventually move towards a multicultural direction.

> Ben: Initially, they (English-speaking congregation) came either due to their parents' insistence or their ethnic Chinese identity. However, over the years, many have left and moved away. As I said before, the second- and third-generation members have no need to come to an ethnic Chinese church.
>
> (After they left this church, where did they go?)
>
> Ben: Most went to a multicultural Canadian church. There are some Canadian churches with multiethnic congregations. In such churches, you would find members who are Chinese, Indian, Caucasian, and so on. Many of our former members now attend these types of churches.
>
> Ben: I would like for this church to become a multicultural church. I am aware that the future is limited for the Cantonese-speaking ministry. It will be no different for the English-speaking congregations if we keep our Chinese identity. We see that the second- and third-generation members are slowly disappearing or moving away. As I said, unless we are able to reach out beyond the Chinese or start a separate Mandarin ministry, this church will not survive.

According to Ben, the ethnic-specific churches will have to make changes to stay viable into the next generation and beyond. Given the emerging preference for becoming a multicultural church, particularly amongst the English-speaking congregants, Ben believes that the ethnic-specific churches can survive once they open up to "others," or those of other ethnicities, and strive for a multicultural congregation.

As we discussed in chapter 7, our vision for a multicultural church seems not only timely, but also biblical and theological. Likewise Melia, an English-speaking interviewee, envisions a multicultural church that seeks to embrace people of all ethnicities, and not just Asians. She believes that in Christ we open our eyes and hearts to "others"; in Christ our church can become naturally multicultural and be a witness to God's transforming power. She elaborates as follows:

> I think it would be multicultural. Very multicultural. I think as God, so this is kind of what I've observed. As God transforms our hearts to be more like him, we begin to see our, I guess, our identity as more in Christ. And as it's more in Christ, he puts in our heart for more to open our eyes, my heart is not only for the Asian people, but it's also for all nations. And as he puts that in our hearts, um, our church will naturally become more and more multicultural.

Kate also thinks that our church will become a church for all, the mosaic of people God created, from the sociological perspective—considering the multicultural composition of our society at large: "I think English ministry will be forefront of the North America—of the, I guess, church, because we live again in a North American society where it's multicultural, English is the main language, English is, I think because of that I'm hoping our English ministry will be more multicultural and not just, not just Filipinos and Malaysian people but really seeing like a mosaic of people."

Ruth envisions a multicultural church for a different, yet practical reason, suggesting that a multicultural church is part of the natural evolution of her generation and beyond due to the increase in the intercultural or interracial marriages: "It'll be more multicultural and that's just going to be, that's just natural evolution of uh generations. I mean, my generation, I'd say half my friends married Koreans, but the other half didn't, and then our children."

It is interesting to note that a number of first-generation interviewees share the second generation's vision for a multicultural church. Jae Min hopes that his church will move in a multicultural direction with more active local involvement in a missional sense, thereby shifting away from being an isolated ethnic-specific church to a locally integrated community church. He puts it this way: "My church will become a multicultural church and actively involved with the local community. I believe my church will become less distinctly Korean in the future to become an integrated community church, with members from diverse backgrounds." Ga Eun has a similar vision for her church, citing the same reason, namely the transition towards a missional church based in the local community: "I think my church would be more multicultural considering our outreach efforts in the local community and contributions to local missions . . . If the church is to become more multicultural, we should be more understanding and considerate of those coming from different cultures."

Abraham, an English ministry pastor, dreams of his church becoming a multicultural church with the English-speaking congregation leading the church, as inspired by his missional understanding: "I am hoping that this church will become multicultural . . . the EM congregation will become the leading congregation of the church in twenty-five years. This is to ensure that my church develops into an open-minded church serving and ministering to all people." Likewise, the majority of lay and clergy interviewees express their desire to establish multicultural congregations within their ethnic-specific churches, meaning they would like to move in the multicultural direction while preserving some of their ethnic distinctiveness.

We can identify several biblical and theological reasons for a multicultural church. All human beings, regardless of color and ethnic affiliation, are created in the image of God. Thus we are all connected in God's image. Paul stresses that there are many members of the one body. Regardless of our ethnic, sexual, and social status in society—whether we are Jews or Greeks, male or female, slaves or free—we are all one in the Spirit and share one body of Christ, albeit with different gifts and functions (Rom 12:4–5; 1 Cor 10:17; 12:12–27; Gal 5:26–29). According to the story of Pentecost (Acts 2:1–13), the birth of the church brought together diverse groups of people with varying language proficiencies. Nevertheless, these people gathered from every nation in Jerusalem were able to understand the spirit in their native languages. The story of Pentecost helps us imagine the apocalyptic vision of John (Rev 7:9–10): "Before the throne and before the Lamb there was a great multitude 'from every nation, from all tribes and peoples and languages.'" God's kingdom would include people of all colors and languages. Through the work of the Holy Spirit, all nations, tribes, and peoples become one body of Christ, visible and invisible. The love of God for all people (John 17:20–23; Acts 11:19–26; 13:1; Eph 2:11—3:6) requires us to go beyond our own ethnicity. It is natural for the church on earth to be diverse in terms of ethnicity and languages. This is a difficult feat that is considered critical for the advancement of the gospel in the twenty-first century and beyond. While we may relate to different cultures based on our ethnic affiliation, we are still related to one another and bound together via our connections in the body of Christ.

In the present millennium, there have been some dramatic social demographic changes at both the local and global levels, particularly due to transnational migration. For example, the Greater Toronto Area (GTA) demographic has changed significantly over the last few decades and is still undergoing rapid changes. In the GTA, visible minorities are now the majority, at over 50 percent of the entire population. With these demographic changes in our social fabric, the multicultural or multiethnic church is emerging. The multicultural church would likely become the "new norm," "cultural evolution," and "inevitable," serving as a sign of changing times of the new millennium. Deymaz claims that our churches are now in the early adopter stage in terms of becoming multicultural churches, and predicts that by 2020 in the United States, about 20 percent of churches will have 20 percent ethnically diverse members in their congregations. And by 2050, 50 percent of churches in the United States will have 50 percent ethnically diverse members in their congregations.[1] Although we have yet to gather comparable statistics in Canada, we find many churches claiming to be multicultural churches on the internet. A multicultural church is reflective of God's will as observed in the changing society that is becoming ever more culturally and ethnically diverse. In other words, the emerging multicultural church should not been seen as a challenge, but rather as an opportunity to serve God and strengthen God's kingdom on earth.

Our Asian immigrant churches need to move towards a multicultural church, not only for theological, Biblical, and sociological reasons, but also for existential and missional reasons, seeing as we cannot entirely depend on the new immigrants and children of immigrants for future survival. In the early days, the English ministry was comprised primarily of the children of first-generation immigrants. Over the years with the decreasing immigration rate, we have seen a corresponding decrease in the membership of both the ethnic-language and English-speaking ministries of our churches. However, we would like to continue working towards the actualization of the kingdom vision on earth, just as Jasmin aspires: "More colored faces, different nationalities." About two thirds of English-speaking lay interviewees, along with several ethnic-language-speaking lay interviewees, and more than half of the clergy interviewees envisage a multicultural church for our church's future. When we imagine our church pews filled with a cultural mosaic of people, praising, and worshiping God together in the same

---

1. Deymaz and Li, *Ethnic Blends*, 28.

worship hall, a question comes to mind: How can we become a multicultural church, and still be able to retain and celebrate certain characteristics of our own ethnic cultures? Many of our Asian immigrant churches continue to grapple with this question; becoming a multicultural church is easier said than done, even for our English-speaking ministries.

Wrong Assumptions? Challenges? Or Possibilities?

Opening up and Welcoming "Others"

Joan, like many of us, thinks that if we open up to and welcome those of other ethnic backgrounds, our church will naturally become more multicultural. She says, "As long as we are more welcoming to not just those who are Taiwanese- or Mandarin-speaking but also other English-speaking newcomers, our English congregation may become more multicultural." Ben thinks that one of the strengths of his church is the openness of its English ministry (EM) to all ethnic groups. He elaborates as follows: "Even though most of us are ethnically Chinese here, we strive to be welcoming of other ethnic groups. My dream is to have more non-Chinese members in the EM, which has been rather difficult. Sometimes non-Chinese people would walk in and see all these Chinese faces in the pews, which would make them feel like they don't belong here." While being open and welcoming of potential new members from other ethnic backgrounds certainly help them feel at ease upon entering our church doors, from experience we know that we would need to do more to make them stay on as long-term members of the church. More often than not, the non-Asian newcomers walk into our church, smell Asian food being prepared in the kitchen, see a large number of Asian people in close quarters, and feel uncomfortable. So, most would choose to walk out, even before giving us a chance to open up and welcome them to our church. Sometimes the non-Asian newcomers would stay for a few English-speaking services, but they would tell us that they do not see how they can belong to our church. Although it is natural for people to feel more comfortable with those who are more like them, it is quite unfortunate that our church's Asianness has become a barrier for the non-Asian newcomers to give us a fair chance. As a result, our Asian immigrant churches are often misconstrued as being ethnocentric and closedminded.

Merging with a Canadian (Caucasian) Church

Ben, a long-time English ministry (EM) pastor, considered finding a smaller Canadian (Caucasian) church to merge with his church. He thought that this merge would be mutually beneficial for both churches, as the integrated church would end up with a mix of people in the congregation. In reality, this was not easy, either. Ben describes his experience as follows: "I have toyed with this idea some years ago. I was looking around to see whether other churches were interested in merging with us. I could not really find any church which wanted to do that. It is not easy because the Caucasian churches are not really interested in mergers." These churches would have had different reasons why they turned down Ben's merger proposal. First, they are not used to sharing of power in church leadership, and thus not yet ready to form a church with ethnically Chinese congregation. This is similar to what Jeung claims in his book *Faithful Generation*: "While Asian Americans are familiar with predominantly white settings, whites are less likely to feel comfortable on the periphery of a group's relational networks, even if they have a leadership role."[2]

Merging with a Multicultural Church Near Us

Then we might consider merging with one of the multicultural churches nearby, which seems easier at first glance. But how realistic is it to facilitate a merge between Asian immigrant churches and local multicultural churches? Ben continues his speculation on merging with a multicultural church in order to become more multicultural:

> It is not easy because they don't want to merge. They would probably welcome our members with open arms. But they would not want to merge in terms of leadership. They have certain ways of doing their ministry. They wouldn't want me to come in and join their pastoral staff, unless I was called to serve there and become their minister. It is always difficult when you merge two churches due to governance."

When we take a closer look at the churches currently claiming to be multicultural churches, their leadership positions are held mostly by Caucasian Canadians, despite the majority of congregation members being so-called "visible minorities." In the absence of multicultural leadership, how can these churches claim to be truly multicultural? Although more

---

2. Jeung, *Faithful Generation*, 157.

multicultural churches are on the rise, not many seem to fully understand what a multicultural church is.

Taking a Non-ethnic Church?

This is still a very hard task for us. Given that the laity and clergy alike desire to form a multicultural church, is there a way for the existing Asian Canadian immigrant churches to actually become a multicultural church? Ben speculates again, "As I said previously, it is no easy feat to merge two churches together, and even harder for two different ethnic congregations. This is the challenge. Perhaps a Chinese pastor can go and take a non-Chinese church to build a multicultural church. This wouldn't be easy, but he/she can try." This is Ben's conclusion regarding how to make a multicultural church, drawing from his experience as a long-time ethnic English-speaking minister. Indeed, it is not easy to merge two churches together. Then, would it be easier for Asian Canadian ministers to be called to a non-ethnic-specific church and build a multicultural church from within? How realistic and applicable are any of the options discussed above for Asian Canadian immigrant churches?

We acknowledge that the English-speaking second-generation members can engage well with members from diverse backgrounds to create a unique, integrated multicultural worship service in English. Although our churches emphasize that the English service is open to everyone, is there a way in reality to be a church for all the diverse ethnic groups in Canada? Why does our Asian-ness become the barriers and limitations to forming a multicultural church? Do these barriers and limitations come from the subtle or unconscious discrimination against ethnic minorities in North America—in this case, Asians in Canada? In her book, *A Faith of Our Own*, Sharon Kim describes her research on twenty-two Korean American second-generation churches in Los Angeles, specifically how difficult it is to plant and grow a multiracial church. In her research study, six second-generation pastors planted monoethnic Korean American churches; sixteen second-generation pastors planted pan-Asian churches. The latter grew well over time. Ten out of sixteen ministers serving pan-Asian churches wanted to expand their ethnic boundary to become a multiethnic or pan-ethnic church including non-Asians. However, their attempts at attracting non-Asians to their church were largely unsuccessful, and thus none of these churches could transition to a multiracial church.[3] In this regard, Kim's study closely resembles Pastor Cho's case, whose church had

---

3. Kim, *Faith of Our Own*, 141.

close to one thousand non-Asian visitors, yet only twelve who stayed on as long-term members.[4] In his book, *Faithful Generations*, Russell Jeung confirms the same with his study on the fifty English-speaking ministers based in the Bay Area of the United States. Jeung interviewed and categorized them into four groups: twenty ministers as ethnic-specific; six as ethnic and pan-Asian, sixteen as pan-Asian, and eight as desiring to become multicultural.[5] Jeung explains that "the new multiethnic churches have not been truly successful in becoming multiracial in membership . . . only two of the eight multiethnic congregations studied here may be considered truly multiethnic or multiracial."[6]

Even as we begin to see some mix of ethnicity in our English-speaking congregation, most newcomers are of Asian backgrounds. For example, one Korean immigrant church has 20 percent non-Korean English-speaking congregants, most of whom came from other parts of Asia. If we really want to become a multicultural church, we would need to consider not only how we think and do things around the church, but also what we are not yet aware of. Gerry, an English ministry pastor serving a Taiwanese immigrant church, puts it this way: "It is difficult to find someone who is not ethnically Taiwanese or even Asian to come in and want to stay and cultivate a sense of belonging to our church. There are still a lot of Taiwanese elements to our church culture. Even the food we eat together is always Asian food." Then is it impossible to form a multicultural church, if we do not give up our own ethnic culture altogether. In other words, we are faced with this dilemma between wanting to become a multicultural church and preserving our own cultural heritage at the church. So Young shares her concerns with regards to this dilemma: "Non-Koreans should not be prevented from coming to my church. But I also think that my church should not strip its distinct Korean characteristics to become a multicultural congregation." Ji Hun, a Korean ministry pastor, believes that "[t]he ethnic Korean churches can open their doors to welcome more non-Koreans . . . I think the Korean immigrant churches can retain their unique ethnic identity even after welcoming non-Koreans into the church." Spencer is wary of the challenges associated with building a multicultural church: "The vast majority of churches, even 'black majority,' face enormous challenges when it comes to creating and maintaining an ethnically diverse membership. I believe this happens because how our churches look, or are perceived to be, will often dictate who feels

---

4. Kim, *Faith of Our Own*, 150.
5. Jeung, *Faithful Generation*, 17.
6. Jeung, *Faithful Generation*, 155.

able to come through the door."⁷ One of the underlying challenges associated with building a multicultural church might be due to racism and racial discrimination in North America. If we give up our own ethnic culture, or our Asian-ness altogether, in order to appear more multicultural, the resulting church would not be multicultural in a real sense of the word. Let us now consider what a "multicultural" church is.

What Is a Multicultural Church?

According to Emerson, in sociology "any congregation in which less than 80 percent of the members share the same racial background"⁸ counts as a multicultural church. That means in a culturally mixed congregation, one dominant cultural group would account for less than 80 percent of the total, and other cultural groups would account for more than 20 percent. Garces-Foley affirms "the multicultural church is not the mere presence of diversity within its walls, but the interaction between those inside."⁹

A multicultural church is more than a presence of cultural mosaic of people in the congregation. A multicultural church is characterized by embracing and respecting the differences of other cultures, maintaining the uniqueness of each culture, and celebrating one another's cultures, just as Brian aspires: "My personal take on it is not to get rid of, but to add to. So right now we may be a Taiwanese church, and instead of getting rid of the Taiwanese-ness, we should be celebrating the Taiwanese-ness. At the same time, also celebrate every culture." The goal of a multicultural church is the integration of cultures, but not assimilation to the dominant culture. In the multicultural church, every unique ethnic cultural heritage is a "gift" to be celebrated. The church becomes a place to create opportunities, a community hub of sorts to nourish and appreciate each other's cultural heritage.¹⁰ At the multicultural church, people from different cultures encounter one another and discover each other's unique cultures as a gift given by God to be shared with others. For this integration of cultures to happen, we would need to create the third spaces between different ethnic groups. And at a multicultural church, members of diverse ethnic backgrounds worship, praise, pray, have fellowship, and reach out to one another under the name of the Triune God. In a multicultural church, leadership and power are

---

7. Spencer, *Building a Multi-ethnic Church*, 95.

8. Emerson and Kim, "Multiracial Congregations," 217; Deymaz and Li, *Ethnic Blends*, 24.

9. Garces-Foley, "New Opportunities," 212.

10. Garces-Foley, "New Opportunities," 216.

shared equally among different cultures and ethnic groups. In this chapter, "multicultural" and "multiethnic" are used interchangeably, though we prefer to use "multicultural" because even in a single ethnic group, there could be cultural differences. With this understanding, let us consider the steps for moving towards becoming a multicultural church.

Moving towards a Multicultural Church

One Family of God

In order to transition to a multicultural church, first we would need to change our understanding of what it means to be a human being. In his book *Coming Together in the 21st Century*, DeYoung stresses the fundamental oneness of humanity, and points out the importance of accepting our shared humanity and our unique cultural identities.[11] According to DeYoung, the starting point of any discussion on diversity is the oneness of humanity and the universality of God's love, rather than the differences of cultural expression. Culture is a particular and distinct way of life of a group of people, beginning with a family, a geographical region, ethnic group, and/or nation. Culture has a dynamic character. It never stays the same. Human beings change culture constantly by reforming, making and remaking it. This is particularly true in today's globalized world, as in all the areas of the world where cultures have become hybrid. The essence of human nature never changes, however.

The beginning of multicultural church should be based on an affirmation of the commonality of all human beings, regardless of ethnicity, skin color, nationality, gender, class, or geographical location. That understanding should be our starting point for a multicultural church. In his book, *In Living Color: An Intercultural Approach to Pastoral Care and Counselling* (1997), the well-known practical theologian, Emmanuel Y. Lartey, affirms a "trinitarian" understanding of human personhood as follows:

1. "We are like all others": there are universal characteristics which all human persons have in common.
2. "We are like some others": as humans we are shaped, influenced, and patterned to some extent by the community within which we are socialized.
3. "We are like no other": each individual is unique.[12]

---

11. DeYoung, *Coming Together*, 3.
12. Lartey, *In Living Colour*, 12.

Lartey stresses the importance of intercultural pastoral care and counseling in maintaining a balance between these three aspects of a human being, raising them as three kinds of questions about persons and situations, although he understands inter-culturality fundamentally in terms of inter-relatedness and interconnectedness.

However, the foundational operating premise for multicultural church should be "we are like all others." All human beings are of one human race, no matter what the cultural and skin-color differences of the "other-us." In order to be open to and welcome all people to our church, and to treat all people in a society of cultural diversity equally, a multicultural church must begin from the universal commonality of human beings. Cultures are indeed different, based on where people are geographically, the period of time they are living in, certain areas of the world, etc., but the essence of humanity, of human beings, remains the same. All humans are one human kind as we believe that God created all human beings in God's image. Spencer asserts, "There is only one race—the human race."[13]

It is clear that "race" is not a biological term of variation; it is instead a social, cultural, and political term that has long been used in this world, particularly by people who were or are privileged, in order to categorize others in terms of geographical origin, culture, ethnicity, skin color, or even eye color. In terms of these racial categories, dehumanizing racial discrimination has long prevailed in human history. And racial discrimination is still prevalent, becoming ever more violent all over the world. The word "race" has caused people to assume there are different kinds of humans: superior and inferior. This discrimination in Canada also brought about the birth of ethnic churches. Also, the word "ethnicity," used to differentiate different groups of people according to shared origin, culture, tradition, and social background, has most often been applied to ethnic minority groups of different physical appearance.[14] Ethnicity is used to distinguish invaluable shared origins, cultures, and traditions among certain group of peoples. That is the reason in this book we have not used the word "race"; instead, we have used the words "multiethnic" or "multiculture," although we are aware of racial discrimination in social reality.

Living in Canada, we meet different ethnic peoples in our neighborhood at any given moment. At first glance, we tend to see only the cultural differences of others, such as apparent behaviors, physical appearance, language, customs, clothes, and certain values. Then we fear the "other-us" on account of these differences. Yet, as the relationship develops, we see less

13. Spencer, *Building a Multi-ethnic Church*, 4.
14. Dein, "Race, Culture and Ethnicity," 68.

difference in the "other-us," and more of the commonalities of people: The human being itself. How delighted we are to discover sameness in the midst of difference! That commonality then serves to connect our deep heart with those of "other-us," and cultural differences become an attractive point in the connecting. All are created by God in God's image, yet all are sinful, all are in need of the grace of God. Brock reflects about her change of theological perspective on the Genesis text of the creation of humankind: "I had always been taught to see the creation of opposites, male and female. But as I looked at it more carefully, I saw that it speaks deeply of sameness in the midst of diversity, of how we are created humankind, the same spirit in God's image, even when we are different."[15]

In a multicultural church we envisage a fully connected community as one family of God based on embracing all ethnic groups equally beyond the differences of appearance or gifts or cultural expressions, brought together with new possibilities.

Wrong Motivations for a Multicultural Church

Before transitioning to a multicultural church, we would need to reflect on our motivations for wanting to move in that direction. Are we seeking to become a multicultural church from the biblical and theological hermeneutical motivation, just as we discussed earlier in this chapter? Or are we moving in that direction for the sake of our own survival in the future, as immigration rate continues to drop and more second- and third-generation congregants assimilate to the mainstream Canadian society? If we would like to build a healthy multicultural church, we need to have the right motivations to begin with: To please God by becoming one body of Christ with people of diverse backgrounds, and to benefit "other-us" who are brothers and sisters in Christ in a missional understanding.

What would be considered a wrong motivation for wanting to build a multicultural church? First, we would be considered wrongly motivated if we use other ethnic Christian groups for our own church's vested interest, that is, if we bring in another ethnic group in order to shift the focus of our church's current crisis, problems, and issues. This is an example of functional and survival-oriented motivation. In fact, once a church moves in a multicultural direction under such motivation, the ongoing crisis and problems would not be mitigated—they would worsen over time. The church itself would not grow healthily; the church will become stagnant, and may even cease to exist. Likewise, we would be considered wrongly motivated if we seek to simply fill

15. Brock et al., *Setting the Table*, 140.

our church pews, boost church membership, and ensure church's financial stability overnight by becoming a multicultural church. This is another example of functional and survival-oriented motivation.

Another example of existential or survival-oriented motivation for wanting to become a multicultural church is seeking to use newfound multiculturality of our church as a coping mechanism, specifically as a way to escape from our ethnic history and roots, and also from our experience of racial discrimination and "otherness" in the mainstream Canadian society. Although we did not address this directly in our interviews, we wonder whether some interviewees are more inclined to build a multicultural church because deep down they want to run away from their ethnic identity and history, or perceived "Asian-ness." What's worse, some of us seek to blend in with others in a big "multicultural" church as a way of masking our aversion to "otherness" in a good way. We would convince ourselves into thinking that we have formed "one body" with other racial and ethnic groups in the congregation, when in fact this would be just another wrong motivation. Hence, it is very important to have an honest and open discussion to critically examine our motivations for wanting to move in a multicultural direction as a church.

Two Different Approaches to Becoming a Multicultural Church

1. Church-to-Church Merging Approach: This approach entails having an ethnic-specific church merge with one or more other churches in the neighborhood, as Ben once tried to do. Ben attempted to merge with Caucasian churches near his own church, but none seemed interested at the time. Based on Ben's experience, we may want to locate other ethnic-specific churches in the neighborhood for merger proposals, instead of focusing on non-ethnic minority mainline churches. In many parts of Canada including the Greater Toronto Area (GTA), there are a number of ethnic immigrant churches looking for their own place of worship on Sunday. They are often on the lookout for a place to hold fellowship and other services during the week. On any given Sunday, we can easily locate foldable, makeshift church signs on the local streets and around public places in the neighborhood, such as schools and community centers. An Asian immigrant church with its own church building may want to start by approaching these churches in the neighborhood, to initiate a conversation regarding the possibility of merger.

    Of note is that several Asian immigrant churches in Canada already allow other smaller ethnic-specific churches, such as the

Vietnamese church, Syrian church, and Egyptian church, to use the church facilities for free on Sunday. In that case, instead of being two independent churches in a host-guest relationship, why not consider joining together as an interdependent multicultural church, thereby becoming equal partners in the house of God? Coming together to create one interdependent church would also help us disclaim our ownership of the church. The resulting church would have multiple ethnic-language congregations based on demands, along with a single unified English-speaking congregation, all independent in terms of finance and governing system. Meaning, there would be one English worship service for the children, youth, and English-speaking adults from different ethnic groups in the church.

The resulting church would operate in a similar manner to our current church model of accommodating two or three language congregations based on language preferences—that is, while remaining independent in terms of finance and governing systems, they would be interdependent in other areas of the church including mission projects, education programs, services, and events. These combined church-sponsored activities may vary from church to church such as church bazaar, church picnic, overseas mission trips, joint worship services, and so on, but nevertheless allow the different congregations under the same church banner to come together occasionally, and celebrate their oneness in Christ. In particular, the ethnic first-generation congregations can serve as bridge-builders to create one unified English-speaking congregation at the church. This English-speaking congregation would be multicultural by default, and eventually become the leading congregation of the church, naturally paving the way for multicultural church in the next generation and beyond.

While at first glance this approach to becoming a multicultural church might seem relatively simple—with its primary focus on the combining of services for the second-generation members from diverse backgrounds—there will still be numerous issues, challenges, and barriers associated with this merger approach. First, as we have experienced under our current church model of having two or three different-language congregations sharing the same roof, we would need to make compromises between the different congregations before, during, and after joining together as a multicultural church. We would need to continuously negotiate amongst ourselves. While doing so, we would need to be respectful and loving towards one another; we would also need to treat all members equally as the same brothers and sisters in Christ, without exercising "power" and "privilege."

If the resulting multicultural church is able to negotiate through the issues, challenges, and barriers that arise post-merge, this would be one of the most efficient and ideal approaches to becoming a multicultural church, especially for Asian immigrant churches in Canada with their own church buildings. With this approach, we would be able to remove the "label" of being an Asian-specific church for the Chinese, Korean, and Taiwanese in Canada. It would not be advisable to rush into the merge process, but rather take as much time as needed to consider the voices of the church community, from leaders to laity, before deciding to merge. But even before that—before initiating a conversation regarding merger as a church—we would need to tread carefully with small steps, and begin by building relationships between congregations, facilitating church-to-church interactions, organizing special joint-worship services, hosting joint programs such as summer camp, conferences, retreats, picnics, sports days, and so on. Having these joint activities together may spark a conversation regarding a merger very naturally, and make the transition towards a multicultural church that much more seamless.

2. Individual-based intentional approach: This approach entails inviting individual members of the community to the English-speaking service of our church through the intentional efforts of congregation members. With this approach, congregation members undertake intentional actions for the purpose of becoming a multicultural church, such as keeping the church doors open on Sunday, inviting friends and neighbors to the English-speaking service, holding a workshop on changing the church culture to be more inviting and inclusive, and welcoming new visitors with open arms regardless of their language proficiency, cultural heritage, and ethnic affiliation. Our church building belongs to no one single person or group, because it belongs to God and God alone. We are in the house of God when we come to church for worship on Sunday. Therefore, everyone is welcome to worship with us in our church. The church adopting this approach needs to actively publicize themselves to the community by developing relevant programs and services for the community, which would help motivate local residents to come out to the church. In other words, the church needs to focus on creating more opportunities for the non-churched neighbors to step inside the church building. And the church needs to empower its members to invite their friends and neighbors, while seeking to serve as a hospitable and missional church for the broader local community. Each church is ultimately built on relationships. It is

up to each congregation to develop close relationships with the local residents and community to which it belongs.

This second approach would gain momentum at a slower pace with fewer issues than the first, requiring innovative thinking and intentional and proactive actions to provide an inviting atmosphere for all people, from the signpost outside to the heart and life of congregation—that is, living a way of Christian life outside and inside the church. One of the most important tasks of the Asian immigrant church is to help other cultural groups feel at home while nurturing their sense of belonging to our church community—thereby overcoming the label of being an "Asian-specific" church. It is up to the leaders and members of our church to make everyone who walks through the door feel loved, included, and embraced, thus embodying the essence of the gospel.

Of course, there is another approach: the English-speaking congregation may choose to leave the ethnic-specific church of its origin and plant a multicultural church of its own, which was a common occurrence in the United States, and less so in Canada. For example, in the Greater Toronto Area (GTA), some independent churches offering English-only worship services have been planted by ethnic second-generation ministers who aspired to grow a multicultural or pan-Asian church. For the most part, their efforts have not borne fruit; only a handful of such churches have been successful in becoming a multicultural or pan-Asian church. In this book, we do not delve into this scenario of leaving and planting a multicultural or pan-Asian church, completely independent from the ethnic specific church of origin. From the outset, we were interested in writing a book for those who wanted to work together to build a healthy church of the future, while remaining a part of our current Asian Canadian immigrant churches. Given the two approaches discussed in detail above, let us now explore the implications for our churches seeking to build a multicultural church from within.

Implications for Moving towards a Multicultural Church

Whatever approach we decide to adopt for our church, we would need to be intentional about becoming a multicultural church. A multicultural church does not happen overnight by itself, considering that most of our churches are still very much ethnic-specific. From both our experiences and Ben's testimony, we know that our church culture itself—what people see and feel upon entering through the door—often intimidates people who are "different" from us ethnically and culturally. The utmost priority should be given to making such people feel comfortable and safe with us.

1. Our Asian Canadian immigrant churches envisioning a multicultural church need to have learning opportunities about biblical and theological mandates for a multicultural church, and intercultural learning opportunities, such as workshops and seminars. There are clear mandates for churches to transition to multicultural churches, beginning with what the church is. We need to reexamine the meaning of the church. As we have discussed in chapters 4, 5, and 6, we may have and identify with different cultures at the church, even amongst the people of same ethnicity and generation. We need to have more than classroom-based educational opportunities for cultural sensitivity or cultural competency. For example, the joint gatherings of two or three language congregations would aid in the understanding of each other's cultures, such as how we do things differently and similarly, and become an opportunity to share our thoughts on certain issues, values, and church priorities. This interaction would turn into a mutually beneficial learning opportunity for the different generations and language groups at the church. Then, we should extend these cultural learning opportunities to other ethnic cultures, using tools such as cultural sensitivity training, awareness training, and learning about other culture's traditions and customs. We need to understand that people of other ethnic backgrounds may act and respond differently in a given situation. For instance, it is okay to have children running around and playing by themselves during fellowship in some cultures, while the same would not be condoned in other cultures.

2. Our Asian Canadian immigrant churches envisioning a multicultural church must determine what things are necessary and what are not necessary from both the inside and outside of the church to invite and include other ethnic groups to our church. That means creating a church culture of welcoming, inviting, and being hospitable to people of different cultures. We must think and share ideas on how both the inside and outside of our churches can appear more friendly and inclusive of other ethnic groups. For example, the decorations inside the church may include elements of other cultures, in addition to our own. The church name should also be displayed in both English and ethnic languages. Likewise, the Sunday worship times on the church worship signboard need to be clearly displayed in both English and ethnic languages. Posting a short friendly English phrase on the church signboard such as "A Church for All Nations!" would help us appear

more welcoming and inclusive. This would also help us reaffirm our welcoming and inclusive church culture. Along with the signboard, our church website should clearly indicate that people of all ethnicities are invited to join us for worship—and that our church is striving for a multiethnic/multicultural congregation.

3. Our Asian Canadian immigrant churches envisioning a multicultural church need to strive for a specific vision of the multicultural church in faith. This vision needs to appear on the church bulletin every Sunday, on the church website, and any other official medium the church name might appear. After creating the vision for multicultural church, the church needs to develop specific strategies, coupled with an action plan, for becoming a multicultural church. Our action plan would help us move towards becoming a multicultural church, step-by-step.

4. Our Asian Canadian immigrant churches envisioning a multicultural church need to be intentional about helping congregants develop crosscultural relationships amongst members and peoples outside of the church. We should provide ample opportunities to foster active engagement and mutual understanding both within and outside of the church. Furthermore, we should seek to practice "radical hospitality" to those who are different from us, particularly the new immigrants to this land. Choi defines radical hospitality as "the full embrace of the otherness of the strangers, and as the reduction of political, economic, and cultural privileges."[16] In radical hospitality the host becomes the guest and guest becomes the host. In faith they become one another and build mutual relationship.[17] If we offer more hospitality as we would to our own people, the people of same ethnicity, then we will be able to build an authentic multicultural community based on our faith in Christ.

5. Asian Canadian churches envisioning a multicultural church need to learn at least a few words and phrases in the languages of other ethnic groups at our church and in our neighborhood. When we engage in a conversation with a local newcomer from a different ethnic background than our own, speaking a few words or phrases in his/her language would be taken as a friendly gesture of welcoming.

Deymaz declares, "Compared with other social institutions, the church, far from representing the diversity and unity of the kingdom of God, was actually the primary institution perpetuating systemic racism in

---

16. Choi, *Postcolonial Self*, 138.
17. Choi, *Postcolonial Self*, 141.

our society."[18] One of the ethnic minister interviewees is in agreement with Deymaz: "This is the direction that we should be headed, to welcome all who comes through our doors. However, I think it will be difficult to get rid of our ethnic color completely. As long as racism exists in this society, there will be a need for ethnic churches."

Nevertheless, Asian Canadian immigrant churches are well-equipped to strive for a multiethnic/multicultural congregation due to our own experiences living as ethnic minorities in Canada, and certain characteristics of our "Asian-ness." First, we as Asians have endured systematic discrimination and racism in Canada. Our experiences living as ethnic minorities in Canada, as strangers in a strange land, help us build a common ground and mutual understanding with those of other minority groups. This is an important first step towards establishing a multicultural/multiethnic church. Second, we as Asians are the people of *jeong*, as discussed in one of the previous chapters. This makes us unique in terms of our collective thinking, altruistic mindset, and community-oriented spirit, all of which have had an overall positive influence on the Asian Canadian immigrant churches. Our collectivism, along with our community-oriented spirit, allows us to place the church first in our life before all else. So once we overcome the barriers between the different cultures, we will be able to extend our *jeong* relations to "other-us." Third, our collective thinking helps our faith to become missional, or missionally driven, as reflected in our church priorities. Although the second- and third-generation Asian Canadians are considered "less Asian and more Canadian" compared to their first-generation counterparts, they still carry certain traits and characteristics associated with our "Asian-ness." After all, many of them were raised by ethnic-language-speaking first-generation parents, and regularly attended Asian immigrant churches growing up. Therefore, we believe that Asian Canadian Christians are ready to move towards building a multicultural church for the kingdom of God. Currently, several resources are readily available to assist, in addition to established networks offering support and connections for churches seeking to move in a multicultural direction, including Mosaix.[19] All we need to do is move towards our kingdom vision step-by-step, even if it takes a long time. While striving to become a multicultural church might not be an option for all of us, in due time it might be an inevitable option for some Asian Canadian immigrant churches seeking changes for better future outcomes.

---

18. Deymaz and Li, *Ethnic Blends*, 24.
19. Deymas and Li, *Ethnic Blends*, 27, 219.

Reflection and Discussion Questions

1. What have you learned from Ben's multicultural trial, namely his experience of approaching other neighboring churches for merger proposals?

2. How would you define a multicultural church? What does it mean for you?

3. What biblical and theological foundations motivate you or your church to move towards a multicultural church?

4. Have you had a chance to critically assess your own motivations for wanting to become a multicultural church? If yes, what are they? If not, please take a moment to do so and share your assessment with others.

5. What changes would your church need to make in order to welcome "others"? What can you and your church do to help them feel at home at the church?

Conclusion

COMING OUT OF THIS research study, we acknowledge that the lay members and leaders of Asian Canadian immigrant churches (ACIC) identify first as the people of faith, and second as the people of *jeong* (*qing*). The congregants of ACIC are able to worship God in their preferred language amongst the people of same ethnicity, and along the way they share *jeong*, or a piece of their beautiful heart (*qing*). Being able to do so has been our source of strength and joy in this strange land that we call home right now, which is completely different from our countries of origin in terms of time zones, geography, language, culture, history, customs, values, and such. Andy, a second-generation English ministry (EM) pastor, admits that much like their first-generation counterparts, the "Canadianized" second-generation congregants often feel at home in their own ethnic-specific churches, given their significantly ethnic home life and church life growing up. The second-generation members find the ethnic environment provided by their Asian immigrant churches, and its associated "Asian-ness" comforting, especially in the presence of ethnic English-speaking ministers with whom they can establish a common ground based on shared feelings and experiences. So it would appear that both the first- and second-generation Asian Canadian Christians have long considered ACIC as their home—a home base if you will, for seeking spiritual guidance, moral support, cultural solidarity, and psychological/emotional help.

However, if we do not carefully plan and prepare ahead of the future, there will be no guarantee of the continued survival of ACIC into the next generation and beyond. Considering the generally agreed-upon assumptions among ACIC—that the future church will look completely different from what they are now—we want to be equipped with the right skills, resources, and guides that can help increase our church's chances of survival in the future. But we want to do more than survive; we would like to continue thriving as a church for generations to come in this fast-paced changing world. This is one of the reasons why we decided to conduct this research study in the first place, to help ease the transition process of all ACIC in the next twenty-five years.

Let us now imagine what our churches would look like in the future. How different would they be from the current ACIC? First, our church names might not include the term "immigrant" or simply be known as Asian Canadian churches. We may also see many different types of Asian Canadian churches, including pan-Asian churches, multicultural churches, and of course the currently widespread ethnic-specific churches with two or three different-language congregations. The difference is that the ethnic-specific churches of the future would be English-dominant, with the English congregation serving as the leading congregation. There might also be new emerging church types in the future, such as house churches, cyber-churches, intentional communities, simple churches, or missional churches. Regardless of the types of church that may emerge and proliferate in the future, we predict the following: First, our churches will be universally English-dominant unless changes are observed either in the immigration trends or Canada's official languages; second, our churches will be led by the lay leaders and clergy from the second generation, or the generations after that. Our second generation will create a hybrid third space in the church for multiple generations of congregants comprised of diverse ethnic groups.

What the first- and second-generation leaders need to do is initiate a serious conversation about the right time to turn our keys over to the second-generation leaders of ACIC. In other words, it is the time to prepare for the transition of our church leadership. For this transitional phase, the copastors model or the partnership model would be preferred over the senior pastor model or the so-called "Duplex" or "Triplex" model, as discussed previously. The "Duplex" or "Triplex" model is traditionally one-language dominant—either English or ethnic language—and similar to the townhouse model of having two independent churches loosely connected under the same roof. Currently, most ACIC would be considered a "Duplex"/"Triplex" church or townhouse church. All the different-language congregations under such models of church need to come together and envision their future as a church, which ideally would be close to our "Open Concept House" model. What future directions would your church like to embark on this leadership transition process?

Each church has varying needs within its unique contexts and circumstances. Hence, each church must take into account its own unique contexts when deciding on future directions. The leaders of each church—from both the laity and clergy—need to take enough time to review and agree on the best type or model of church for their contexts going forward. While many leaders and lay members expressed a desire to pursue the multiethnic or multicultural direction for their ethnic immigrant churches in the future, it must be noted that not all Asian ethnic churches can turn into multicultural churches. Nor can they all become pan-Asian churches. Even though the new immigrants and visitors to Canada may not be increasing greatly in number, there will still be a need for ACIC, given that certain support services and ethnic-language worship service are only available at ACIC. This will be the case as long as Canada receives immigrants and visitors from around the world, including countries in Asia.

The ethnic immigrant churches need to be further diversified, offering various subtypes of churches that meet the needs and preferences of as many congregants as possible. Each church needs to discern the future on its own, considering and reflecting on the local community where the church is situated and its members' desires and preferences. Along with our own visions for the church, we need to have a clear understanding of what God is calling the church to be and to do in the future.

This need to discern God's calling comes from our faith in him, rather than *jeong (qing)*—from our deep love for the church itself, the body of Christ, and God who is the source of all things. And in the process of doing so, we are hoping to serve as an example for the future leaders and members of the church who love and seek to serve God just as much as we do. At times we may need to set our *jeong (qing)* aside for the sake of our church, that is, the strong attachment to "our" church and a sense of ownership arising from all the time, energy, resources, and financial contributions we have spent over the years. We must consider first how our church can survive and thrive in the future, not only as a place to worship God in the community, but also as a place to call home for many generations to come.

Bibliography

Aarim-Harriot, Najia. *Chinese Immigrants, African Americans, and Racial Anxiety in the United States, 1848–82.* Urbana: University of Illinois Press, 2003.

Abel, Andrew. "Favor Fishing and Punch-Bowl Christians: Ritual and Conversion in a Chinese Protestant Church." *Sociology of Religion* 67 (2006) 161–78.

Alumkal, Antony W. "Being Korean, Being Christian: Particularism and Universalism in a Second-Generation and Congregation." In *Korean Americans and Their Religions: Pilgrims and Missionaries from a Different Shore*, edited by Ho-Youn Kwon et al., 181–91. Pennsylvania: Pennsylvania State University Press, 2001.

Beckman, Jim, and Eric Gallagher. *Discipleship Focused Youth Ministry: A Getting Started Guide for Parishes.* Lexington: Discipleship Focused Youth Ministry, 2016.

Bekerman, Zvi, and Ezra Kopelowitz, eds. *Cultural Education—Cultural Sustainability: Minority, Diaspora, Indigenous, and Ethno-Religious Groups in Multicultural Societies.* New York: Routledge, 2009.

Belzer, Tobin, et al. "Congregations That Get It: Understanding Religious Identities in the Next Generation." In *Passing on the Faith*, edited by James L. Heft, 103–22. New York: Fordham University Press, 2006.

Berry, John W. "Immigration, Acculturation, and Adaptation." *Applied Psychology: An International Review* 46 (1997) 5–68.

Borland, Helen. "Intergenerational Language Transmission in an Established Australian Migrant Community: What Makes the Difference?" *International Journal of the Sociology of Language* 180 (2006) 23–41.

Brock, Rita Nakashima. "Critical Reflection on Asian American Religious Identity: Response—Clearing the Tangled Vines." *Amerasia Journal* 22.1 (1996) 181–86.

Brock, Rita Nakashima, and Naomi Southard. "The Other Half of the Basket: Asian American Women and the Search for a Theological Home." *Journal of Feminist Studies in Religion* 3.2 (1987) 135–50.

Brock, Rita Nakashima, et al., eds. *Setting the Table: Women in Theological Conversation.* St. Louis: Chalice, 1995.

Cha, Peter, et al., eds. *Growing Healthy Asian American Churches: Ministry Insights from groundbreaking Congregations.* Downers Grove: InterVarsity, 2006.

Chai, Karen J., et al. *Competing for the Second Generation: English-Language Ministry at a Korean Protestant Church, Gatherings in Diaspora: Religious Communities And the New Immigration.* Philadelphia: Temple University Press, 1998.

Chan, Anthony B. "Chinese Canadians." https://www.thecanadianencyclopedia.ca/en/article/chinese-canadians.

Chan, Chung-Yan Joyce. "Recovering a Missing Trail in Canadian Baptist Footprints in the Northwest: Stories of Chinese Baptists in Western Canada." *Baptist History and Heritage* 39.3 (Fall 2004) 20–35.

Chee, Maria W. L. *Taiwanese American Transnational Families: Women and Kin Work*. New York: Routledge, 2005.

Chen, Carolyn. "From Filial Piety to Religious Piety: Evangelical Christianity Reconstructing Taiwanese Immigrant Families in the United States." *International Migration Revie* 40 (2006) 573–602. doi: 10.1111/j.747-7379.2006.00032.x.

———. *Getting Saved in America: Taiwanese Immigration and Religious Experience*. Princeton: Princeton University Press, 2008.

———. "The Religious Varieties of Ethnic Presence: A Comparison between a Taiwanese Immigrant Buddhist Temple and an Evangelical Christian Church." *Sociology of Religion* 63 (2002) 215–38.

———. "A Self of One's Own: Taiwanese Immigrant Women and Religious Conversion." *Gender and Society* 19.3 (2005) 336–57.

Chen Feng, Jessica, et al. "Intergenerational Tension, Connectedness, and Separateness in the Lived Experience of First and Second Generation Chinese American Christians." *Contemporary Family Therapy* 37.2 (May 2015) 153–64. doi: 10.1007/s10591-015-9335-9.

Chiang, Lan-Hung Nora. "Return Migration: The Case of the 1.5 Generation of Taiwanese in Canada and New Zealand." *China Review* 11.2 (2011) 91–123.

Ching, Julia. "The House of Self." In *Journeys at the Margin: Toward an Autobiographical Theology in American-Asian Perspective*, edited by Peter C. Phan and Jung Young Lee, 41–61. Collegeville, MN: Liturgical, 1999.

Cho, Grace M. *Haunting the Korean Diaspora: Shame, Secrecy, and the Forgotten War*. Minneapolis: University of Minnesota Press, 2008.

Cho, Lily. *Eating Chinese: Culture on the Menu in Small Town Canada*. Toronto: University of Toronto Press, 2010.

Choi, Hee An. *Korean Women and God*. Maryland, New York: Orbis, 2005.

———. *A Postcolonial Self: Korean Immigrant Theology and Church*. Albany: State University of New York Press, 2015.

Choi, Joseph Y., and W. Jae Lee. *Hiring an English Ministry Pastor & Beyond: In an Asian American Church Context*. Columbia, Maryland: JnJ, 2011.

Chong, K. H. "What It Means to Be Christian: The Role of Religion in the Construction of Ethnic Identity and Boundary among Second-Generation Korean Americans." *Sociology of Religion* 59.3 (1998) 259–86.

Chuang, D. J. *MultiAsian.Church: A Future for Asian Americans in a Multiethnic World*. N.p.: CreateSpace Independent Publishing Platform, 2016.

Chung, Christopher K., and Samson Cho. "Significance of 'Jeong' in Korean Culture and Psychotherapy." https://www.semanticscholar.org/paper/Significance-of-%E2%80%9C-Jeong-%E2%80%9D-in-Korean-Culture-and-Chung-Cho/b492d8398d95aadefe1cf99f3782621cf6a55cb6.

Chung, Ruth H. Gim. "Gender, Ethnicity, and Acculturation in Intergenerational Conflict of Asian American College Students." *Cultural Diversity and Ethnic Minority Psychology* 7 (2001) 376–86. doi: 10.1037//1099-9809.7.4.

"Church Records: Methodist." https://guides.vpl.ca/ccg/church_records/#tabs-3.

Dein, Simon. "Race, Culture and Ethnicity in Minority Research: A Critical Discussion." *Journal of Cultural Diversity* 13.2 (Summer 2006) 68–75.

Deymaz, Mark, and Harry Li. *Ethnic Blends: Mixing Diversity into Your Local Church*. Grand Rapids, MI: Zondervan, 2010.

———. *Leading a Healthy Multi-Ethnic Church: Seven Common Challenges and How to Overcome Them*. Grand Rapids, MI: Zondervan, 2013.

DeYoung, Curtiss Paul. *Coming Together in the 21st Century: The Bible's Message in an Age of Diversity*. Valley Forge: Judson, 2009.

Dhingra, Pawan. "'We're Not a Korean American Church Any More': Dilemmas in Constructing a Multi-Racial Church Identity." *Social Compass* 51.3 (September 2004) 367–79.

Ecklund, Elaine Howard. *Korean American Evangelicals: New Models for Civic Life*. New York: Oxford University Press, 2006.

Emerson, Michael O., and Karen Chai Kim. "Multiracial Congregations: An Analysis of Their Development and a Typology." *Journal for the Scientific Study of Religion* 42.2 (2003) 217–27.

Evans, James A. "The Impending "Silent Exodus" of Canadian-born Chinese Christians from the Canadian Chinese Church." DMin diss., Fuller Theological Seminary, 2008.

Everist, Norma Cook, and Craig L. Nessan. *Transforming Leadership: New Vision for a Church in Mission*. Minneapolis: Fortress, 2008.

Firkatian, Mari. "Retaining Ethnic Identity: The Armenians in Bulgaria." In *Cultural Education-Cultural Sustainability: Minority, Diaspora, Indigenous, and Ethno-Religious Groups in Multicultural Societies*, edited by Zvi Bekerman and Ezra Kopelowitz, 181–99. New York: Routledge, 2009.

Formosan Christian Church in Toronto in Commemoration of its 30th Anniversary (1966–96). *The Establishment and Development of the Church*.

Formosan Grace Christian Church in Toronto in Commemoration of its 50th Anniversary. *Church History: Formosan Christian Church in Toronto*.

Foskett, Mary E., and Jeffrey Kah-Jin Kuan. *Ways of Being, Ways of Reading: Asian American Biblical Interpretation*. St. Louis: Chalice, 2006.

Francis, Leslie J., and Yaacov J. Katz, eds. *Joining and Leaving Religion: Research Perspectives*. Leominster: Gracewing, 2000.

Garces-Foley, Kathleen. "New Opportunities and New Values: The Emergence of the Multicultural Church." *The Annals of the American Academy of Political and Social Science* 612 (July 2007) 209–24.

Gu, Chien-Juh. *Mental Health among Taiwanese Americans: Gender, Immigration, and Transnational Struggles*. New York: LFB Scholarly, 2006.

Hammett, Edward H. *Spiritual Leadership in a Secular Age: Building Bridges Instead of Barriers*. St. Louis: Lake Hickory Resources, 2005.

Han, Huamei. "Unintended Language Maintenance: the English Congregation of a Baptist Chinese Church in Western Canada." *International Journal of the Sociology of Language* 2013.222 (2013) 101–29. doi: https://doiorg.myaccess.library.utoronto.ca/10.1515/ijsl-2013-0034.

———. "'Westerners,' 'Chinese,' and/or 'Us': Exploring the Intersections of Language, Race, Religion, and Immigrantization." *Anthropology & Education Quarterly* 45.1 (March 2014) 54–70.

Harris, Heather, and Mary Sun. *The Chinese Canadians*. Scarborough, ON: Nelson Canada, 1982.

Heo, Chun Hoi. *Multicultural Christology: A Korean Immigrant Perspective*. New York: Lang, 2003.

Heschel, Abraham Joshua. *The Sabbath: Its Meaning for Modern Man*. New York: Farrar, Straus & Giroux, 1951.

Hickey, M. Gail. "New Worlds, Old Values: Cultured Maintenance in Asian Indian Women Immigrants' Narratives." In *Cultural Education-Cultural Sustainability: Minority, Diaspora, Indigenous, and Ethno-Religious Groups in Multicultural Societies*, edited by Zvi Bekerman and Ezra Kopelowitz, 181–99. New York: Routledge, 2009.

Huang, Evelyn, and Lawrence Jeffery. *Chinese Canadians: Voices from a Community*. Vancouver: Douglas & McIntyre, 1992.

Hurh, Won Moo, and Kwang Chung Kim. "Religious Participation of Korean Immigrants in the United States." *Journal for the Scientific Study of Religion* 29 (2009) 19–34.

Hwang, Wu-Tong. *A History of the Development of Taiwanese Christian Churches in North America*. Los Angeles: Taiwanese Christian Church Council of North America, 1986.

Jeung, Russell. "Asian American Pan-ethnic Formation and Congregational Culture." In *Religions in Asian America: Building Faith Communities*, edited by Pyong Gap Min and Jung Ha Kim, 215–44. Walnut Creek, California: AltaMira, 2002.

———. *At Home in Exile*. Grand Rapids: Zondervan, 2016.

———. "Evangelical and Mainline Teachings on Asian American Identity." *Semeia* 90/91 (2002) 211–36.

———. *Faithful Generations: Race and New Asian American Churches*. New Brunswick, NJ: Rutgers University Press, 2005.

Korean Canadian Cultural Association. *History of Korean Canadians*. Toronto: Korean Canadian Cultural Association, 2013.

Kibria, Nazli. "College and Notions of 'Asian Americans': Second-Generation Chinese Americans and Korean Americans." In *The Second Generation: Ethnic Identity among Asian Americans*, edited by Pyong Gap Min, 183–208. Walnut Creek, California: AltaMira, 2002.

Kim, Bok-Lim C., and Eunjung Ryu. "Korean Families." In *Ethnicity & Family Therapy*, edited by Monica McGoldrick et al., 349–62. 3rd ed. New York: Guilford, 2005.

Kim, Dae Sung. "New Missions with a New Generation: The Experiences of Korean American Churches and Missions." *International Bulletin of Mission Research* (2019) 1–9. doi: 11.1177/2396939319838911.

Kim, Henry, and Ralph Pyle. "An Exception to the Exception: Second-Generation Korean American Church Participation." *Social Compass* 51.3 (September 2004) 321–33.

Kim, Matthew D. "Possible Selves: A Homiletic for Second Generation Korean American Churches." *Homiletic* 32.1 (Summer 2007) 1–17.

———. *Preaching to Second Generation Korean Americans: Towards a Possible Selves Contextual Homiletic*. New York: Lang, 2007.

Kim, Rebecca Y. *God's New Whiz Kids?* New York: New York University Press, 2006.

Kim, Sharon. *A Faith of Our Own: Second-Generation Spirituality in Korean American churches*. New Brunswick, NJ: Rutgers University Press, 2010.

———. "Shifting Boundaries within Second-Generation Korean American Churches." *Sociology of Religion* 71.1 (January 2010) 98–122.

Ko, Min Ho. "Recognizing and Bridging Common Intergenerational Differences in a Korean American Congregation." DMin diss., Drew University, 2010.

Kuo, Ben C. H. "Coping, Acculturation, and Psychological Adaptation among Migrants: A Theoretical and Empirical Review and Synthesis of the Literature." *Health Psychology and Behavioral Medicine: An Open Access Journal* 2 (2014) 16–33. doi: 10.1080/21642850.2013.843459.

Kuo, Ben C. H., and Jian Guan. "Risk and Protective Factors of Depression among Older Chinese Immigrants in Canada: Acculturation, Relationship with Children, Social Support, and Perceived Service Barriers." *34rd Annual Scientific and Educational Meeting of the Canadian Association on Gerontology*. CAG, 2005.

Kuo, Ben C. H., et al. "Multicultural Coping: Chinese Canadian Adolescents, Male Gender Role Conflict, and Psychological Distress." *Psychology of Men & Masculinity* 7.2 (April 2006) 83–100.

Kwak, Jennica Y. "Between Two Cultures Within One Race: Korean-American Youth in Search of Identity through Literary in Korean Church Communities." PhD diss., Camden Rutgers University Press, 2011.

Lai, Daniel W. L. "Prevalence and Correlates of Depressive Symptoms in Older Taiwanese Immigrants in Canada." *Journal of the Chinese Medical Association* 68.3 (2005) 118–25.

Lai, David Chuenyan, et al. "The Chinese in Canada: Their Unrecognized Religion." In *Religion and Ethnicity in Canada*, edited by Paul Bramadat and David Seljak, 89–110. Toronto: Pearson Education Canada, 2005.

Larocque, Alain. *Losing 'Our' Chinese: The St. Enfance Movement*. Toronto : University of Toronto-York University Joint Centre for Asia Pacific Studies, 1987.

Lartey, Emmanuel Y. *In Living Colour: An Intercultural Approach to Pastoral Care and Counselling*. London: Cassell, 1997.

Lee, Evelyn, and Matthew R. Mock. "Asian Families: An Overview." In *Ethnicity & Family Therapy*, edited by Monica McGoldrick et al., 276. 3rd ed. New York: Guilford, 2005.

Lee, Helen. "Silent Exodus: Can the East Asian Church in America Reverse the Flight of Its Next Generation?" *Christianity Today* 40.9 (1996) 50–53.

———. "Silent Exodus No More." *Christianity Today* (2014) 38–47.

Lee, Inn Soon, and Timothy D. Son, eds. *Asian Americans and Christian Ministry*. Eugene, OR: Wipf & Stock, 1999.

Lee, Jung Young. *Marginality: The Key to Multicultural Theology*. Minneapolis: Fortress, 1995.

Ley, David. "The Immigrant Church as an Urban Service Hub." *Urban Studies* 45.10 (September 2008) 2057–74.

Li, Julia Ningyu, eds. *Canadian Steel, Chinese Grit: A Tribute to the Chinese Who Worked on Canada's Railroads More than a Century Ago*. Translated by John Howard-Gibbon and Jan Walls. Toronto: Paxlink Communication, 2000.

Li, Peter S. *Chinese in Canada*. 2nd ed. Toronto: Oxford University Press, 1998.

Lies, Tat-Siong Benny. *What Is Asian-American Biblical Hermeneutics? Reading the New Testament*. Honolulu: University of Hawaii Press, 2008.

Lin Ott, Sophia. "Taiwanese Americans: Protestant Christianity, Acculturation, and Ethnic Identity." PsyD diss., Alliant International University, 2008.

Ling, Huping. *Chinese St. Louis: From Enclave to Cultural Community.* Temple University Press, 2004.

Ling, Samuel. *The "Chinese" Way of Doing Things.* Phillipsburg: P&R, 1999.

Loo, Dennis. "Why an Asian American Theology of Liberation?" *Church and Society* 64 (January–February 1974) 51.

Lowe, Lisa. "Heterogeneity, Hybridity, Multiplicity: Marking Asian American Differences." In *Asian American Studies: A Reader,* edited by Jean Yu-wen Shen Wu and Min Song, 423–42. New Brunswick, NJ: Rutgers University, 2000.

Lyght, Ernest S., et al. *Many Faces One Church: A Manual for Cross-Racial and Cross-Cultural Ministry.* Nashville: Abingdon, 2006.

Macdonald, Stuart. "Presbyterian and Reformed Christians and Ethnicity." In *Christianity and Ethnicity in Canada,* edited by Paul Bramadat and David Seljak, 168–203. Toronto: University of Toronto Press, 2008.

Matsumoto, David, and Linda Juang. *Culture and Psychology.* 5th ed. Belmont, CA: Wadsworth, 2013.

Matsuoka, Fumitaka. *Out of Silence, Emerging Themes in Asian American Churches.* Cleveland: United Church, 1995.

Matsuoka, Fumitaka, and Eleazar S. Fernandez, eds. *Realizing the America of Our Hearts: Theological Voices of Asian Americans.* St. Louis: Chalice, 2003.

Medina, Nestor, et al., eds. *Reading In-Between: How Minoritized Cultural Communities Interpret the Bible in Canada.* Eugene, OR: Wipf & Stock, 2019.

Min, Pyong Gap, and Dae Young Kim. "Intergenerational Transmission of Religion and Culture: Korean Protestants in the U.S." *Sociology of Religion* 66.3 (October 2005) 263–82.

Myers, Ched, and Matthew Colwell. *Our God Is Undocumented: Biblical Faith and Immigrant Justice.* Maryknoll: Orbis, 2012.

Nagata, Judith. "Christianity among Transnational Chinese: Religious versus (Sub) ethnic Affiliation." *International Migration* 43.3 (August 2005) 99–130.

Nakka-Cammauf, Viji, and Timothy Tseng, eds. *Asian American Christianity Reader.* N.p.: Pacific Asian Americans & Canadian Christian Education and Institute for the Study of Asian American Christianity, 2009.

Ng, David. "A Path of Concentric Circles: Toward an Autobiographical Theology of Community." In *Journeys at the Margin: Toward an Autobiographical Theology in American-Asian Perspective,* edited by Peter C. Phan and Jung Young Lee, 81–102. Collegeville, MN: Liturgical, 1999.

Ng, David, ed. *People on the Way: Asian North Americans Discovering Christ, Culture, and Community.* Valley Forge: Judson, 1996.

Ng, Franklin. *The Taiwanese Americans.* Westport, CT: Greenwood, 1998.

Ng, Greer Anne Wenh-In. "Land of Maple and Lands of Bamboo." In *Realizing the America of our Hearts: Theological Voices of Asian Americans,* edited by Fumitaka Matsuoka and Eleazar S. Fernandez, 99–114. St. Louis: Chalice, 2003.

———. *Our Roots, Our Lives: Glimpse of Faith and Life from Black and Asian Canadian Women,* Toronto: United Church, 2003.

———. "Pacific-Asian North American Religious Education." In *Multicultural Religious Education,* edited by Barbara Wilkerson, 190–234. Birmingham: Religious Education, 1997.

Ng, Wing Chung. "At America's Gates: Chinese Immigration during the Exclusion Era, 1882–1943." *Journal of Asian Studies* 64.1 (Feb 2005) 159–61.

Ngan, Lai Ling Elizabeth. "Neither Here nor There: Boundary and Identity in the Hagar Story." In *Ways of Being Ways of Reading: Asian-American Biblical Interpretation*, edited by Mary F. Foskett and Jeffrey Kah-Jin Kuan, 70–83. St. Louis: Chalice, 2006.

Noh, Marianne S. "Contextualizing Ethnic/Racial Identity: Nationalized and Gendered Experiences of Segmented Assimilation Among Second Generation Korean Immigrants in Canada and the United States." PhD diss., University of Akron, 2008.

Noh, Samuel, and William R. Avison. "Asian Immigrants and the Stress Process: A Study of Koreans in Canada." *Journal of Health and Social Behavior* 37.2 (June 1996) 192–206.

Noh, Samuel, et al. *Korean Immigrants in Canada*. Toronto: University of Toronto Press, 2012.

Norton, Henry K. *The Story of California From the Earliest Days to the Present*. Chicago: McClurg, 1924.

Ooka, Emi. *Growing Up Canadian: Language, Culture, and Identity among Second-generation Chinese Youths in Canada*. Microform.

Park, Andrew Sung. "The Formation of Multicultural Religious Identity within Persons in Korean-American Experience." *Journal of Pastoral Theology* 13.2 (Fall 2003) 34–50.

———. *From Hurt to Healing: A Theology of the Wounded*. Nashville, TN: Abingdon, 2004.

———. *Triune Atonement: Christ's Healing for Sinners, Victims, and the Whole Creation*. Louisville: Westminster John Knox, 2009.

Park, Kil Kae. "Yellow on White Background: Korean American Youth Ministry and the Challenge of Constructing Korean American Identity." *Journal of Youth Ministry* 4.1 (Fall 2005) 23–37.

Park, M. Sydney, et al., eds. *Honoring the Generations: Learning with Asian North American Congregations*. Valley Forge: Judson, 2012.

Park, Seong Man. "The Role of Ethnic Religious Community Institutions in the Intergenerational Transmission of Korean among Immigrant Students in Montreal." *Language, Culture and Curriculum* 24.2 (July 2011) 195–206.

Penner, James, et al. *Hemorrhaging Faith: Why and When Canadian Young Adults are Leaving, Staying and Returning to Church*. Toronto: Evangelical Fellowship of Canada, 2011.

Phan, Peter C. "Betwixt and Between: Doing Theology with Memory and Imagination." In *Journeys at the Margin: Toward an Autobiographical Theology in American-Asian Perspective*, edited by Peter C. Phan and Jung Young Lee, 113–33. Collegeville: Liturgical, 1999.

Phan, Peter C., et al., eds. *Journeys at the Margin: Toward an Autobiographical Theology in American-Asian Perspective*. Collegeville: Liturgical, 1999.

Poon, Vincent, et al. "Pastoral Counseling Among Chinese Churches: A Canadian Study." *The Journal of Pastoral Care & Counseling* 57.4 (Winter 2003) 395–403.

Purvis, Connie. "Tales of Taiwanese Churches." *The Presbyterian Record* 132.10 (November 2008) 12–13.

Rajkumar, Peniel, eds. *Asian Theology on the Way: Christianity, Culture, and Context*. Minneapolis: Fortress, 2015.

Reimer, Sam, et al. "Christian Churches and Immigrant Support in Canada: An Organizational Ecology Perspective." *Review of Religious Research* 58.4 (December 2016) 495–513.
Samovar, Larry A., et al. *Intercultural Communication: A Reader.* 13th ed. Boston: Wadsworth, 2012.
Shin, Benjamin C., and Sheryl Takagi Silzer. *Tapestry of Grace: Untangling the Cultural Complexities in Asian American Life and Ministry.* Eugene, OR: Wipf & Stock, 2016.
Son, Angella. "Jeong as the Paradigmatic Embodiment of Compassion (Hesed): A Critical Examination of Disparate and Dispositional Jeong." *Pastoral Psychology* 63 (2014) 735–47. doi: 10.1007/s11089-014-0611-7.
Song, Nam Soon. "Demythologizing the Silent Exodus: Asian-Canadian Protestant Young Adults." *Journal of Youth Ministry* (Fall 2019) 11–33.
———. "Youth Ministry that Matters: Voices of Korean Canadian Youth." *The Journal of Youth Ministry* 15.2 (Spring 2017) 97–120.
Spencer, Linbert. *Building a Multi-ethnic Church.* London: Society of Promoting Christian Knowledge, 2007.
Sugikaw, Nancy, and M. Sydney Park. "Formation of Servants in God's Household." In *Honoring the Generations: Learning with Asian North American Congregations,* edited by M. Sydney Park et al., 120–47. Valley Forge: Judson, 2012.
Suh, Suh Kyoung. "Toward the Recovery of Effective Youth Ministry for Korean Ethnic Churches in the United States." DMiss diss., Asbury Theological Seminary, 1996.
Sun, Shirley Hsiao-Li. "Housework and Gender in Nuclear Versus Extended Family Households: Experiences of Taiwanese Immigrants in Canada." *Journal of Comparative Family Studies* 39.1 (Winter 2008) 1–9.
Swinton, John, and Harriet Mowazt. *Practical Theology and Qualitative Research.* 2nd ed. London: SCM, 2016.
Taiwan Justice and Grace Christian Church in Toronto in Commemoration of its 10th Anniversary. *Church History: Taiwan Justice and Grace Christian Church in Toronto.*
Taiwanese United Church in Toronto 5th Anniversary Booklet (1983–88). *The Church History.*
Tan, Jonathan Y. *Introducing Asian American Theologies.* Maryknoll: Orbis, 2008.
Tira, Sadiri Joy. "The Local Church and Mission to the Diaspora: Examples in the Christian & Missionary Alliance in Canada." *Missio Nexus* (2017) 1–17. https://missionexus.org/the-local-church-and-mission-to-the-diaspora-examples-in-the-christian-missionary-alliance-in-canada/.
Todd, Matthew R. S. *English Ministry Crisis in Chinese Canadian Churches: Toward the Retention of English-Speaking Adults from Chinese Canadian Churches through Associated Parallel Independent English Congregational Models.* Eugene, OR: Wipf & Stock, 2015.
Toronto Central Taiwanese Presbyterian Church 20th Anniversary Publication (1983–2003). *The Church History.*
Tsang, Wing. "Integration of Immigrants: The Role of Ethnic Churches." *Journal of International Migration and Integration* 16.4 (November 2015) 1177–93.
Tse, Justin K. H. "Making a Cantonese-Christian Family: Quotidian Habits of Language and Background in a Transnational Hongkonger Church." *Population, Space, and Place* 17 (2011) 756–68. doi: 10.1002/psp/640.

Tseng, Timothy. "Asian Pacific American Christianity in a Post-Ethnic Future." *American Baptist Quarterly* 21.3 (September 2002) 277–292.

Tuan, Mia. *Forever Foreigners or Honorary Whites? The Asian Ethnic Experience Today.* New Brunswick, NJ: Rutgers University Press, 1998.

Wang, Jiwu. "Organised Protestant Missions to Chinese Immigrants in Canada, 1885–1923." *Journal of Ecclesiastical History* 54.4 (October 2003) 691–713.

———. "Religious Identity and Ethnic Language: Correlations between Shifting Chinese Canadian Religious Affiliation and Mother Tongue Retention, 1931–1961." *Canadian Ethnic Studies* 34.2 (June 2002) 63. http://www.confmanager.com/main.cfm?cid=128&nid=1805.

Wong, Enoch, et al. *Listening to Their Voices: An Exploration of Faith Journeys of Canadian-Born Chinese Christians.* N.p.: CCCOWE Canada, 2018.

Wu, Cheng-Tsu, eds. *Chink: A Documentary History of Anti-Chinese Prejudice in America.* New York: Meridian, 1971.

Wu, Frank. *Yellow: Race in America Beyond Black and White.* New York: Basic, 2001.

Yamada, Frank M. "Constructing Hybridity and Heterogeneity: Asian American Biblical Interpretation from a Third-Generation Perspective." In *Ways of Being Ways of Reading: Asian-American Biblical Interpretation*, edited by Mary F. Foskett and Jeffrey Kah-Jin Kuan, 164–77. St. Louis: Chalice, 2006.

Yang, Fenggang. *Chinese Christians in America: Conversion, Assimilation, and Adhesive Identities.* University Park: Pennsylvania State University Press, 1999.

Ye, Jing. "Protestant Missionary Work among the Chinese in Canada, 1880s–1930s: With a Focus on the Toronto Area," *Journal of the Canadian Church Historical Society* 48 (2006) 5–54.

Yep, Jeanette, et al. *Following Jesus Without Dishonoring Your Parents: Asian American Discipleship.* Downers Grove: InterVarsity, 1998.

Young, Jacob Yongseok. *The English-Speaking Ministry Based on Collective Korean American Autobiography, Korean, Asian or American?* Lanham: University Press of America, 2012.

Yu, Joanne Li, ed. *Chinese Presbyterian Church 100th Anniversary: Inspired by Our History, Invigorated for the Future.* Toronto: N.p., 2010.

Zhou, Min, and James V. Gatewood. *Contemporary Asian America: A Multidisciplinary Reader.* New York: New York University Press, 2000.

www.ingramcontent.com/pod-product-compliance
Lightning Source LLC
Chambersburg PA
CBHW062020220426
43662CB00010B/1415